Dreaming Black/Writing White

Dreaming Black/Writing White

The Hagar Myth in American Cultural History

Janet Gabler-Hover

THE UNIVERSITY PRESS OF KENTUCKY

Publication of this volume was made possible in part by a grant from the National Endowment for the Humanities.

Copyright © 2000 by The University Press of Kentucky

Scholarly publisher for the Commonwealth,
serving Bellarmine College, Berea College, Centre
College of Kentucky, Eastern Kentucky University,
The Filson Club Historical Society, Georgetown College,
Kentucky Historical Society, Kentucky State University,
Morehead State University, Murray State University,
Northern Kentucky University, Transylvania University,
University of Kentucky, University of Louisville,
and Western Kentucky University.
All rights reserved.

Editorial and Sales Offices: The University Press of Kentucky
663 South Limestone Street, Lexington, Kentucky 40508-4008

04 03 02 01 00   5 4 3 2 1

Library of Congress Cataloging-in-Publication Data

Gabler-Hover, Janet.
    Dreaming black/writing white : the Hagar myth in American cultural history / Janet Gabler-Hover.
      p.   cm.
    Includes bibliographical references (p.   ) and index.
    ISBN 0-8131-2143-4 (alk.paper)
    1. American fiction—19th century—History and criticism.
2. Hagar (Biblical character)—In literature. 3. American fiction—Women authors—History and criticism. 4. American fiction—White authors—History and criticism. 5. Southworth, Emma Dorothy Eliza Nevitte, 1819-1899—Criticism and interpretation. 6. Stephens, H. Marion (Harriet Marion), 1823-1858. Hagar the martyr. 7. Hopkins, Pauline E. (Pauline Elizabeth). Hagar's daughter. 8. Clay, Charles M., 1829-1895. Modern Hagar. 9. Women, Black, in literature. 10. Race in literature. I. Title.
PS374.H27G33   1999
813'.309351—dc21   99-26982

This book is printed on acid-free recycled paper
meeting the requirements of the American National Standard
for Permanence of Paper for Printed Library Materials.

Manufactured in the United States of America

For My Mother

"On Eagle's Wings"
Mary Ellen Johnston Gabler
January 14, 1927–November 1, 1996

Contents

List of Illustrations   ix

Acknowledgments   xi

1. Hagar and John Audubon: American Hybridity   1

2. Hagar: The Nineteenth-Century Myth   25

3. The Resurrected South: Hagar in Southworth's *The Deserted Wife*   38

4. Hagar's Demise in Southworth: *Virginia and Magdalene*   55

5. The Scandal of Race: Stephens's *Hagar the Martyr*   76

6. Hagar Splitting: Clark's *Modern Hagar*   95

7. Prodigal Daughters: Hopkins's *Hagar's Daughter* and Black Female Identity   122

Conclusion   158

Notes   164

Bibliography   180

Index   190

Illustrations

1. Jean-Baptiste-Camille Corot, "Hagar in the Wilderness" 12
2. Benjamin West, "Hagar and Ishmael" 13
3. Barocci(?), "Hagar and Ishmael" 14
4. Pierre-Paul Prud'hon, "And the Angel of God called to Hagar out of Heaven." 15
5. Charles Eastlake, "Hagar" 16
6. Christian Koehler, "Hagar and Ishmael" 17
7. Artist unknown, "The Departure of Hagar" 19
8. Hagar and Ishmael, from a painting by Hugues Merle 128
9. Alexander Skeete, Hagar jumping from a bridge 133
10. Edmonia Lewis, "Hagar in the Wilderness" 136

Acknowledgments

This book was an ongoing discovery aided by close friends. I thank Carolyn Denard for responding to my question "Who is Hagar?"—as I was reading *Hagar's Daughter*—by lending me *Sisters in the Wilderness: The Challenge of Womanist God-Talk*. Carolyn's counsel on issues of race relations while I was writing this book was timely and wise.

I also wish to acknowledge my friend Patricia Ferrara, an antique dealer, who sent me Southworth's *Ishmael*. Noelle Baker alerted me to the fact that the heroine of Southworth's *The Deserted Wife* was named Hagar. Cindy Cunningham reminded me that Hagar is mentioned in Herman Melville's *Pierre*. Psychologist Louisa Branscomb initiated discussion of the role of black women in white feminist psychoanalysis. Martha Kropf, LPC, provided ongoing encouragement and information on Jungian archetypology.

Many other people provided encouragement. Colleagues who read parts of my manuscript include Christine Gallant, Margaret Mills Harper, Matthew Roudané, and Marta Werner. Thanks also to my department chair, Robert Sattelmeyer, and the former chair, Virginia Spencer Carr, for their administrative support of my work. The project began with a partially funded year's leave granted by the Board of Regents of Georgia State University through the recommendation of these professors and the approval of the Dean of Arts and Sciences, Ahmed Abdelal. Since then I have been provided with course release, summer funding, and graduate assistantship.

The book could not have been accomplished without the dogged and relentless assistance of the Interlibrary Loan Department at Georgia State University. Marjorie Patterson is patient, supportive, and determined to get the sources that GSU faculty need.

The readers from Kentucky were superb. Thanks especially to Dana Nelson for her constructive suggestions about cultural studies sources to incorporate in the work. Professor Nelson provided invaluable criticism in a detailed and engaged reading that offered constructive advice on reworking parts of the manuscript, as well as enthusiasm for the project. I am grateful. I would also like to thank J. Lee Greene for a close and supportive reading of race consciousness in the text and for his guidance toward other relevant research.

Thanks also to Kirk Nuss, a talented graduate assistant in our department, who has worked on the final production of three books in this past year in the department; I was fortunate to snag him for the index and proofreading.

I acknowledge the following libraries and museums for their permission to reproduce Hagar illustrations in this book: the New York Metropolitan Museum of Art (Corot's "Hagar in the Wilderness" and West's "Hagar and Ishmael"); the Stattliche Kunstsammlungen in Dresden, Germany (Barocci's[?] "Hagar and Ishmael"); the Special Collections, Miller Nichols Library University of Missouri-Kansas City University (Prud'hon's *Christian Parlor* illustration); Washington University Library (Eastlake's "Hagar"); Duke University Rare Book, Manuscript, and Special Collections Library (*Peterson's* "Departure of Hagar"); the University of Georgia Libraries (*Woman in Sacred History*); and the National Museum of American Art, Smithsonian. Gift of Delta Sigma Theta Sorority, Inc. (Lewis's "Hagar"). I would also like to thank Deputy Chief Curator George Gurney at the National Museum for a personal tour and education on the museum's Edmonia Lewis's holdings.

On a more personal note, my neighbor Jean Bryant opened her heart to me and was always there for coffee klatches, antiquing adventures, discussions on Hagar, and unconditional love—she is gone now. I will never stop missing her, but I am sure she is relieved that this work is done. On a lighter note, my cat, Pasha, made my study his home during the initial composition of this manuscript and provided a requisite levity and sense of companionship. My father, Robert Gabler, offered encouragement and insight from his prolific career as author and editor of geographical publications. I thank with all my heart my incredible husband for his evaluative skills, patience, faith, love, and domestic skills. Bill is my compass center, my most keen supporter, and my best friend.

This book, finally, honors my students. They have, over the years, welcomed me into their thoughts, opened their hearts to the works, and never stopped inspiring. To list just a few: Geneva Baxter, Jacqueline Carmichael, Linda Fleming, Angel Joy Harper, Dwan Henderson, Jerelle Hendon, Deslyn Hendrickson, Geisha Hollingsworth, Robert Jackson, Natalie Maxwell, Delia Matthews, Diana Miles, Crystal Petway, Lynn Scott Simpson, Venessa Sims, Venika Sims, Shawn Starr, Devoc Walker, Krisna Walker . . . and so many more.

1
Hagar and John Audubon
American Hybridity

While African Americans have contributed significantly to the making of America, white America has staged the disappearance of some of those contributions in a privileged writing of American history. Sometimes a rumor—an intriguing bit of information previously unheard—can expose, through enigma, what was hidden in the pages of history. One such enigma—the historical riddle of John James Audubon—serves as a parable to introduce the topic of this book: the prominent place in nineteenth-century American art and literature of the biblical heroine Hagar, and the way in which Hagar's biblical status as an African woman is exploited by nineteenth-century American artists while at the same time being radically disavowed.

Why does art historian David Driskell include the allegedly white Audubon in his *Two Centuries of Black American Art*? The legend of Audubon (1785–1851), the famous naturalist, painter, and lithographer, seems to be of a white man's man—a real "frontier" white American as represented in the James Fenimore Cooper Leatherstocking tales that Audubon loved.[1] Audubon is remembered as a pioneer whose gifts as a naturalist contributed to scientific progress in later Victorian America. At age eighteen, he sailed from France to America to take over a family business; failing at that, he traveled through the wilderness he loved and drew and classified nature, for which he gained fame and his country's admiration. This is the Audubon legacy familiar to most white Americans, but it is a story that excludes racial complexities in Audubon's history.

Audubon self-fashioned a high-Victorian Anglophone identity that "hid" not only his illegitimate birth but, more intently, his ties with African ethnicity. Illegitimacy was a serious taint on Victorian respectability;

it exposed sexual desire not properly contained within the laws of Victorian propriety. As Audubon well knew, the additional "taint" of racial admixture—"blackness" coupled with illegitimacy—would toll the death knell on his inclusion in white America. After all, Victorian America equated illicit sexual desire with African American ethnicity, an equation that served as a convenient means of excluding allegedly over-sexualized black Americans from white society. The black woman, in particular, was stereotyped as a desiring "Jezebel"[2]. Audubon's connection with a mixed-race mother would ruin his ambition to be canonized within white Victorian myth. The American myth of *inherent* white superiority was, as J. Lee Greene convincingly demonstrates, instilled in history by pseudo-documentarians from Thomas Jefferson onward in such a way as to make American whiteness seem *inherently* superior.[3]

Like the Duke and the King in *Huckleberry Finn*, Audubon took advantage of (by not disputing) the prominent rumor that he was of royal European blood, the last Dauphin, son of Louis XVI and Marie Antoinette. Eager to inflate his Victorian status, he also carried a letter of introduction to Europe proclaiming his father a French admiral instead of the lieutenant that he actually was. He fostered further illusions by claiming, in the extended version of his posthumously published *Ornithological Biography* (1893), that he was born in Louisiana. By obscuring his past, he sought Anglo American legendary status through a myth of transcendence that distorted, if not virtually erased, his illegitimacy as well as a culturally stigmatized ethnicity that was a part of his family history. In the early twentieth century, Audubon's first formal biographer, Francis Hobart Herrick, set out to "lift the veil . . . cast over the birth and parentage of Audubon."[4]

Herrick determined to lay to rest rumors of Audubon's royal birth and to expose "the unwelcome fact of [Audubon's] illegitimacy."[5] He established that Audubon was born in Santo Domingo, the son of French merchant and sugar planter Jean Audubon and a French creole woman named Mlle Rabin, who died shortly after his birth. Audubon's father took his illegitimate son to his ancestral home in France, where he and his legal wife, Anne, older and childless, "adopted" him for the appearance of propriety.

Audubon's illegitimacy would have been disruptive enough of his status as a white American male hero,[6] but the transplantation of his birth to foreign ground placed his status as "white" in greater peril in ways probably unintended by Herrick. While Herrick claims that Jean, or Jeanne, Rabin was a white French woman, recent art historian David

Driskell, noting that "a great deal of confusion obscures the details of Audubon's birth,"[7] describes him as "the famous mulatto naturalist and illustrator," stating that Audubon's mother was either "a creole or mulatto servant who worked for the Audubons at their large plantation on Aux Cayes, Haiti." Driskell cites both Herrick's biography and that of Alice Ford.

How does Driskell derive his deduction from either biography, since neither suggests that Audubon was of mixed parentage?[8] Herrick provides the clue. Mixed-race status is suggested by Herrick's ambiguous use of "creole" to refer to both Sanitte Bouffard (the mother of Audubon's half-sister, Rose), a "'*creole de Saint Domingue*,' who subsequently went to France," and Jean Rabin. He calls both of them "'creole[s] of Santo Domingo,' that is, . . . born on the island and of French parentage," and makes no ethnic distinction between them. In addition, he refers to John James also as a "'*creole de Saint-Domingue*.'" Neither Rabin nor Bouffard is racially inflected by her identification as "creole"; indeed, the question of *which* ethnicity belongs with "creole" only emerges in Herrick's one-time mention of "African creole[s]" in the biography. Thus the word "Creole" becomes invested with racial ambiguity, an ambiguity retained in Herrick's discussion of Audubon's matriarchal descent from the La Fougeres, who by Herrick's day "all [had] negro blood."[9] "Creole" connoted racial mixture as early as the 1850s, when the French race theorist Joseph Gobineau noted the appealing sexuality of "many mulatto, Creole, and quadroon women." Robert Young notes that Gobineau's wife was a creole "whose unadulterated whiteness would always remain open to doubt."[10]

The racial ambiguity inherent in Herrick's use of "creole" suggests that Driskell may well have read Audubon's mulatto status from Herrick, whose biography is counterbalanced by Alice Ford's strategic narrativizing of mulatto status *away* from John James Audubon and onto his half-sister, Rose. Ford participates in what Audubon began, the mythification of his status as inherently white—and hence inherently superior—through the disavowal of what Homi Bhabha would call his own psychic "splitting." "Splitting" is the Jekyll and Hyde of self-identity, a psychic state of imbalance in which, as Bhabha explains, "the shadow of the other falls upon the self."[11] This Jekyll is not, as Freud would have it, the pathological site of unconscious psychic "darkness" that needs to surface in consciousness in order for the conscious psyche to be healed. Instead, this "Jekyll" is the product of cultural labeling: "Jekyll" is an arbitrary rendering of cultural "otherness" by the colonial power structure.

Robert Young's definition of "racial" hybridity matches Bhabha's definition of psychic splitting, a cultural/racial hybridity that could replicate on a personal level what Bhabha calls for in a "transnational" ideal of cultural identity.[12] The entertainment of hybridity is that point of suspension within the self that denies "denial" and therefore does not perpetuate the creation of an imperialist self by displacing ambiguity onto a marginalized "other." Ford supports Audubon's disavowal of his racial hybridity—his self-divisive "otherness"—by sloughing off his blackness onto a marginalized ethnic other, his half-sister, Rose. This radical disavowal mythifies white cultural superiority as a transcendent essential rather than a culturally constructed accident; Audubon's cultural contributions to American science and art are invariably attributed to his whiteness.

Alice Ford's biographies (1964, 1988) seem intent on rescuing Audubon from mixed-race parentage. She argues that Audubon Senior fled with his children during the Haitian rebellion, taking John James and his four-year-old sister Rose (Sanitte's child) to France for adoption by himself and his legal wife, who was older and childless, while Sanitte and her other child, a son, were left in Haiti. Cultural others that serve to define white male power through their oppositional status (women, ethnic others) are also, paradoxically, put "under erasure" as less than human and/or "fix[ed] in the ideological construction of [reductive] otherness."[13] Audubon provides a good illustration of how personal psychology is indivisible from cultural politics; by erasing his "otherness," he recapitulated the public American myth of white cultural superiority.

Ford protects this image by meticulously dispelling the historical problem that in the ship's charters it was Rose, not John James, who was listed as white. The ship's roll that transported the children identified Rose as the "natural daughter and orphan of [white] Demoiselle Rabin," while John James was listed as one of the sons of an unknown "Monsieur Montou." Ironically, Ford reads "Rabin" as a hidden code to cover up "the damning truth" of Rose's mixed-race status. She argues that the addition in the log of "white" after Rose's entry is "conspicuous . . . in a ledger where ordinarily only 'black' and 'mulatto' were designated," adding that "white" "does not recur in a whole shelf of ledgers for the era." Ford implies that John James is made the scapegoat for Rose's coding as "creole and white"; note that "creole," in Ford's account, belongs exclusively to whiteness, a subtle erasure of Herrick's point that Sanitte Bouffard was also a "creole," a terse denial of cultural hybridity and its potential to dispel cultural power imbalances.

Ford "rescues" John James, placing him staunchly in Anglo-European tradition: "The first Romans had arrived at just about the same spot where the boy of the burning hazel eyes, golden-brown curly hair, and restless grace came ashore."[14]

Regardless of the factuality of Ford's research, the text registers an implicit white racial narcissism in the way black blood is removed from John James Audubon and transfused into Rose. Ford's zeal transcends devotion to historical verity. One is struck, rather, by the narrative voice calling blackness "damning," with no narrative detachment from this cultural judgment. Ford also engages empathetically with the mind of "white" Jean Rabin, who to Ford's mind has far more reason than the socially "invisible" black Sanitte to fear the wrath of Audubon's wife: "What thoughts must have passed through the mind of one of such pious upbringing? She may have wondered whether by some merciful stroke of fortune the childless Anne, twenty-six years her senior, might not live to know what an unthinkable tragedy had befallen her. That Audubon Senior had spent scarcely four of the past eleven years with his aging wife did not ameliorate the dread of her finding out. The presence of a *black mistress* was one thing, the imagined intrusion of a *white woman*. . . quite another." [italics added][15]

This imaginative identification replicates the psychology of colonial imperialism. Ford sets up the white woman as a subject with status, one worthy of the wrath of an imagined opponent, while the "native" black woman becomes, for Ford, a colonized object with no status, a "no thing" in the estimation of white women. Further, the marginalized "no being" is predictably objectified as the eroticized "other" representative of the "uncontrollable sexual drive of the non-white races and their limitless fertility"; she is the object of the aversive fascination of the colonial white with "people having sex—interminable, adulterating, aleatory, illicit, inter-racial sex."[16] Ford fantasizes Sanitte as one of those "alluring dusky girls in their long, full, striped or figured skirts and bright bandanas set off by brass earrings. Audubon [Senior] counted himself lucky to be amongst them, enjoying their warm smiles, their grace, their delicious *calaloux* redolent of garlic and pimiento. On their heads they often bore trays of pomegranates, figs, bananas, oranges, and sweetmeats." Ford makes Sanitte figural and picturesque, an objectivized part of a quaint and eroticized setting as a "dark siren."[17]

The Audubon story reveals the process of disavowal by which nineteenth-century white America denied the substantive cultural contributions of black Americans to American cultural identity. Our story in this book—the Hagar story in nineteenth-century America—reveals on a grander scale how black Americans funded the cultural identity formation of America in the nineteenth century while simultaneously white Americans disavowed their contribution. Not coincidentally, the process by which black identity is disavowed is again through the stereotyping of black women as inherently promiscuous and thus separated from sexually restrained "whiteness." It is not surprising that Audubon's story is also a Hagar story; Sanitte, as Hagar, in the Old Testament and in nineteenth-century American novels, is made to "disappear"; she is made outcast through her sexuality.

It will be recalled that Hagar is depicted in Genesis as (apparently) the daughter of the Egyptian pharaoh who attempted to seduce Sarah, who is, unknown to him, the wife of the patriarch Abraham. When informed of his error, the pharaoh gives Hagar to Sarah as a handmaid to atone for his attempted seduction. Hagar is commanded by Sarah to bear a child with her husband, Abraham, for Sarah is old and childless and needs a son to inherit her legacy. Meanwhile, God gives Sarah a child (Isaac) in her old age. After Hagar voluntarily runs away to the desert to escape Sarah's cruelty and is remanded to Sarah by God, Sarah makes Abraham banish Hagar and her child Ishmael to the desert. Here God gives Hagar water to save her child and reveals that Ishmael will be a warrior, hunter, and ruler of a great race (Genesis, 16:1–16, 21:9–21).[18]

Throughout African American tradition, Hagar has been understood to be black because of her Egyptian affiliation. Whether the founders of Egyptian civilization were African was, as chapter 3 discusses, one of the central controversies of pro- and antislavery politics in antebellum America. Delores Williams notes that African American "sculptors, writers, poets, scholars, preachers and just plain folks have passed along the biblical figure Hagar to generation after generation of black folks," and notes that in the nineteenth century, African American poet Paul Laurence Dunbar wrote about "the Afro-American Sons of Hagar Club."[19] The name "Hagar" connotes African American ethnicity, seemingly beyond the boundaries of African American recognition. A Hagar poem written in 1845 by the white writer Anne Charlotte Lynch, for example, calls Hagar "the dark-browed child of Egypt." In nineteenth-century America, "dark-browed" was a metonym for African, as can be seen in the reference to the "dark-browed and enthusiastic speaker" who urges African Americans to return to Africa in the November 1859 *Anglo-African Magazine*. The name "Hagar" was among the 102 black women's names posted in the *Massachusetts Mercury* on September 16, 1800, in a warning to African Americans to leave the commonwealth. In the 1850s, slaveowner Elizabeth Clitherall records mourning the loss of "her own 'faithful old Hagar' who had begun life's journey with her." The 1907 slave narrative of Susie King Taylor reminisces that Taylor's grandmother named her children James and Hagar Ann in the 1830s.[20] Not only black but white women clearly understood the name's ethnic connotations. Harriet Beecher Stowe uses the name Hagar in a stereotypical sense to identify a black slave mother about to lose her child at a slave auction in *Uncle Tom's Cabin* (as I will discuss below).

Both nineteenth-century African and Anglo Americans knew that the black ethnicity of Hagar and her son Ishmael in the Bible served as a major source for the proslavery imperative to exclude African Americans from America's white power base. J. Lee Greene points out that the expulsion of Hagar and her son from Abraham's home served the notion of a white American Eden from which African Ishmael [obviously, Hagar also] was "naturally" excluded.[21]

This overwhelming cultural "reading" of Hagar as African creates a stunning enigma: a number of pre–Civil War white artists in America depicted Hagar as white. This depiction is further complicated by the sympathetic and often heroic depiction of Hagar. Of course, despite the religious context from which Hagar emerged, American readers during this time were comfortable with the secularization and embellishment of biblical characters in popular fiction.[22] Surprising as it may seem in these Victorian times of strict sexual rules, Hagar, the outcast bondswoman banished into the wilderness with her illegitimate son, gains iconic status in popular culture as a sympathetic figure. Hagar's hold on nineteenth-century American popular culture is implied by the numerous domestic fictions, poems, and graphic art depictions of Hagar. And, of course, her popularity was not exclusive to this place or time. A number of Hagar novels were written during the nineteenth century in Britain, including Fergus Hume's *Hagar of the Pawn-Shop: The Gypsy Detective* (London, 1897) and Eliza Tabor Stephenson's *Hagar* (London, 1870). Hagar plays were also produced in nineteenth-century America and London during the *fin de siècle*.[23] Obviously, her symbolic value survived the century as well. Hagar engaged a number of lesser-known writers during the first half of the twentieth century and emerged as the central figure in major fiction by two Canadian writers (Margaret Atwood's *The Handmaid's Tale* and Margaret Laurence's *Stone Angel*) and as references in Maya Angelou's poem "The Mothering Blackness" and in Toni Morrison's *Song of Solomon,* which includes a character named Hagar.[24]

In contrast to these less frequent, although no less profound, contemporary treatments of Hagar, at least thirteen Hagar novels were published in America between 1850 and 1913. In the chapters that follow, I will be addressing the core of that tradition, beginning with the first Hagar novel, E.D.E.N. Southworth's *The Deserted Wife* (*Hagar, or the Deserted Wife* [1849]), and continuing with Alice Carey's *Hagar: A Story of Today* (1852), *Hagar the Martyr; or, Passion and Reality* (1855) by Harriet Marion Stephens, Mary Jane Holmes's *Maggie Miller; Or, Old Hagar's Secret* (1859), *The Modern Hagar* by Charlotte Moon Clark (1882), Pauline Hopkins's *Hagar's Daughter* (1901–1902) and Mary Johnston's *Hagar* (1913). In the antebellum selections from this list, Hagar is white, but, as the century progresses, she evolves, through gradations, into full racial hybridity that marks her, in American society, as black. Significantly, I will argue that even in the first Hagar novel, Southworth's *Deserted Wife*, Hagar is *covertly* depicted as black—that is, of mixed race, rendered black by the presence of black blood.

Despite—in fact *because* of—the latent ethnic ambiguity of the Hagar heroine, it is no coincidence that the nineteenth-century American Hagar "canon" begins and ends with southern writers. In its paradigmatic form, the nineteenth-century American Hagar novels that fall most closely to the center of the canon were written by, or at least about, southern women, with the tale of Hagar closely bound to woman's position in the antebellum South. In fact, it is the women's Hagar novels, typically southern and proslavery, that present a positive Hagar. The irony of a black heroine turned white, although covertly black, and presented as the heroine of proslavery novels is tough to miss. Certainly the single African American author on our list of nineteenth-century Hagar novelists, Pauline Hopkins, was aware of this irony. Hopkins radically responds to the racial merger and ultimate exclusionary ethics of the white women's Hagar novel in her reclamation of Hagar in *Hagar's Daughter* (as discussed in chapter 7 below.)

Why did southern white women writers during proslavery times select Hagar as their heroine? A study of Hagar novels reveals that the women who wrote them were deliberately playing on the cultural recognition of Hagar's blackness. Indeed, Hagar's ethnic complexity—Is she white? Is she black?—provided a tantalizing opportunity for southern women under the thumb of a restrictive patriarchy to reimagine themselves in richer and more admirable identities through their black Hagar heroines. Why Hagar? She was, in her blackness, imagined to have a sexuality outside the permissible boundaries of femininity. In the Hagar works in this study, Hagar's freer sexuality—her passion—is presented as integral to other freeing and empowering qualities; in particular, the combination of sexual passion and artistic creativity serves as a conduit toward women's taking on male roles of economic power in American society.

These women writers probably selected Hagar because they wished to write novels exceeding the boundaries of the woman's domestic novel in mid-century America. The domestic novel—or the "woman's novel," as Nina Baym (to dignify the genre) relabels it in her work of the same name—does share some features with Hagar novels. The heroine's self-reliance in her transition from orphanhood into empowered femininity is paradigmatic in Hagar novels as well. But Hagar novels fail to qualify for one central attribute of the woman's novel heroine—her female chastity. The woman's novel depicts sexual women, especially "fallen women," as peripheral and antithetical to the story's main plot and heroine.[25] Hence, Hagar novels more rightly belong to what Baym describes in *Novels, Readers, and Reviewers* as the "sensational novel": "a feverish, florid, improbable, melodramatic, exciting genre" that included what one contemporary reviewer called "lurid exhibitions of unbridled passion."[26] It goes without saying that the sexual desire of the Hagar heroine appears frequently; because of their passion, the heroines temporarily falter—into questionable secret marriages or into even more dubious liaisons that result in pregnancy and abandonment: "Hagar has become the martyr of love, the wreck of womanhood, the outcast, the worse than slave!"[27] Unprecedented in the domestic novel of the time, this "wreck of womanhood" in *Hagar the Martyr* emerges victorious as an accomplished author who achieves marriage with her lover, the social catch of her upright society.

This resistance to the desexualized domestic novel was adventurous for antebellum southern women authors, who lived in a world in which sexual standards were even more restrictive than they were in the North.[28] Southern white women writers dared to explore this taboo ground by creating heroines, in Hagar, who were ethnically ambiguous: white enough to allow white women authors and readers to imagine themselves in the role of sexual and political rebellion against the patriarchy, but at the same time black enough to provide them with an escape hatch through which such rebellion could be safely disavowed. The victory of Hagar in the above example, for instance, is contingent on the defeat of the accusation that she is black. But the author, Stephens, first relies on suggestive insinuations that her heroine is indeed of mixed race.

The idea that blackness could empower a woman to transform the universe reveals at least two things. First, white authors of Hagar novels imagined black women archetypally in uneasy juxtaposition with the real-life historical situation of black women's enslavement. Second, Hagar fictions were essentially absurd and ideologically convoluted; they contained complicated narrative mechanisms by which a proslavery author could fictively stage the redemption of the old proslavery South by imagining herself to be black!

What exactly did white women writers get when they used Hagar as their heroine? Novels with Hagar heroines were much more actively feminist than the usual woman's novel.[29] Both white and black women across centuries have understood Hagar to be a model of feminist resistance to patriarchal forces. The white contemporary Jungian psychotherapist Marion Woodman calls Hagar the "black goddess" who "becomes [white women's] bridge between spirit and body." She argues that this dream image impels the destruction of the patriarchal "power principle whose goal is to keep [white women] in a gas oven until they die." This "Black Madonna" archetype "is Hagar, the dark Egyptian, the freed bondwoman of Abraham, who is cast out into the desert."[30] Similarly, two black feminist theologians, Delores Williams in *Sisters in the Wilderness: The Challenge of Womanist God-Talk* (1993) and Savina J. Teubal in *Hagar the Egyptian: The Lost Tradition of the Matriarchs* (1990), point to Hagar as the seminal presence that eclipses the "patriarchal plotline" of the Old Testament.[31] Teubal in fact identifies the patriarchal prohibition of Hagar's sexuality in the Old Testament as *the* moment when female rule in the world is eclipsed, since God gives Sarah (in her chastity) a child and initiates the exclusion of the sexual surrogate Hagar and her child from Abraham's "garden."[32]

The numerous graphic illustrations of the biblical Hagar that abounded in nineteenth-century America aptly illustrate this patriarchal "plot" to remove the power of Hagar's sexuality; one of the ways artists did this was to depict Hagar as white, an exemplary visual analogue to the eventual "whitewashing" of the Hagar heroine. Nevertheless, the graphic illustrations revealed the motive for white women writers to deploy Hagar as their model. In doing so, they constructed a feminist resistance to the desexualization of Hagar by Western artists, a resistance to the patriarchal repression of women's sexuality visible in Hagar art. In the nineteenth century, female sexuality was part of a continuum of female qualities, including passion, sensation, creativity, and emotional affect.[33] To proscribe female sexuality, therefore, was to proscribe the formative elements that could empower female identity. In removing Hagar's blackness, while in some instances covertly rendering it, graphic artists replicated the disavowal portion of white women writers' covert deployment of Hagar's black identity. But in presenting Hagar within the sentimentalized frame of mother, as opposed to mistress, Hagar graphic artists were antifeminist in the sense that "motherhood" in nineteenth-century America typically symbolized the desexualization of women.[34]

Two typical scenes dominate the artistic depiction of Hagar throughout history: the farewell scene in which Hagar and Ishmael depart from Abraham's home and the desert/wilderness scene in which Hagar pleads with God for water to sustain Ishmael's life. In nineteenth-century America, the scene in the wilderness becomes prominent because it emphasizes Hagar's role not as sexual outcast but as loving mother; this portrayal elicits sympathy for Hagar in her weakened role as loving mother/beseeching nurturer rather than that of sexualized creator of life.

Hagar art proliferated in nineteenth-century America, when the wider dissemination of artwork beyond elite patrons and private collections was made possible through graphic reproduction, such as steel engraving, lithography, and chromolithography. From the 1840s onward, periodical art in the form of increasingly refined graphic reproduction made "the aesthetic available to everyone."[35] In America it was the paintings of Hagar in the desert, rather than the farewell scene, that elicited the most attention. Among earlier paintings, Giovanni Benedetto Castiglione's romantic "Hagar and the Angel" brings us closest to the ubiquitous elements of the wilderness scene that characterize Hagar in popular nineteenth-century American artistic representation: a powerfully drawn, lamenting Hagar in fluid robes kneeling a "bowshot" (Genesis 21:15) away from her thirst-parched son, an emptied water vessel lying at her feet.

At least seven Hagar works were probably seen by many nineteenth-century Americans in the form of paintings, engravings, or lithographs. Americans early in the century may have been familiar with Corot's art, although there was no full exhibition of his paintings in this country until 1946, in Philadelphia.[36] The famous French lithographer Celestin Nanteuil (1813–1873) engraved Corot's 1835 "Hagar in the Wilderness" (Figure 1). Since French lithography was frequently imported to the United States during the early years of the century, it is at least possible that Americans saw Corot's Hagar as an engraving.[37]

One Hagar painting that would have been familiar to nineteenth-century American gallery visitors was Benjamin West's "Hagar and

Figure 1. Jean-Baptiste-Camille Corot, "Hagar in the Wilderness" (1835), a painting probably familiar to some nineteenth-century Americans. All rights reserved, The Metropolitan Museum of Art, Rogers Fund, 1938. (38.64)

Ishmael" (1803)[38] (Figure 2). The first overt periodical reference in America to a Hagar painting *in* America is the "Baroccio" engraving named as the inspiration for a poem entitled "Hagar" in the April 1840 *Southern Literary Messenger*.[39] This is a probable reference to Barocci, a sixteenth-century Italian painter and printmaker, which suggests that some Americans may have been aware of his painting "Hagar and Ishmael" (Figure 3).

Prud'hon's untitled engraving (Figure 4) accompanied an essay entitled "Hagar in the Wilderness" in the June 1844 *Christian Parlor Magazine*, an attempt by the religious periodical press to compete with popular secular periodicals. The next year brought Charles Eastlake's "Hagar" in the keepsake volume the *Diadem for 1845: A Present for All Seasons* (Figure 5). The famous Philadelphia publishing firm of Carey and Hart produced the giftbook, and Carey apparently owned the Eastlake Hagar painting from which the engraving was taken. *Godey's Lady's Book* for June 1847 mentions the inclusion of Eastlake's Hagar in the "Carey Collection" at the Philadelphia Academy.[40] One of the few departure

Figure 2. Benjamin West, "Hagar and Ishmael" (1803), which was on display at the Philadelphia Academy of Art from 1851 through 1864. All rights reserved, The Metropolitan Museum of Art, Maria De Witt Jesup Fund, 1923. (95.22.8)

Figure 3. A painting, possibly by Barocci, denoted as "Hagar and Ishmael" by the Staatliche Kunstsammlungen, Dresden.

Figure 4. Pierre-Paul Prud'hon, untitled painting, reproduced in the *Christian Parlor Magazine* in June 1844. The inscription reads, "And the Angel of God called to Hagar out of Heaven." Used by permission of the University of Missouri-Kansas City Libraries, Special Collections Department.

scenes in American depictions appeared in *Peterson's Ladies' Magazine* in September 1852. Finally, a chromolithograph of Hagar executed from an 1843 painting by Christian Koehler was included in Harriet Beecher Stowe's *Woman in Sacred History* (1873), published by New York's J.B. Ford and Company (Figure 6).

The Hagar art seen by nineteenth-century Americans elicits what Mieke Bal would call "recognition" based on the Bible as a given idiom; that is, certain well-known elements from the biblical story are expected in the picture.[41] In reading Hagar art, the viewer "understands" the positions of Sarah, Abraham, Hagar, and Ishmael from their places in the Bible; equally, the stories of Hagar and Ishmael's departure and wilderness experiences are "naturalized," read in a deterministic way, by their familiar biblical meaning. The image of the bow/archer, Hagar's water vessel, the barren landscape, and Hagar's arms raised heavenward beseeching water for Ishmael also continually reappear in Hagar wilderness paintings.

But sometimes painters (or "readers" of paintings) unfreeze the

Figure 5. Charles Eastlake, "Hagar" (1843–45), which was exhibited at the Philadelphia Academy in 1847. This engraving appeared in the *Diadem for 1845: A Present for All Seasons* (Philadelphia: Carey and Hart, 1845). Courtesy of Washington University Library.

conventions of a picture by deviating from the expected. For example, as mentioned, one of the prominent features that occurs in these Hagar illustrations is the vessel. In terms of the biblical story, this vessel can be read literally as the absence of water, a dutiful repetition of the original facts; Hagar lacks water for her son—her vessel of water has been drained—and she turns to God in supplication. Of the engravings available in America, only Christian Koehler chose not to depict the vessel in his supplicatory "Hagar and Ishmael," and Eastlake's depiction of the vessel as full is a notable deviation from typical representation. In fact, Eastlake had painted an earlier version of "Hagar and Ishmael" for the British Royal Academy in 1830 in stereotypical terms, with the vessel lying empty on its side and Hagar reclining hopelessly with her eyes cast upward, her son lying insensibly on her lap. Eastlake's later Hagar deconstructs the former, revealing that the depiction of the vessel as empty is an individual and, I would suggest, culturally imprinted choice.[42]

In contrast to white women's Hagar fiction, nineteenth-century

Figure 6. Christian Koehler, "Hagar and Ishmael" (1843), which appeared as a chromolithograph in Harriet Beecher Stowe's *Woman in Sacred History* (1873). Courtesy of the University of Georgia Libraries.

Hagar art implicitly endorses the loss of women's power by sanctioning (and sentimentalizing) the subordinate and supplicatory position of women. If we follow Teubal's hypothesis that Hagar's loss of status marks the ascendancy of Western Christian religion in collusion with the patriarchy, then the status of the water vessel in Hagar paintings either encodes or challenges the loss of woman's power. It is interesting that in Jungian archetypology, "at the center of the feminine elementary character in which the woman contains and protects, nourishes and gives birth, stands the vessel." The vessel, according to Erich Neumann, is the central image of the woman as body-vessel herself, "bearing the child 'within' her and [the] man entering into her in the sexual act." The most elementary (unconscious) experience of the feminine is symbolized by the vessel, "for as the Great Round ["uroboros," or undifferentiated psyche where the feminine is experienced as the "all"], it is the vessel that preserves and holds fast. But, in addition, it is the nourishing vessel that provides the unborn as well as the born with food and drink."[43]

The vessel in the Hagar paintings can be understood in this way as a long-encoded symbol of the female power reread into the Hagar story by Teubal. The "lack" embedded in the vessel is represented in Prud'hon's *Christian Parlor Magazine* engraving, where the vessel is depicted lying on its side, obviously empty, as it is in the painting by West. In the *Peterson's* engraving (Figure 7), the vessel sits prominently in the foreground, an ominous foreshadowing of the imminent loss of feminine power. In feminist theory, the vessel represents the female organ that is sexual and reproductive in an undifferentiated, amoral matrix. Teubal argues, for example, that before patriarchal revision—the onset of Christianized Western civilization—sexuality was not a moral category liable to ethical judgment.[44] When God gives Sarah a child in the Hagar story, Old Testament patriarchy renders women superfluous; women's sexuality is ethically imprinted and condemned and women's generative power is occluded.

In archetypal terms as well, the wasted landscape, which is so prominent a feature in the Hagar works by Eastlake, Prud'hon, Corot, and West, also symbolizes the depletion of "The Great Mother's" nurturing potential, for in matriarchal creation myth, as derived from the observation of neolithic and paleolithic statuary, the Great Earth Mother creates all vegetation; "she brings forth all life from herself."[45] Here, Hagar and her son are the victims of a barren landscape over which Hagar has no creative power.

Feminist theorist Judith Butler deconstructs the essentialism of the male myth of female depletion by showing its patriarchal inscription in

Figure 7. "The Departure of Hagar," artist unknown, was published in *Peterson's Ladies' Magazine* in September 1852. Courtesy of Duke University Rare Book, Manuscript, and Special Collections Library.

significant cultural/historical moments. She exposes Plato's philosophy of forms as patriarchal; the woman/mother is Plato's analogy for the "receiving principle," while the father is a "source" or a "spring." The woman is thus dematerialized as "no form" that is referred to analogically as "'bastard thinking.' In this sense the human who would know this [Mother] nature [in any materialized sense] is dispossessed of/by the paternal principle, a son out of wedlock [like Ishmael], a deviation from patrilineality and the analogical relation by which patronymic lineage proceeds." The Platonic "no form" of woman—the empty vessel—is contrasted in Butler's explanation with the "phallic Form that reproduces only and always further versions of itself, and does this through the feminine, *but with no assistance from her*" (italics mine). This is precisely the male fantasy inscribed in the Old Testament's shifting of reproductive power from Hagar to God. As Butler writes of Plato, "This fantasy of autogenesis or self-constitution is effected through a denial and cooptation of the female capacity for reproduction."[46]

It is important to note that, in contrast to mythological thinking that would reinstate the feminine as originative, Butler debates any myth of essentialism. Instead, she seeks to focus on "the *de*constituting possibility in the very process of [historical/cultural] repetition, the power that undoes the very effects by which 'sex' is stabilized, the possibility to put the consolidation of the norms of 'sex' into a potentially productive crisis."[47] Butler seeks to derail Freud's and Lacan's essentialization of the vagina as lack and the penis as presence, "to insist, on the contrary, on the transferability of the phallus." Butler argues that Lacan's replacement of "penis" with the more vague and universalizing "phallus" imparts wholeness to male identity in its deflection from the morphological reality of "penis" as a fragmented body part. Butler suggests an alternative reading of "phallus" as a floating signifier from which one can question "why it is assumed that the phallus requires that particular body part [the penis] to symbolize, and why it could not operate through symbolizing other body parts [such as female erotic zones]."[48]

The transferability of the phallus—equally, thus, of source/body as opposed to empty receptacle—is suggested by Teubal's shift of bow imagery to Hagar from the Old Testament's connection of it with Ishmael: "Emblems of two crossed arrows (and sometimes a shield) became the symbols of the huntress-goddess Neith of Sais in the Delta. A stela of Queen Meryet-Neith was found at Abydos bearing the insignia of crossed arrows. . . . Could the queens whose name contained the element *neith* and whose symbol incorporated arrows have any relevance to the woman, lost in the desert, who measured distance by the length of a bow-shot (Gen. 21:15)?"[49]

Mieke Bal notes that Ishmael's hunting equipment in Rembrandt's "Hagar's Dismissal" is "a textual detail that becomes much more significant in the visual tradition." Bal locates Ishmael's hunting equipment in a textual reference from Genesis 21:21: "he became an archer." He concludes that "the quiver is enough to recognize Hagar's departure" in further drawings: "We must recognize Hagar here because we have seen her so often in company of the quiver bearer."[50]

Although Bal himself cautions that Hagar's presence can easily be overread simplistically rather than polysemically, we can "underread" the free play of the art text registered, for example, in a gesture of despair that Rembrandt elects to portray on Hagar's face. Bal's own interpretation of the quiver as affixed to the presence of Ishmael is too simplistic. The allusion to Hagar's bowshot measurement alternatively suggests that hunting references imply a phallic/feminine knowledge actually transferred onto Ishmael by Hagar.

The bow/quiver (and its container) can be conjectured as a penetrative arrow/shaft and thus as phallic; note the shape of the arrow container in Figure 5. Accordingly, Hagar's originative bow suggests a female phallus, and the biblical/artistic depiction of the bow as Ishmael's is an appropriative gesture away from polysemic sexuality. In our set of illustrations, only Eastlake employs the archer imagery that Bal identifies with Hagar farewell scenes. Eastlake's original wilderness "Hagar" portrayed Hagar reclining hopelessly with her eyes cast upward, her son lying insensibly on her lap. The full vessel in her hands in Eastlake's second version achieves a balance with the phallic vessel that is depicted on Ishmael's waist. Eastlake's art is often understood as the high Victorian expression of American and British bourgeois sentimentality. His final Hagar might be understood to neutralize, or mystify, the struggle for originative power encoded in the Hagar wilderness paintings. It is also a tidy partitioning off of woman's sexuality from her reproductive/nurturing capacities. Eastlake's "Hagar" mystifies the source of Hagar's water by showing the vessel full instead of empty. Hence the Old Testament tension between Hagar and God as originative sources—and the transfer of power from Hagar onto a white male God—is erased in the repressive tableau of Victorian codes of sexuality. Hagar is the mother/nurturer and Ishmael the earthly form of God's originative power. Hagar loses her sexual cachet; the phallus is fixed.

Judith Butler resists the celebration of woman's reproductivity because what is left out of this equation is woman's sexuality as an expression, in and of itself, of desire. Hagar's request for water from God is not so much a symbolic relinquishing of her power to reproduce as it is her acceptance of her subordinate position in a patriarchal world. Central to white male hegemony is a culturally encoded division between women's sexual reproductivity and sexual desire. The woman's experience of sexual desire is placed under a restrictive taboo that presents such desire as illegitimate, improper, less than human.

The link between the patriarchal repression in Hagar graphic art in nineteenth-century America and the use of Hagar for feminist empowerment in Hagar novels of the same period explains what white women got out of using Hagar for their feminist novels. In nineteenth-century America, women who experienced sexual desire or a more general passion were thought "unnatural." Since white women were deployed as ideal asexual mothers, not surprisingly women's sexuality was racialized. White women were regulated by what G.M. Goshgarian calls "the doctrine of female passionlessness." But "womanology," or "the scientific study of the weaker sex," expressed the possibility that "woman's purity was shadowed by a potential for depravity even greater than man. . . . the whore, that is, lurked in the madonna."[51] There exists in the pictorial Hagars the inverse "shadow" of the Madonna: in Koehler's Hagar one sees the Virgin Mary cradling her child, yet there is an implicitly inverted parallelism between one mother, holy and chaste, with child, and one "fallen" mother who must bow to a patriarchal god to plead nurturance for her child. Jungian archetypology actually deflates the dream of a sexualized Great Mother/Creation Goddess by its insistence that this archetype is a virgin. Neumann explains that sexual promiscuity was an early and ongoing part of life, but pregnancy was dissociated from sexual love, and "the woman always conceived by [means of] an extrahuman, transpersonal power."[52] Marina Warner argues the inherent destructiveness for women of holding up the impossible goal of chastity in motherhood—emblematized in the Virgin Mary—as the Christian ideal for womanhood.

The exclusion of sexuality in the Great Mother/Great Goddess archetype is intensified in the Christian contribution, according to Warner, since preexisting creation goddesses had been neither condemned nor praised for their sexual abstention until the advent of the Christian Virgin Mary. In the Catholic tradition, pains were taken throughout history to emphasize how Mary's virginity was kept *in partu* and *post partum*. Mary's lack of problems during childbirth and childbearing was ascribed to her lack of sexual desire in Christ's conception. According to medieval theologian Francisco Suarez, Mary did not experience "that troublesome weariness with which all pregnant women are burdened" because "she alone did not experience who alone conceived without pleasure." As Warner explains, "Through the virgin birth Mary conquered the post-Eden natural law that man and woman couple in lust to produce children. Chaste, she escaped the debt of Adam and Eve." St. Augustine went so far as to extol the sexless marriage of Mary and Joseph as the perfect marriage. As Warner puts it, "A mutual vow of abstinence from sex was the highest good in marriage." Strange, then, that a shadow image of the Virgin Mary in Hagar pictorial representation elicited sympathy. But Marina Warner observes the presence of "the penitent whore" figure of Mary Magdalene (another inverted analogue of the Virgin Mary) that rose in popularity during the High Middle Ages and Counter-Reformation as an "important lacuna" for the "image of human error" and as a model for the repentance of sexually active women. Both Marion Woodman and Marina Warner view analogical inversions of the Virgin Mary more positively as means for white women to discover their own creative "pregnancy"—for example, through the Black Madonna, a variant of the Virgin Mary worshiped from the Middle Ages by the Benedictine Monks of Monserrat.[53]

Nineteenth-century white women writers of Hagar fiction used a historical black Hagar as the catalytic wellspring from which to appropriate a sexual continuum of creative powers culturally unavailable to them. But it was risky for white feminists to activate, even temporarily, a sexualized Hagar in their portrayal of "white" Hagar heroines; patriarchally invested Victorian women readers, as well as male readers, deplored the inscription of women's sexuality.

Unfortunately proslavery white women writers of Hagar fiction depended on the stereotyping of black women as sexual to instigate in their texts an ultimate disavowal of their white heroines' ethnic ambiguity once empowerment had been achieved. White women writers would not have written Hagar fiction unless they could have relied ultimately on the alibi of racist constructions of white and black female identity. The opposition between chaste white and sexualized black women was ethnically inscribed in nineteenth-century racist "science" on female reproductivity. The American gynecologist Robert T. Morris articulated the racial politics invariably attached to female "deviancy" when he argued that female surgery should be determined by ethnicity: "the proportion of white women with normal sexual organs is small," he reasoned, and surgery actually might be required to improve white women's sexual receptivity, but "among black and Indian women . . . he was sure that the clitoris was 'free,' leading to their greater sexual responsiveness."[54]

Unfortunately, components of the complex and ambiguous merger between women's sexual self, creativity, and rebellion against male domination that compels Hagar's endurance as a feminist symbol are singled out and split asunder in Hagar fiction. In *Location of Culture,* Homi Bhabha maintains that colonial power fractures ("splits") internally when ethnic minorities bulldoze their way into the consciousness of those in power with their ethnic similarity. In Hagar novels, white women writers consciously seek the merger with black identity to gain qualities that they imagine they lack. The potential power of the merger, back to Bhabha's coinage of "transnational identity," suggests a positive taking in rather than the expulsion of racial otherness by white women. Southern white feminist Hagar fiction, however, dramatizes a painful historical convergence between the prebiblical reconstruction of Hagar as an African woman who is sexual in a positive and powerful way, a biblical African Hagar who is sexual by virtue of oppression forced upon her (although she "survives"), and the hyperbolically sexualized black woman stereotyped by racist white America as an apology for black women's sexual and social oppression. Only to the degree that sexuality can be recognized as positive and empowering do white proslavery feminists deploy the complex ambiguity of Hagar. Just as antebellum white feminists deployed the analogy of slavery to empower white rather than black women, so proslavery writers of Hagar fiction throughout the nineteenth century used a black Hagar as a means to an end. These writers risked the temporary deployment of Hagar's "black" sexuality/creativity to "dream" their own. Usually, when Hagar's freedom is achieved in this fiction, her "tabooed" sexuality becomes "tamed" and is projected onto her equally disappearing (disavowed) blackness.

2
Hagar
The Nineteenth-Century Myth

With a few rare exceptions, Hagar's popularity in the lithographic art of the nineteenth century evolved alongside the outright emphasis on her sexuality in domestic fiction.[1] The sheer force and endurance of Hagar as a symbol of largely southern female oppression in white women's literature can be seen in the appearance of a Hagar lithograph in "Old Mrs. Harris," by early twentieth-century writer Willa Cather. This story appeared in 1938 in the *Ladies' Home Journal*. In it, two families in late nineteenth-century America have migrated west to Colorado. The story is filtered in part through the Jewish German immigrant Mrs. Rosen, who admires Grandma Harris, the matriarch of the Tennessee Templeton family. The Templetons have relocated from Tennessee, with Grandma Harris feeling severed from her roots. Grandma Harris accepts this fate, however: she "didn't believe that women, especially old women, could say when or where they would stop." She feels obliged by southern custom to exchange her former role as ruling matriarch for her now-menial role as family servant and to accept geographical displacement as she moves west with her daughter's family. Her sad life, especially as filtered through Mrs. Rosen, is one of heartbreaking pathos.

Grandma Harris brings totems of southern tradition with her, including *Tom Sawyer*, which she reads to her grandchildren, as well as "the Bible or the continued story in the Chicago weekly paper." Her tastes, a cross-section of deep-seated middle-class southern values, include two pictures brought along to embellish the parlor: what she calls "oil chromos," "'Hagar and Ishmael in the Wilderness,' and 'The Light of the World' [Christ]."[2] Cather's use of the Hagar chromo verifies Hagar's centrality as an emblem of female dispossession within the South. Hagar connects Mrs. Rosen's outcast position—her geographical dislocation from "home"—with Grandma Harris's descent into the back-kitchen "slave" role determined, she perceives, by southern tradition.

That Cather does not activate the sexual stereotype of Hagar may arise from her focus on grandmotherly women, but it may also suggest that she was recalling Harriet Beecher Stowe's use of Hagar to symbolize racial injustice in *Uncle Tom's Cabin* (1852). Stowe's, the first overt representation in Anglo American literary history of Hagar as African American, is a desexualized Hagar. Stowe's fictional use of Hagar as the self-sacrificial mother is anticipated by the "Poet's Corner" of the *Boston Recorder* (untitled) on November 23, 1822:

> Did not the tear in Hagar's eye,
> As o'er her dying son she knelt,
> In speechless, silent agony,
> Show what the anxious mother felt?
> . . . .
> O, there's a something in the tear,
> That dims a mother's kindling eye,
> A charm so fraught with love—so dear,
> We weep—we know not—care not—why.[3]

Hagar is portrayed similarly as a self-sacrificial mother in the pages of the *Christian Parlor Magazine* (1844), a religious periodical that included publications by Stowe's father, Lyman Beecher: "The mother—her own famishing state forgotten—thinks only of her son. She has no hope—probably no wish to live, but she cannot endure to see that son die."[4] Stowe must have felt—either consciously or otherwise—that an abolitionist treatment of Hagar must necessarily repress her risky sexuality in order to appeal safely to a Victorian audience. As Fred G. See explains in his reading of Stowe's fiction, her theological treatment of maternity as a form of spiritual transcendence suggests "'an impossible elsewhere'—a maternity which hedges the ludic denial, validates the heart, and rescues [sexual] desire from its play and its scandal."[5] As we recall from the discussion of Eastlake's lithograph of Hagar and Ishmael in chapter 1, the focus on Hagar's motherhood can deflect strategically from her sexual—and powerfully creative—woman/goddess role.

Stowe refers to Hagar in *Uncle Tom's Cabin* to elicit unambiguous sympathy from a conservative Victorian audience. The slave Eliza, Stowe's principal heroine in the novel, is about to lose her son to cruel slavetraders when she desperately escapes to save her child. Stowe links Hagar and Eliza obliquely when an Ohio senator's wife empathizes through a similar loss with "the delicate woman who sits there by the lamp, dropping slow tears, while she prepares the memorials of her own lost one for the *outcast wanderer*" [italics mine].[6]

We pick up on this comparison in a later debate on scripture between Eliza's fugitive husband, George, and the good-natured but wrong-minded white manufacturer Mr. Wilson, who contemplates turning George in: "Why George, no—no it won't do; this way of talking is wicked—unscriptural. . . . you know how the angel commanded Hagar to return to her mistress, and submit herself under her hand" (134).

Stowe refers twice to a character named Hagar in the slave auction scene that includes Tom. A woman named Hagar expresses her terror at losing her son:

> The men and women to be sold sat in a group apart, talking in a low tone to each other. The woman who had been advertised by the name of Hagar was a regular African in feature and figure. She might have been sixty, but was older than that by hard work and disease, was partially blind, and somewhat crippled with rheumatism. By her side stood her only remaining son, Albert, a bright-looking little fellow of fourteen years. The boy was the only survivor of a large family, who had been successively sold away from her to a southern market. The mother held on to him with both her shaking hands, and eyed with intense trepidation every one who walked up to examine him.
>
> 'Don't be feard, Aunt Hagar,' said the older of the men, 'I spoke to Mas'r Thomas 'bout it, and he thought he might manage to sell you in a lot both together.' (144)

Of course the abominable occurs: Albert is sold away from his mother. "'Trust in the Lord, Aunt Hagar,' said the older of the men, sorrowfully. 'What good will it do?' said she, sobbing passionately" (146).

Stowe's conflation of Hagar's African ethnicity and her self-sacrificial motherhood is a potent rhetorical attempt to transfer onto African American women the empathy and adulation accorded ideal womanhood in Anglo American culture. Stowe is apparently oblivious to the latent sexual content in the Hagar biblical paradigm.

Her awareness appears to have grown, however, by the time she wrote *Woman in Sacred History* (1873). In this later work, Stowe defames Hagar as a "proud, hot-hearted, ungoverned slave-girl," a "violent, desolate creature," an "imperious rival" who should but does not accept her subservient role as a "dependent, who owed all the elevation on which she prided herself to the good-will of her mistress." Given her earlier, more famous deployment of an Africanized Hagar to champion abolition, it is simply stunning to see Stowe's later Hagar, marked and condemned by her passion and found equally culpable because of her "insubordination."[7]

The key to this shift may lie in the very poem that Stowe selected to accompany the Hagar lithograph in *Woman in Sacred History*. Nathaniel Parker Willis's "Hagar in the Wilderness," first published in 1827, was the famous and frequently reprinted poem that most likely catalyzed highly wrought white women's Hagar fiction. Willis edited the *American Monthly Magazine*, the *New York Mirror*, and the *Home Journal* and wrote prolifically for women's giftbooks, the *New York Ledger*, the *Ladies' Companion*, and *Godey's Lady's Book*. Though better known today as the heartless widow-deserter depicted by his sister Sara Parton (Fanny Fern) in *Ruth Hall*, Willis was instrumental in constructing American female culture until his death in 1867.[8] He introduced not only Hagar's motherhood but also her sexuality into Hagar discourse, something to which Stowe may have been blind but many other writers were not.[9] Willis's Hagar is proud and also passionate: "Her lips were pressed / Till the blood started; and the wandering veins / Of her transparent forehead were swelled out, / As if her pride would burst them." Willis's Hagar rejects the victimization implicit in self-sacrificial motherhood:

> Should Hagar weep? May slighted woman turn
> And, as a vine the oak hath shaken off,
> Bend lightly to her leaning trust again?
> O no! by all her loveliness, by all
> That makes life poetry and beauty, no![10]

Willis anticipates Hagar fiction by making Hagar proud and thus empowered by her passion. He also insinuates Hagar's blackness with the same covert marks of exoticism: although her complexion is described as transparent, she is clearly tied to "my own land of Egypt, the far Nile."

What happened to Stowe in the twenty-one years that transpired between her sympathetic portrait of Hagar in *Uncle Tom's Cabin* and her scathing indictment in *Woman in Sacred History*? The latter work came shortly after her *Lady Byron Vindicated* (1870), a fervent defense of her heroine's divorce on the grounds of Byron's incestuous promiscuity. Critics accused Stowe of impropriety in her position as a "lady," as they had after the publication of *Uncle Tom's Cabin*. Joan Hedrick explains that Stowe was "not prepared for the storm of abuse that broke on her," since her vindication of Lady Byron was based on "the Victorian strategy of passionlessness."[11] Thus, the adverse response marked Stowe's first and last venture into feminist prose.

In the domestic fiction she wrote after *Uncle Tom's Cabin*, Stowe condemned Hagar's sexual nature. This defamation can be understood as a narrative strategy for recuperating her own literary persona as a Victorian "lady." Somewhere along the line, Stowe had become familiar with Willis's passionate *Hagar* poem, which was reprinted with greatest frequency in the middle of the century, during Stowe's active period as an author.[12] Undoubtedly by this time Stowe had also read her friend E.D.E.N. Southworth's *Deserted Wife* and the *Hagar* by her acquaintance Alice Carey, both of which focus on Hagar's passion.[13] Stowe's later condemnation of a sexual Hagar whom she had identified in *Uncle Tom's Cabin* as African may be the result of her own concern for the public perception of her sexual propriety. Since Stowe clearly conceives of Hagar as African, her proscription of Hagar's sexuality may be read as a purposeful public deflection of her own sexually imperiled status onto a black female other. Stowe's personal motivation for splitting Hagar's image is an ominous foreshadowing of what happens when white women dream black women in Hagar fiction.

In fact, both white and black feminists have constructed a myth of Hagar from which feminists have urged female empowerment. Hagar's biblical story is perceived by feminists as a matriarchal cosmogonic myth that reverses the prevailing myth of white male empowerment in Western civilization. Savina K. Teubal, in her textual deconstruction of Genesis, for example, works to recover an Egyptian origin for the Hagar story that eclipses the "patriarchal plotline"[14] of the Old Testament. The original Hagar story, argues Teubal, told of the collaborative activities of two women, both sacred, one (Hagar) a childbearer for a priestess who had to remain childless because of her higher position. Teubal argues that the patriarchal editors of Genesis excluded Ishmael's birth scene so as to erase the "dramatic image of the intimate relationship necessary between the two women."

The Old Testament patriarchal editors intervened with a divisive rhetoric based on the prohibition of women's sexuality. Through God, Sarah conceives in her chastity, which makes Hagar's sexuality supplementary. Teubal notes that it is the Apostle Paul who ultimately labels Hagar "as 'of the flesh' and therefore inferior to the free woman (Sarah) who, though not 'of the Spirit' herself, is of superior stature for having received 'the promise.'" Before patriarchal revision—the onset of Christianized Western civilization—sexuality was not a moral category liable to ethical judgment.[15]

Teubal's suggestion that Hagar is the matriarchal *origin* of worldly power, creativity, and sexuality is uncannily like Marion Woodman's Jungian argument that Hagar is the "black goddess who becomes [white women's] bridge between spirit and body." Jungian analysts Barbara Mor and Monica Sjoo also argue that "a real, historic blackness of the early goddesses of Egypt and Africa is being recalled" in the "Black Madonna," a Hagar analogue: "The archetype . . . was once an experienced fact of the external world" that is now "stored in our genes."[16] As demonstrated above, Jungian scholars often conflate history with origin. Robert Clark labels this the essentialization of myth as inherently natural[17]—so that the *early* "Black Madonna" "stored in our genes" seems a myth of cosmogony, a tale of origin. Notably, both black and white contemporary feminists are here reading Hagar as African, spiritually and sexually empowered, and as the arbiter of the defeat of the patriarchal "power principle."[18]

None of these authors, however, addresses how the archetypal Hagar fits explicitly into the specific historical dynamics of the antebellum and postbellum South, where black women were clearly not thus empowered. For a more "real-time" link between Hagar as biblical archetype and black slave women, one can turn to Delores Williams's *Sisters in the Wilderness: The Challenge of Womanist God-Talk*, in which she argues that Hagar's biblical archetype is a good model for black women from the antebellum period through the present day, as a figure not quite of matriarchal ascendancy but of female survival. In Hagar, Williams sees exemplified the forced concubinage of black women by slaveowners, the ongoing exploitation of black women's sexuality, and the continued devaluation of black women's social status.[19] Like Woodman and Teubal, Williams also seeks to revitalize Hagar in opposition to Abraham as the feminist focus for the Hagar story in Genesis. In so doing, she argues for an empowered place for black women in the church and in history that is not celebrated in the church's patriarchal model of Moses. While Moses, Williams argues, forces the African American church into identification with white male "liberators" and capitalist oppression, Hagar represents the "*survivalist/quality-of-life tradition of African American biblical appropriation*"—the "real-life" conditions, in other words, of African Americans in history.[20]

For the purposes of this Hagar study, it is absolutely crucial to note that although Williams celebrates a different archetypal aspect of Hagar from that of the Jungian analysts, all of these feminists mythologize Hagar, in an originary sense, as a sexual being who is hierarchically lesser because of her sexual functions. Even in Teubal's account, Hagar, the childbearer, is the lesser priestess of the two female collaborators. More ominously still, Delores Williams's argument that Hagar stands for survival is flawed by her seeming need to justify the fact that Hagar, in her sexuality, is somehow "less than" in the eyes of God. While Teubal questions God's part in the moral indictment of women's sexuality as imagined by Old Testament patriarchal editors, for Williams the Old Testament God is transcendent; his actions/judgments exist *outside* patriarchal history. Ironically, Williams employs Hagar's relation to God as the crux of her argument about black women's empowerment. She acknowledges that Hagar's sexuality is problematic in the Old Testament God-centered universe through her focus on Hagar as a "sipha"—virgin—in the biblical story. That God actually stages Hagar's loss of virginity—Sarah says that "the LORD hath restrained me from bearing: I pray thee [Abraham] go in unto my maid [Hagar]" (16:2)—remains unmentioned by Williams. Instead, she notes the concessions that God makes to Hagar as a sexual surrogate: Hagar has the unique privilege of granting God a name, and God decrees her son a future ruler.

Of the three accounts, not coincidentally, Hagar appears least empowered in Williams's. Her Hagar is not a precultural symbol; she is already under the sign of the patriarchy. Hence Hagar's sexuality, which may seem so safely powerful and wondrously complex in the language of myth, becomes the very basis of her victimization. For this reason, it is dangerous to mythify Hagar at all. The real question is not what happens when white women "dream" Hagar but what happens when white women who are intensely invested in the disempowerment of "real" black women dream a black, sexualized Hagar in their own narratives of white self-empowerment.

Undoubtedly the ahistorical ubiquity of a black goddess archetype that goes against the grain of the actual-fact world makes its own case for a transcendence that resists history and goes back to a level playing ground, so to speak—an origin *against* the grain of white male oppression. On the other hand, a culturally dominant myth, such as the myth of inherent white male superiority, can assimilate any resistant myth to its preservationist goals of white male "racial purity, cultural priority."[21] Williams's Hagar, although granted concessions in the midst of her adversity, represents the "lack" inscribed by the racial/sexual supremacist onto the subordinate "other." In supremacist terms, Hagar, both as a woman and as an African, is doubly determined as the fetish of white colonial supremacy.

As such, Hagar may be thought to pervade the white literary imagination in ways unsuspected. In her role as fetish, as an imaginary "space" for sexual desire against white male proscription, Hagar can be hypothesized as the actual source behind the white male "isolato" of American romance fiction. Melville's opening line of *Moby-Dick*, "Call me Ishmael," is not incidental to the argument that the matter of the New England canonical romance appropriates the matter of the South—indeed, that Ishmael, the black man excluded, forms the heart of *Moby-Dick*, with its critical appropriation of "outcast" as the white hero's status. James Baird's description of the Ishmael foundational myth in Melville calls Melville's deployment of Ishmael an "autotype," a personally engendered private symbolization that "does not *transcend* the individual."[22] Nothing could be farther from the truth. By Melville's time, not only was "Ishmael" ubiquitously deployed in American culture but his blackness was actually a biblical/cultural commonality. The typical hero of white male romance, argues Robert Clark, is a conflation of the outcast and the colonial expansionist in his pairing with an exotic "other" who obscures the hero's complicit role in white male supremacy. But Melville's Ishmael does not require a Queequeg for racial conflation. He is himself a racial hybrid. Such "blackness" at the heart of New England literary romance suggests Toni Morrison's utterance that "the contemplation of . . . black presence is central to any understanding of our national literature and should not be permitted to hover at the margins of the literary imagination."[23]

Recovering the Hagar heroine in domestic fiction is in fact a project of double reclamation, for it entails the recognition that not only blackness but also black womanness may be at the heart of the white literary imagination and that Hagar's presence in popular culture created a literary space for the white male hero. Melville, for example, affirms Hagar as a more authentic madonna figure in "The Two Temples": "A Puseyitish painting of a Madonna and Child, adorning a lower window, seemed showing to me the sole tenants of this painted wilderness—the true Hagar and her Ishmael." And Hagar is the "lack" Pierre longs for, his "maternal Hagar" in Melville's *Pierre, or The Ambiguities*.[24]

Melville's simultaneous insinuation and erasure of Ishmael's blackness (a nineteenth-century motif in its own right) invokes another, more originary "absence": Ishmael's goddess-mother, the African Hagar. As well, an African American Hagar presence may be similarly avowed and disavowed in Nathaniel Hawthorne's *Scarlet Letter,* where Hester's sexuality is patriarchally prohibited and she is "cast out" from her child's father into the wilderness margins of Puritan civilization. According to Kristin Herzog's reading of *The Scarlet Letter,* Hawthorne and Melville were the first American writers to seek character complexity in exoticism—Hawthorne, to give his heroine, Hester, special powers invested in her Oriental and Native American traits. Women, often connected with the primitive in nineteenth-century American literature, are presented by these authors, along with primitive peoples, "as neither saints nor demons but as ambiguous human beings." And, argues Herzog, "No American author before Hawthorne had described a woman as powerful as Hester Prynne."[25]

But a possible source for Hester's powerful exoticism is the first novel with a Hagar heroine in this study, E.D.E.N. Southworth's *Deserted Wife,* which appeared in the *Saturday Evening Post* in seventeen installments from August through December 1849. Perhaps not so coincidentally, Nathaniel Hawthorne began a feverish renewal of his writing career with *The Scarlet Letter* in September 1849.[26] Southworth's second installment, chapters 4–7, appeared in the August 25, 1849, issue of the *Post*. An early character in the novel, Hagar's seventeen-year-old aunt and caretaker, Sophie, feels averse to the courtship of a minister and finds an apt place for gloomy reflection in the parlor wallpaper patterned on Fox's *Christian Martyrs*.[27] Hester Prynne, persecuted by *her* own community of ministers, emerges from prison to stand on a scaffold with her babe in her arms. The two following passages evoke a resonance. From *The Deserted Wife:*

> Sophie was silent. He [the minister/suitor] had now taken a seat by her side on the settle under the window. Sophie's eyes were riveted abstractedly on the opposite wall, papered with the martyrdom of St. Petronella and the four noble Roman ladies who suffered with her; the scene represented the martyrdom at the moment when life was offered the young saint as she stood upon the scaffold, on condition of her recantation. She stood in the centre of the scaffold . . . . behind her, leaning on his axe, whose end rested on the block, stood the executioner; on her left hand stood the group of imperial officers, with their offer of mercy; on her right knelt her aged father with his grey locks streaming on the wind, his face up-

> turned to hers in the anguish of supplication, holding towards her a babe of a few days old—*her* babe, of which she had been delivered in prison—appealing to her . . . to recant her faith, and to live for them.[28]

And from *The Scarlet Letter:*

> The door of the jail being flung open from within [marked] the grim and grisly presence of the town-beadle, with a sword by his side and his staff of office in his hand . . . . Stretching forth the official staff in his left hand, he laid his right upon the shoulder of a young woman, whom he thus drew forward; until, on the threshold of the prison-door, she repelled him, by an action marked with natural dignity and force of character, and stepped into the open air, as if by her own free-will. She bore in her arms a child, a baby of some three months old . . . acquainted only with the gray twilight of a dungeon, or other darksome apartment of the prison.[29]

Before Southworth turns to Hagar in the fourth installment (September 1, 1849), Sophie is the major heroine and, as such, anticipates Hagar in Southworth's strategy of racial confusions: she has a "mulatto" complexion, misidentifies the spectre of an abandoned wife as a runaway slave, and imagines *herself* persecuted on the scaffold. Hagar takes over Sophie's role as racially ambiguous, but not before Sophie goes on to marry a minister who in his accelerating madness becomes ever more eloquent in his sermons to an unsuspecting and increasingly appreciative public. Then the racial suggestiveness transfers onto Hagar who, as Hawthorne suggests of Hester, is the dark madonna analogue. Hawthorne's geographical elsewhere for a more sympathetic view of Hester—Europe—has an American analogue in the South, which had a large Catholic (or, in Hawthorne's terms, Papist) component.

That the Hagar tradition was intertextual is equally suggested from Harriet Marion Stephens's heavy borrowings from Hawthorne's *Scarlet Letter* for her *Hagar the Martyr* (1855). In addition, specific textual comparisons are not needed to see that nineteenth-century American Hagar heroines in the woman's tradition follow a trajectory more common to the hero of the white male romance than to the heroine of the women's domestic, or sentimental, fiction. The Hagar heroine is clearly excluded from domestic fiction's taboo on female sexuality. As noted by Nina Baym, in the woman's novel, "however they have fallen, women characters whose bodies are marked by sexual passion—whether their own or the man's—have no place in woman's fiction except as occasional recipients of protagonist sympathy."[30]

The outcast position of the Hagar heroines, by virtue of their tabooed sexuality, reroutes them out of the domestic frame into the wilderness of male romance; *their* orphanhood, as opposed to that of the domestic orphan, is tied to quest imagery. Although Hagar fiction features the quality of self-reliance and ultimate closure in domesticity that figures prominently in woman's fiction, the Hagar orphan is the warrior orphan, the renegade, the avatar of rebellion. Nevertheless, although Hagar heroines ride horses and keenly hunt, their "romance" victory is reconfigured from the white male victory of "killing their first deer at the threshold of manhood"[31] to a feminist victory of creative self-engenderment, where sexuality is ambiguously merged with their growth into the creativity that ultimately empowers them.

The fact that Hagar is a consistently southern heroine suggests, again, the intertexuality of the Hagar novels and the New England literary romance. Certainly the romance trope of America as Eden with the white male hero as an American Adam in communion with nature originated not in the New England Puritanical context of the American wilderness as savage but rather in the image of nature as Paradise. The ideological and literary "Matter of the South," so formative in Southworth's Hagar fiction in particular, is the historical moment of the colonial South. Even more specifically, it is pre-federalist, federalist, and post-federalist Virginia, envisioned by southern intellectuals such as Thomas Jefferson to be Eden. This is the trope that J. Lee Greene rightly demonstrates to be *the* origin myth of America—"America as earthly paradise" (1490s-1770s), "America as a civil utopia" (revolutionary and early national periods), the "South as a plantation idyll" (1800s-Civil War)—reconstituted onward through American history.

Greene locates the roots of the Anglo American exclusionary myth of Eden in America's South, where the concept of the land was pastoral as opposed to the Puritans' conception of the land as a "desolate wilderness" inhabited by Indians, "Satan's children."[32] American Hagar fiction doubly employs the myth of colonial Virginia as an "original" Eden and the later South as a Puritan wilderness that requires redemption. The colonial Edenic South is imagined as a prelapsarian Paradise supposedly uninhabited by "savages" or, more accurately, somehow mysteriously untainted by the blood guilt of the colonizer that lay at the heart of the "fallen" white American consciousness. Greene notes that "building upon the image of America as a New Eden, Anglo Americans from the colonial period onward appropriated, transformed, and conflated passages from the Judeo-Christian Bible to justify their exclusion of Africans and descendants of Africans from the American family."[33] The Puritan myth of the savage—now southern slave—as the cause rather than the victim of this guilt allowed proslavery apologism the rationale by which to exclude blacks from their imagination of Eden.

Greene contends that when white American romance writers such as Hawthorne and Melville shifted to the southern (as opposed to Puritan) construction of Eden, the "Matter of the South" became the "Matter of the North" in the great renaissance of American fiction writing in mid-nineteenth-century New England.[34] If, as Greene claims, the biblical origin myth of Abraham, Isaac, and Ishmael is the foundation of the agrarian southern Eden, it is also the foundational myth of the nineteenth-century American New England literary canon. Moreover, myths North and South exclude as well as include African presence as a necessary empowerment for Anglo American identity. Arguably, Melville's Ishmael gains his isolato status from this myth.[35]

Just as Delores Williams argues that black churchmen displace Hagar through their focus on Ishmael, Melville in *Moby-Dick* appropriated the Ishmael story away from Hagar. In *Moby-Dick*, Hagar's sexual desire becomes fixated onto the morphology of the male body, as in Ishmael's celebration of male sexual fluids in chapter 94, "A Squeeze of the Hand." By contrast, white women writers of Hagar fiction preserve gender identification with Hagar that makes the real-life identity of contemporary black women more difficult to slough off. Even though antebellum white feminists used the African heroine Hagar as a means to empower white rather than black women, an identity merger with "real" black slave women through this process was almost inevitable. Indeed, plot convolutions abound in Hagar fiction to wish away this "trans-ethnic" identification.

Anxiety over Hagar's ambiguous ethnic mixture usually resulted in an equally covert method of warding off the incipient dangers of Hagar immersion. After publication of *The Deserted Wife,* in fact, authors became more attuned to the implications of Hagar's ethnic ambiguity. They were aware that portraying Hagar as the offspring of miscegenation—Ishmael's role in the Bible—put them on the wrong side, as proslavers, of the stormy debates about racial "purity" and mixed race "contamination" that occurred in both antebellum and postbellum America. Their problem became how to keep the women's rights dimension of Hagar separate from her status as minority ethnic other—in particular, African American other.

The fear of "contamination" that emerges from these white writers' risky appropriation of blackness results in a backlash against black women. Not only is risky feminism (sexual passion) projected onto black women, but those black women—splintered off bad Hagars—are also made to disappear with a vengeance, while white Hagar clones remain with the "goods" of Hagar's artistic creativity. By century's end, the colored Hagar heroine disappears altogether in the white Hagar fiction of Lizzie Holmes and Mary Johnston. Johnston's work takes one of those side avenues into female liberation through the encouragement of female—and unquestionably white—female chastity. The ethnic bleaching of a woman's-rights Hagar, in the instance of Johnston and Lizzie Holmes, parallels the abandonment of black women by white women in the post–Civil War women's rights movement. It also parallels the failure of northern white women to support black women on the question of woman's suffrage; rather, they reconciled with southern white women at the expense of the "real" black Hagar. Simultaneously, these women (such as Johnston) were demonizing sexuality and playing right back into what Teubal calls the "patriarchal plotline." Paula Giddings notes that "by the turn of the century, [Susan B.] Anthony and other suffrage veterans were making way for a new generation of activists in NAWSA [National American Women's Suffrage Association]. Included were Southern white women, and others who had not been weaned in the abolitionist or natural-rights tradition." Southern delegates were allowed "to hammer out a strategy to make woman suffrage 'a means to the end of securing white supremacy in the state.'"[36] *Fin-de-siècle* Hagar fiction reveals at what price white feminists disavowed black female identity.

The project for the critic of proslavery Hagar fiction is to restage the appearance of the richly ambiguous hybridized Hagar, the Hagar who is finally resurrected by Pauline Hopkins in her revisionist African American novel *Hagar's Daughter*. By virtue of this hybridized appearance of Hagar in the fiction of white women, the memory of their twinned relationship with black women *as* women cannot be fully erased. This is the dramatized history of the betrayal of black women by white feminists in nineteenth-century America, and it is also a testament to the foundational nature of black presence in the construction of Anglo American cultural identity.

3
The Resurrected South
Hagar in Southworth's THE DESERTED WIFE

E.D.E.N. Southworth's *The Deserted Wife* (1849) (or, as it was titled in England, *Hagar; or The Deserted Wife*) was the inaugural entry into the canon of proslavery Hagar literature that would speedily follow in the succeeding decades. Although seldom explicitly labeled a southern novelist,[1] Emma Dorothy Eliza Nevitte argued in her Hagar fiction (which included also *Ishmael* and *Self-Raised*) that proslavery agrarian idealism was morally superior to northern urban capitalism. Her anagram—E.D.E.N—made her either a canny or an uncanny personification of the Jeffersonian South, which must have struck her as showing the hand of divine intervention. One can only add that having the surname Southworth must have made this writer feel even more uniquely ordained to produce a "worthy" fictional paradigm of a revitalized South.

Critics do not usually point out the proslavery dimensions of Southworth's fiction. To begin with, in her personal life in Washington, D.C., she was intimately connected with the most ardent abolitionists. She first published in the *National Era*, edited by the prominent abolitionist Gamaliel Bailey,[2] and was a good friend of John Greenleaf Whittier and Harriet Beecher Stowe. Southworth used her Washington home, Mt. Prospect "cottage," to provide nursing, food, and shelter for Union soldiers. She liked to boast about the fact that Abraham Lincoln actually slept at her home during a Union campaign.[3]

Despite Southworth's public defense of abolition, her fictional construction of an exclusionary white Eden in *The Deserted Wife* places her in the camp of antebellum proslavery apologism. She is at odds, however, with other southern women writers in her advocacy of a feminism far more ardent than was ever deemed acceptable in the antebellum South. This resistance to the South is revealed in her use of Hagar in her proslavery fiction. In it, Southworth embeds a discourse for the empowerment of women that invariably threatens the coherence of the proslavery argument. There is a paradoxical tension in her texts between her "taking in" of blackness and the racist assumption in the South that blacks are inferior and whites superior. Southworth's use of a covertly black Hagar heroine for feminist purposes produces racial ambiguities that are inherent in the project of hybridizing a black/white Hagar heroine. Although Southworth attempts to evade this difficulty by using an archetypal black goddess-heroine to empower her white heroines, she nonetheless recognizes black women's—and black people's—suffering in the present moment of the antebellum South. This identification with blackness "taints" her mythological construction of a pre-African American Edenic South, despite her final rhetorical strategy of expelling black identity and reasserting white supremacy and "purity" through a ritual cleansing of Hagar's blackness.

The conscious disavowal of Hagar's hybridity, illustrated in the white pictorial Hagars of the time, is the necessary prerequisite for "dreaming" black Hagar in America. Although this Hagar enables the white woman's idea of "self," her black womanness must be repressed as well as catalyzed so that white women can imagine themselves both empowered and untainted. They seek empowerment *through* the idea of a black sexualized woman who is more rebellious, archetypically creative, and sexually racy than they dare to be in a patriarchal culture. In this reduced sense, black womanhood becomes the evacuated vessel through which white women's creativity is born. This process replicates Judith Butler's gender paradigm about Plato's conception of woman as a "no thing" through which men emerge "to be."[4]

It follows that Hagar's very blackness in *The Deserted Wife* is predictably obscured. Hagar is described as a "slight dark girl" who has been orphaned in her ancestral home and entrusted to her older cousin, Sophie. Sophie unintentionally revictimizes Hagar by marrying an abusive man, at which point Hagar is displaced from her home and doomed to an attic subsistence of little food and little love. In her adulthood, Hagar is victimized a third time by her husband's abandonment. In a cogent reading of Southworth's quest imagery in *The Deserted Wife*, Susan Harris nevertheless underreads Hagar's darkness as an autobiographical reference to Southworth's own childhood as a slight, dark little girl unloved and neglected.[5] Harris may well have found the core of Southworth's perhaps unwitting empathy with black women. But Southworth continually exceeds "dark" whiteness in her obsession with

Hagar's darkness: Hagar is a "black kitten" (40, 74), "dark complexioned" (51); her face is "deep carnation" (83); and she has "purple lips" (69). Her husband calls her a "wild, dark little savage" (101). Even Hagar's horse is "Prince Starlight, the Black Prince" (141).

Southworth also provides the clue to Hagar's Africanized ethnicity by renaming her heroine after the implicitly Africanized biblical model. She is "the orphan heiress of a ruin and desert, the infant Agatha—or, *as from her wild dark beauty,* she was nicknamed *Hagar*" (10) (first italics mine). The desert imagery is clearly biblical; the orphan status is the appropriation of Ishmael's mixed-race, absent-parent status that is endemic to feminist Hagar fiction. The connection between the renaming of Agatha as Hagar and her "wild dark beauty" is a signal of her heroine's Africanized identity.

In Hagar, Southworth crosses ethnic boundaries so as to endow her heroine with archetypal mythological status. For Southworth, Egypt in particular is the originative home of what we can call "power goddesses." Hagar's darkness, Southworth explains, is an "Egypt complexion" (101). In her heroine's triumphant success in epic opera—the vehicle through which she will redeem herself and, ultimately, the patriarchal antebellum South—Southworth describes Hagar dressed in black velvet, with "tresses . . . held back by a serpent whose scales were formed by overlapping emeralds" and whose bare arms have "serpent bracelets twined around them" (168). Snakes in Hagar's hair and entwining her arms suggest many ancient earth goddesses, including the Egyptian Isis.[6] Hagar is apotheosized by her most exuberant admirer, Gusty: "Hagar the Egyptian—the Spirit of Music—the Queen of Song—Hagar of the Lightning. . . . Hagar, the Gypsy—Hagar the Indian" (166). Even more to the point, the narrator suggestively speculates that her wild nature "was transmitted from some Egyptian long since" (43).

The absent reference to African American ethnicity is masked by references to Egypt, the Indian, and the Gypsy; each has an extinct or romanticized status that does not pertain to African American identity in antebellum America. As Ellwood Perry explains, American painters of the Romantic period (1780–1880) depicted "exotic scenes that were far removed from the present time and place," seen as "finally descending into the melancholy twilight of near extinction." On the other hand, black people were painted in a "crudely stylized" form "bordering on the emblematic and calling for preconditioned responses to the question of racial inferiority or racial justice."[7]

The Gypsy, the Native American, the Egyptian are notable stand-ins for African American ethnicity in nineteenth-century America.[8] Of the three, the Egyptian was beyond a doubt the most explosive. Egypt had tremendous power over the minds of Anglo Americans in the nineteenth century because it had been discovered by scientists to be the originative seat of civilization. The Frenchman Jean-François Champollion deciphered Egyptian hieroglyphics early in the century that confirmed convictions about the superiority of Egyptian civilization, and events such as the presentation of an Egyptian sarcophagus to the city of Boston in 1823 led the American public to value Egypt's ancient and civilized nature.[9] Unlike marginalized Gypsy and American Indian ethnicity, Egypt's empire—long extinct—implied a compelling mythos of originative power that actually finessed the American myth of Eden as civilization with its more ancient "before-timeness."

The awe for Egyptian civilization inspired by Champollion's "science" of hieroglyphics could not have come at a more inconvenient time for the proslavery South. The legal argument for exempting African Americans from constitutional privileges hinged on the assertion that nonwhites were less than human. Linking Africans to the ancient civilization of Egypt refuted that idea. The first issue of the *African Repository* (1825) referred specifically to ancient Egypt and to the claim of the Greek historian Herodotus that ancient Egyptians were black to argue that civilization itself originated from the African race.[10] The question of Cleopatra's possible blackness was vehemently debated in nineteenth-century America.[11]

Southworth was playing with fire in linking Hagar to Egypt. Not only did she connect Egypt to Africa in doing so, but she also invested black Hagar with a mythical power that traumatically destabilized arguments used to justify slavery in the South. A whole phalanx of genetic scientists rallied to the cause of denying an Africanized Egypt. Postcolonial scholar Robert Young notes that "Egypt, as the earlier civilization, developed in Africa, clearly represented the major stumbling block to the claim for the permanent inferiority of the black race which, it was alleged, had never created or produced anything whatsoever of value."[12]

Samuel Roberts, a member of the British and foreign Bible Society, argued in 1830 that ancient Africans should be distinguished from ancient Egyptians. The Africans, noted Roberts, were the Old Testament "antidiluvians" who "proceeded scarcely beyond that line of civilization within which we should now include the lowest of our species." The flood, he conjectured, must have wiped out those people, so that they could not be related to the advanced Egyptian civilization.[13]

Egyptologist George Gliddon warned proslavers against the consequences of an African Egypt in his best-selling *Ancient Egypt* (1843). Samuel Morton of Philadelphia published his groundbreaking *Crania Americana* (1839) to establish that Caucasian, American Indian, and African American skulls were different from one another but prototypical to themselves across time. In addition, he argued that the crania showed some races superior to others. Gliddon collaborated with Morton for *Crania Aegyptiaca* (1844) by providing mummy heads that "proved" Egyptians were not blacks, although Africans might have been present in Egypt as servants. Josiah Nott, professor of anatomy at the University of Louisiana, with a medical practice in Mobile, Alabama, asserted that the mulatta was a hybrid less fertile and constitutionally weaker than either of her parents; he thus contributed to arguments against racial miscegenation. The presence of Africans in Egypt, according to these theorists, was the reason Egyptian civilization eventually fell. Nott commented on the results of hybridization: "Positive historical facts prove too, that Egypt has been conquered in early times by various inferior tribes, and the blood of her people adulterated. . . . This adulteration of blood is the reason why Egypt and the Barbary States never can rise again, until the present races are exterminated, and the Caucasian substituted."[14]

The list of ethnic theorists is incomplete without Harvard "natural" history professor Louis Agassiz, who admired Morton and in the 1850s added his prestigious endorsement to the theory of separate creation. Agassiz's slave daguerreotypes, taken in South Carolina and discovered by Harvard's Peabody Museum in 1975, took on the status of "natural facts" as opposed to subjective photographic representations. The implicit standard of the Caucasian ideal that underlay Agassiz's interpretive analysis was rationalized as science, and Agassiz was able to authorize racial types based on a hierarchy of intellect and morality undermining African equality.[15]

Southworth had to have known of the Egypt-Africa debate that was the central pivot for justifying or condemning slavery as a legal and benevolent institution in antebellum America. *The Deserted Wife* is traumatized by the irreconcilable clash between two opposing myths: an originative black Egypt and an originative white colonial Edenic South. The question is: Would Southworth risk compromising the "purity" of her Anglo American Eden by positing its origins in the questionable racial past of Egypt? The answer may be that the value of the Hagar figure for critiquing patriarchy weighed equally with Southworth's desire to uphold the myth of the American South as a divinely invested white Eden.

Charged with such radical ambivalence, the image of Hagar would seem to suggest that white women had little real-life awareness of black women's identity. Southworth's Hagar, apart from her mythologized status in the author's literary imagination, does not substantiate black womanness. Her Hagar "thinks" like an antebellum white woman who assumes entitlement to freedom, mobility, and privilege. It would be possible to assume that Southworth's hybridization of ethnic boundaries is smoke and mirrors, in the way that white feminists conscripted the slavery metaphor for the sake of magnifying white women's suffering.[16] Seen in this light, Southworth's feminist impersonation of the white southern woman Hagar as a slave becomes extremely offensive. The slave connection is made repeatedly. In one of her battles with her husband, for example, Hagar considers that "Yes, it was too true, her liberty was gone. The caress of love had riveted the chain of bondage about the maiden's will—the kiss of love had left the mark of ownership upon the maiden's cheek" (69). The metaphor is strained to the point of trivializing the real pain and suffering of black slave women when Hagar says, "*I have kept my thoughts and feelings down, like wronged, suffering, and desperate captives in the hold of a slave ship, fearing to lift the hatches even, lest they should break forth, spreading pestilence and death*" (119).

Nevertheless, Southworth does not simply manipulate the language of slavery with the result that real black conditions are erased in favor of whiteness. She hybridizes her suffering white woman with ineluctable elements of the "real-life" conditions of black identity. Southworth's legacy to the white woman from her imagined African woman appears to be threefold, emerging both from the cache of Egyptian mythology and from an ineradicable awareness of the enslaved black woman in her historical time. In an archetypal sense, the black woman is imagined to be passionate, wild, and, in direct connection with these two qualities, intensely creative. In the frame of the antebellum present, Southworth's Hagar is prone to self-loathing because of her color, receives double-coded responses of desire and contempt from white people (and from the white narrative voice) on the basis of her color, and is threatened by white male violence. In other words, Southworth appropriates an archetypal but also real-life Hagar slave woman for her white heroines, for whom the destabilized and unconscious identification with African American women is tenuously liberating. This identification *is* so because it unlocks the unconscious content of what the white woman feels prohibited from thinking or saying about her own fear of violence from white men. In the text, this is true for Southworth's earliest heroine in the novel, Hagar's older cousin and guardian, Sophie.

The first three chapters of *The Deserted Wife* introduce the courtship of Sophie by a morose parson (John Withers) sent to Crucifixion Parish in Virginia to replace the deceased husband of Sophie's best friend, Emily. From the beginning, Withers terrifies Sophie, and it is clearly not the terror of male sexuality per se but of male sexual aggression: his "brilliant, basilisk, greenish gray eyes seemed to freeze her eyeballs . . . she felt the glance of those glittering, cold, keen eyes entering her heart, and a chill, an icy chill, ran through all her veins" (15). Near Withers, Sophie feels "a strange pain, dissipating all the intellectual pleasures she was beginning to receive from his society," which "crept into her heart" (22).

Sophie's marriage to the coercive Withers is strangely sanctioned by the narrative voice, which proclaims that white women's purpose is to redeem their husbands through martyred patience and acceptance of their husbands' emotional abuse and economically desecrated pasts. Southworth is immersed here in the southern code that finds obedient southern women essential to the myth of a white Eden reclaimed into innocence. But Sophie's preliminary resistance to this erasure of self is a distinctively feminist voice in the course of the narrative. And it is not at all coincidental that in her often unconscious resistance to Withers, Sophie begins to associate herself with black identity.

Sophie cannot consciously acknowledge her fear of the white, sexually dominant John Withers. But she does know that her favorite painting of the sexually safe Madonna and child (13) cannot protect her from Withers, the rider "in the shadow of the forest." He picked her "up . . . where she was standing on the horse-block, scooped his giant arm, and lift[ed] her lightly to the pillion, drew her arms around his waist and cantered off. Earth and sky swam together in Sophie's vision as they went." We see Sophie momentarily from her friend Emily's point of view: "the cold, dead white face and dilated eyes of Sophie Churchill, with her fingers, which spellbound she scarcely durst withdraw, stiff and pale as tallow candles thrown in the strong relief upon the black broadcloth of the parson's coat." Sophie drops her gloves deliberately, for means of escape: "'*I want to get down and go back and get them*,' said Sophie, in an imploring voice." Unfortunately, Withers will not allow this. He leaves Sophie on the horse and dismounts for the search, sending on the rest of the party. We are told that Withers then "favored the poor girl with a look full in the face that froze the blood in her veins. She thought of the long ride they would now have to take through the forest alone, and her heart died within her" (16). Her fear of sexual violence is implicit.

Sophie is not conscious of this fear. Through Southworth's symbology, the fear is experienced as uncanny, projected outward onto an apparition, "some object crouched in the underwood," that Sophie apprehends has "the wannest, most spectral face that could be conceived, with wild eyes and streaming hair." Southworth makes the reflection complementary; Sophie, too, upon seeing the apparition, becomes "ashy pale" (17). As it turns out, the apparition is Fanny Raymond, John Withers's first wife, who has come to warn Sophie not to marry him. Fanny is technically still Withers's wife, although a wandering outcast for many years. Southworth urges the reader to see that the fate of the female outcast is potentially the fate of every woman. Fanny appears a second time as a "phantom of the forest dell" with "the same wan, spectral face—the same large, intense blue eyes, blazing in their hollow sockets, surrounded by their livid, bluish circle." "*Do not marry him*!" Fanny cries, "Look at me! . . . I *am* a shadow—a memory—a *warning*! I *was* his wife!"

The same apparitional markings appear on Sophie's face the following morning: "Sophie, your cheeks are pale, and a livid blue circle surrounds your eyes; you do not look like yourself—you are ill" (29). When Fanny had earlier cried, "Look at me!" she had "tor[n] the mantel from her breast and displayed a skeleton form, to which the tight skin clung" (28). Fanny implies that her body has been eaten away by Withers's avidity. This episode retains its drama despite later reports of the many years that Fanny has been separated from her husband. The impact lingers. Fanny's display exposes the palpable fear of male physicality shared by other Southworth characters.

The unconscious fear that these white women have of white male violence surfaces on the conscious level as a fear of the fugitive slave. This conscious fear, however, is rendered narratively ambiguous by the conflation of the spectral wife and the fugitive slave (as victims) in Southworth's text. Both loom large at the beginning of the novel. The fugitive slave and the outcast wife are shown as synchronous images; fear of them results from the repression of the heroine's real fear. She "knows," unconsciously, that the real danger is white male brute force and physical/sexual dominance. Of course, the figural significance of the black male slave is complicated by the fact that, as a man, he represents also the potential for sexual dominance feared by these women characters. As the exposed side of the hidden, the black man's sexuality is perceived in caricature; he is, in effect, the spectral manifestation of the "other," the feared—sexuality. Hence the stereotype of black men as sexually dominant is a compensatory displacement of white women's fear of white men's violence—a violence that such women are not supposed to acknowledge within the conventions of southern tradition.

But the weight of the slave/wife comparison obliterates the sexual caricature. When Sophie first describes Fanny's apparition, her friend Emily impulsively—compulsively—identifies it: "a runaway mulatto!" This, after Sophie has described "the wannest, most spectral face . . . and streaming hair" (17). "Wan," meaning pale, and "haggard," meaning gaunt and waste, are used in Southworth's text to describe a white heroine's fluctuating color. But here Sophie has to reemphasize, "I tell you *no*! The face was whiter than snow" (17). This confusion between Fanny and the fugitive slave is followed shortly by Sophie's actual encounter with a fugitive slave. He appears to her during her evening vigil, while she is considering martyrdom (her own, through marriage) and feeling a "vague terror" from her knowledge that "the forest behind was known to be the refuge of a runaway negro—a gigantic fellow, whose depredations in the neighborhood were violent and frequent" (18). In the concrete context of the novel, however, it is a white male suitor from whom Sophie sprinted away in the forest. Interestingly, of all Southworth's putatively white women characters in *The Deserted Wife,* Sophie fits best what would become the stereotypical "tragic mulatta" complexion. Her skin color may or may not hint at Southworth's original intentions for this character: "Sophie Churchill's clear olive complexion looked almost fair, contrasted with her smoothly braided brown hair, her large, melancholy brown eyes, and her brown silk dress" (15). The mulattas Winona, in Pauline Hopkins's tale of the same name, and Reuell Briggs, in Hopkins's *Of One Blood,* are both olive-complexioned, which, according to Claudia Tate, "conforms to the tragic mulatto mold."[17]

Jim Hice, the fugitive slave, appears at Sophie's doorstep during the height of her premonition, when "the rattling branches against the windows seemed the breaking, crushing, crossbar of the burglar, while the glancing of the moonbeams between them seemed like the gliding about of spirits from another world" (17–18). Sophie opens the door unbidden; "there before her, joining her, stood the gigantic negro, with wild, haggard face and bloodshot eyes" (18). With his "gigantic" male physical presence and his "wild, haggard face," Jim Hice is both Fanny Raymond and John Withers. At one point, incidentally, Fanny too is called a "fugitive" (58). As in the presence of Withers, Sophie becomes "petrified," "paralyzed." It is left to Jim to diffuse this presence, which he does by evoking a fatherly image in Sophie's filial memories: "Miss Sophie, Miss Sophie, look at me. [Note that this is the same request Fanny makes of Sophie.] I won't hurt you—how could I hurt you when I can scarcely stand! Give me some victuals—I have not tasted food in four days. Give me some, Miss Sophie!—Oh don't be scared at *me*—who used to ride you on my shoulder when you were a baby—how could *I* hurt you?" (19).

The narrative provides some account of Jim's story amid the brief paranoiac interjection that such fugitives are the "banditti" of the southern states, those who commit "the most heinous crimes" motivated by "revenge, impending starvation, or a passionate desire for liberty." Jim Hice was intercepted in an old friend's refuge by a black overseer whom he had to stab in order to escape. The narrator withholds overt judgment. Jim's escape is effected by Sophie after Withers captures him in Sophie's house by physical force: "Mr. Withers bore him down to the floor, placed his knees upon his breast, crossed his wrists, and hallooed to the old woman to bring a cord to bind him" (19). After some sanctimonious talk about reform, Sophie secretly releases him. The text, marked by racism, nevertheless promotes the identification of a white woman with a black man in a fight against white male violence. Additionally, the conflation of the fugitive slave Jim Hice and the outcast white woman Fanny Raymond foreshadows both Hagar's Africanized hybridity and the radical instability of racial color as an identity determinant. The suggestive interchangeability between black and white threatens to compromise the white racial purity of Southworth's heroines.

The impressions of the black fugitive and the white outcast fuse in the unconscious of the white woman, yet they are split apart in her conscious mind: "I tell you *no*! The face was whiter than snow!" Even this conscious division of white versus black is destabilized in the phantasmagoria of color fluctuations in Southworth's text. Her heroines flush and become wan, and complexion judgments are unstable and precarious. Although Hagar has been described as loathing herself and has been condemned for her darkness, she is reestablished as a dark beauty in various textual moments. Raymond once calls her "beautiful, piquant, and provoking beyond every other woman he ever saw," while not very long before he has called her his "wild, dark little savage" (152, 101). She is experienced by her friend Gusty as "intoxicating . . . like the lightning of a dark, tempestuous night!" (87).

In the text, Hagar's darkness symbolically stands for her resistance to male dominance and for her sexualized being. It bears reiteration that

Hagar's darkness is deliberately Africanized beyond the archetypal linkage to Egypt/Africa in the text. Hagar is twice called a "monkey" by her husband, Raymond, which in the second instance provokes her to ask if she is being enslaved (74, 90). In Southworth's Hagar/Ishmael novels,[18] "monkey" or "gorilla" refers exclusively to an African or African American. Cumbo, the "pure Guinea negress," also dislikes Hagar because of her darkness. As a child, she is "an ugly bad ting" whom Cumbo admonishes, "Go long right trait out dis here kitchen wid yourself. You're so bad I can't a-bear you—but ugly people always *is* bad." Cumbo also calls Hagar her "'piccaninni'" (140). The quotation marks render the marking ambiguous; the label allows Southworth to avow and disavow Hagar's blackness. It may not be overtly iterated, but it is not a coincidence that Cumbo idolizes Hagar's white-skinned, blond-haired, blue-eyed cousin Rosalia as her "putty little angel. . . . *He* [God] made my beautiful, lovely, good little Rose. Some ob dese days she shall be Presiden's wife, and *you* [addressing Hagar]—shall be her waitin' maid cause nobody's ever gwine to marry *you*—you're too ugly and hateful" (48).

Cumbo's evaluations conform to Southworth's fantasized construction of the idealized Mammy of southern proslavery myth, who supposedly adores her mistress's white children while she neglects and often loathes her own, with their dark color. It is a myth deconstructed by "real" history. As Elizabeth Fox-Genovese notes, "Adult slave women demonstrated fierce love for their own children." A short story by Adeline Ries entitled "Mammy" that appeared in *Crisis* (1917) powerfully deconstructs the irony of the Mammy myth. In Ries's story a Mammy's own "black baby" Lucy, her "comfort," is taken away from her to raise the child of Mammy's now grown-up "white baby," Sheila. When Lucy dies in her post, Mammy drowns Sheila's baby in the ocean with the refrain of a "mad-woman": "They took her from me an' she died!"[19]

In the triangular relationship established between Hagar, her husband Raymond, and her sister Rosalia, Hagar perceives that she is abandoned by Raymond and made an outcast because of her darkness. The only champion Hagar had in her young life was Raymond Withers, the son of Sophie's morose minister husband. But when Hagar marries Raymond, he is transformed from a gentle, kind companion to an intractable and cruel husband. He underhandedly sells off Hagar's beloved dogs and horse and insists that Hagar send her babies out for nursing because he is jealous of the attention she gives them. What he wants is Hagar back in his own bed (109). Hagar's resistance comes from what Raymond judges to be her wildness and unregulated passion. He turns to Rosalia, who has come to live with them as their ward, because her docility and emotional availability fulfill his narcissistic need for dominance. He is embarrassingly besotted with Rosalia; "his soul was absorbed" (85).

The equivalence between wildness (in this text synonymous with feminist resistance) and dark skin color is suggested by Hagar's sense that her dark skin color causes Raymond to prefer Rosalia: "[You] prefer her to *me*—could you not love Rosalia better than Hagar? . . . . She is fair, full formed. I am small, thin, and dark" (89). In adolescence, Hagar explains that Rosalia was averse to her own wild habits because Rosalia was a "city baby, used to be nursed by *white* nurses" (44). The implication is that Hagar's being nursed by a black woman caused her wildness, as if the nurse transmitted her supposedly wild blood through the biology of her nursing! By that "logic," Hagar is invariably part black. Southworth obsesses on blood origins in her texts at a historical time when "the language of blood, especially the concepts of 'pure blood' and 'pure race' [were] so deeply associated with the nineteenth-century quasi-scientific study of race."[20]

But in Southworth's textual economy, any white woman who gives in to sexual desire or feminist resistance moves into the position of blackness, as foreshadowed by the conflation of Fanny Raymond (in her outcast role as runaway wife) and the fugitive slave. This pattern is repeated again in Rosalia, who succumbs to Raymond's seduction and runs away with him, thereby moving into the ideological position of African slave formerly occupied by Hagar as the object of Raymond's affections.

Hagar's jealous fear that Rosalia will usurp her husband's affections can be read as the conscious side of her unconscious desire that Rosalia indeed do so. Hagar has been suffering from extreme feelings of marital oppression before Rosalia appears on the scene. In order freely to pursue her fate and achieve self-reliance, Hagar must somehow free herself from her husband's emotional and physical dominance, as well as from her own passion for him. As she has said, these things "enslave" her. Symbolically her freedom is achieved through her ascendance into the triumphant position of the goddess/black woman. Encased in Egyptian/Isis powers in her operatic triumphs, her passion is funneled into musical creativity, and she achieves the stature of a goddess. Hagar's tempestuous emotions create her music, "all impromptus of sudden, irresistible inspiration. . . . They would come, these spasms of inspiration, as the blast comes, and go as it subsides; come as the tide comes, and go as it ebbs. . . . She found her power, though now she played with it only for her pleasure" (117). This onanistic, orgasmic experience of music is tied by Jungian scholar Erich Neumann to "Great Goddess" powers: "Because the ecstatic situation of the seeress results from her being overpowered by a spirit that erupts in her, that speaks from her, or rather chants rhythmically from her, she is the center of magic, of magical song."[21]

But Hagar's ascension into the goddess archetype is achieved only through the sacrifice of the "real" black woman as she exists in slavery. On her quest journey, Hagar moves into the biblical position and power of the goddess triumphant, whose creativity comes from passion—her wildness empowers her operatic singing—and where sexuality as possibility remains outside of history's "taint." Antebellum southern women writers eventually split Hagar to avoid the cultural taint put on sexuality by patriarchal society. This sexuality had eventually to be displaced onto the enslaved side of the biblical model. In other words, woman's sexuality in the context of history—in this instance, the history of Hagar texts—emerges in the stereotype of black slave women as sinfully sexual. Through their alleged desire, they are responsible for their sexual exploitation by white men. Hagar's complexity marks a place of contingency—what Homi Bhabha calls "in-betweenness"—where white women can entertain the possibility of sexual desire through a surrogate otherness of imagined black female identity. Note also that the white woman can transfer the victim role to black female identity during the process of identity merger.

While Southworth, figuratively, intends to cut and run—to get out of the Africanized Hagar archetype only what she wants—her attempt to displace Hagar's disempowered blackness onto a symbolic "other" proves nearly disastrous to her project of endorsing white essentialist female power. Southworth entertains Hagar splitting, displacing Hagar's sexuality onto "blackness" and her empowerment onto "whiteness," but she also deconstructs the myth of white essentialism by maneuvering Rosalia into the outcast Hagar/"Mary Magdalene" role (173). Mary Magdalene is a stand-in for Hagar, as the next chapter on Southworth's *Virginia and Magdalene* will reveal. Southworth transforms Rosalia into the implicitly black Mary Magdalene; her seduction by the white villain Raymond transfers her, in Southworth's textual economy, to the symbolic black woman's role. Since Rosalia's primary symbolism was to represent all the whiteness that Hagar was not, Southworth risks a great deal in toying with Rosalia as the "bad" Hagar. Rosalia is the textual symbol of white female purity—"the serene little Madonna," the "beautiful Virgin Mary" (113). Turning her "black," even temporarily, exposes the radical instability of racial signification as arbitrary, not authoritative, not essential.

Two references enhance the impression of Rosalia's temporary status as a slave. In the first, piracy is connected with slave ships. After Raymond's flight with Rosalia to the seacoast, he finds out that Sophie and her new husband, a naval officer, have engaged with pirates and "captured a slave-ship!" In the nineteenth century, illegal trade in slaves was called "piracy." Rosalia exclaims, "Oh, sweet Providence! Sophie exposed in a battle with a pirate!" (131). In the following scene, Raymond sits with Rosalia in a hotel parlor in Washington, denying his own coercive role in her downfall: "Rose, dear, I am no kidnapper, no pirate" (132).

Southworth does not place her southern belle at risk for long. Rosalia's imperiled status is too threatening for the author to contemplate. She is rescued from her fugitive, wandering state (she has run away from Raymond's seductions) by an Italian countess, who is enchanted with her "lovely, snowy face, with its delicate Grecian profile, half-shaded by the luxuriant tresses of bright golden hair" (165). Her Anglo European complexion, in other words, saves her.

Meanwhile, there is the South to redeem, and Hagar is the woman to do it, if only Southworth can maneuver her heroine away from her Africanized identity now that the archetypal resources of the black Hagar have been expended. In a sense, Hagar has moved upward within the doubly encoded model of black woman as victim/goddess triumphant. After her victorious return to America, however, Hagar still must be ethnically bleached in order to redeem the South as *white* Eden. Ironically, Southworth moves Rosalia into the black Hagar position of sexual subordinateness in order to free Hagar to redeem the patriarchal myth of the South. The resultant threat to white essentialism implicit in rendering whiteness (Rosalia's) racially hybrid causes Southworth to expel blackness radically, to put it under the sign of textual erasure. Remember that Southworth was writing this novel installment by installment, with no ability to edit out her experiments. Hagar's blackness must not be merely displaced because it could always float back; it has to be radically erased. This expulsion is achieved textually through transcendence of Hagar's conflated sexuality/blackness by her ascension into motherhood. After all the attention to Hagar's darkness, this transition is strategically accomplished within the evasive rhetoric of romance speculation: "Now, whether it is the reflection of the white muslin curtains, together with her white dressing robe, or whether her many months sedentary in-door life, and her recent illness had *bleached her into a blonde,* is not known; but certainly she is *many shades fairer,* and much thinner than when we saw her last; her carnation cheek has faded to a pale rose tint; her eyes are not so wild and bright, they are larger, sadder; . . . and see while she stoops over them [her twins] till the ends of her bright ringlets rest upon the counterpane" (105). Hagar, in her illness, has lost a lot of blood; the blackness has been drained right out of her.

To achieve her Edenic South, Southworth must have her Hagar redeem Raymond; indeed, Raymond represents on an ideological level the whole patriarchal, dissipated South. On her return to America as a great, moneyed southern woman, Hagar acts pivotally to bring Raymond and Rosalia back safely within the sanctioned family circle, and she also restores her ancestral Heath Hall and establishes a home.[22] Southworth reveals early on that Heath Hall is representative of the aristocratic Old South "two centuries ago," which had "the oldest-fashioned people, with the oldest-fashioned houses, furniture, and manners in the world." Southworth contrasts these founding fathers with the Puritans, who came to America for "spiritual liberty" while those in Virginia and Maryland sought "material wealth." Ironically, these former southerners' "old ancestral pride . . . habits of idleness, dissipation and reckless expenditure" eventually resulted in northern material success and a South in ruins. Implicitly, it is up to southern women to appropriate the Puritan virtue of labor and fuse it with southern agrarian ideals to create a "garden spot." Through southern womanhood, Southworth achieves her mythological EDEN, which stamps both her place and her name. It must (and can) include white southern men within the cloak of redemption, but it excludes African Americans.

For Southworth, the fount of southern redemption is the New Testament, aligned implicitly with woman's power, rather than the Old Testament, aligned specifically with patriarchal dominance. Hagar's Bible story, her bondage and implicitly her blackness, derive from Old Testament patriarchy. Raymond refers Hagar to Genesis 3:16 to corroborate his conviction that he should dominate her. The text reads: "Unto the woman he [God] said, I will greatly multiply thy sorrow and thy conception; in sorrow thou shalt bring forth children: and thy desire *shall be* to thy husband, and he shall rule over thee."

On the other hand, the New Testament in Southworth's fiction ushers in white women's power. Hagar becomes a feminized Christ figure on her triumphant return to Heath Hall after her successful operatic career in Europe. She welcomes all her stragglers back into the fold with forgiveness. Rosalia calls Hagar "Dearest Hagar! my saviour!" and labels herself Mary Magdalene (173), this fateful image that Southworth develops in her next novel about white/black mariolatry. Heath Hall, we are told, thrives from Hagar's "redemption" (172). Since Southworth implicitly taps into the Puritan value of labor, it is interesting to observe that she actually echoes the Puritans' sense of mission. According to Bercovitch, "The wilderness/garden became their mirror of prophecy. They saw themselves revealed in it as the new Israel that could make the desert bloom as a rose."[23] The allusion is to an Old Testament passage that anticipates New Testament redemption, Isaiah 35:1: "The wilderness and the solitary place shall be glad for them; and the desert shall rejoice, and blossom as the rose" (441). Here is Southworth's version: "In a word, the ruin, the desolation, was redeemed, the wilderness reclaimed and 'bloomed and blossomed like the rose'" (172). Southworth's redeemed South is America's New Jerusalem.

J. Lee Greene's recent study of the southern Anglo American myth of America as Eden includes, among other biblical models, Abraham's outcast son Ishmael as the black Adam excluded from the Garden. This reminds us that Southworth's use of Hagar to promote the Negrophobic Edenic South imagined by revolutionary and post-revolutionary thinkers such as Thomas Jefferson and William Wirt is certainly problematic if not downright ironic.[24] Southworth, like her southern sisters, declares that it must be through women that the South is redeemed, but she goes much further in assigning women power and extending the type of power they have. But Southworth's choice of *Hagar,* a biblical model for black womanhood, to imagine her redemptive southern heroine directly contradicts her southern white Eden from which the black race is clearly excluded.

In *The Deserted Wife,* Southworth's mythologized exclusion of African Americans from the southern Edenic garden comes from her inability to blink away the vision of the white southern family as haunted and cursed by its historical abuse of slaves to gain its profits. The failure and/or betrayal of African American presence in her text is a direct result of her haunted conviction that African American presence must be imaginatively obliterated as a textual condition for the South to be redeemed. Southworth's happy ending, as she seems to see it, depends on it. For how could a black woman redeem the South "*as it already was*" if the paradisiacal past was already premised on slavery? Southworth, despite holding up the Old South as a bygone ideal, acknowledges in other texts (*Virginia and Magdalene*) that the Old South was not really Paradise because it was built on the enforced labor of black people.

Southworth leaves in abeyance whether or not the South can become a New Jerusalem with the blood guilt of the African race on its head. Sacvan Bercovitch argues that the Puritans who sought the New Jerusalem in the wilderness excluded those ethnically different from their list of those who "would make the desert bloom as a rose."[25] Southworth takes the same turn at the end of her text by excluding the ethnic threat to her Paradise. She emphasizes through the words of her character that the money for Heath Hall's "redemption" (172) was all "made in *Europe*" and that German labor has been imported to compensate "a few of the people among whom I made this money" (176). The substitution of the Arian race as a paid labor force constitutes Southworth's symbolic attempt to obliterate the white South's indebtedness to black people, to remove in a fantasy fiction, therefore, the blood guilt that condemns the Old South.

4
Hagar's Demise in Southworth
VIRGINIA AND MAGDALENE

The Deserted Wife implodes from the irreconcilable tension between the Hagar myth of female power and the proslavery myth of southern regeneration. The resultant textual failure brings on a more strenuous reworking of these paradigms in *Virginia and Magdalene; or, The Foster Sisters*, which followed *The Deserted Wife* in the *Saturday Evening Post* in 1851. *The Deserted Wife* concludes with Southworth's obliteration of blacks from the literal southern landscape to silence the dissonance of her African Hagar. But this extermination of blacks and their labor compromises her text as political discourse by severing the connection between myth and reality.

In the utopia that concludes *The Deserted Wife*, Southworth's denial of the material basis—the African American slave production—of the southern economy challenges the novel's value as political discourse. Myth distorts history in the service of an ideological purpose, but it must do so in such a way that historical distortion in effect seems historically real. Myth imitates "natural fact" mimetic representation in order to present a certain political view as authoritatively essential. In other words, if myth shows the seams of its own mythmaking—its tinkering with historical reality—then it loses its illusion of mimesis and therefore its authoritative status. Dematerializing blacks is essential to the antebellum strategy of avowal and disavowal of blackness. But the extermination of blackness in *The Deserted Wife* results in a South without slavery. Exposed gracelessly is the very denial process that enables southern myth to seem essentially "real"; that African Americans both are and are not a material presence in the antebellum South makes them subhuman, "no thing" beings who as a "no-thing" invisible labor force funded the material prosperity of the South as if by an act of magic.

The simultaneous avowal and disavowal of black labor that makes proslavery southern myth appear more "real" is a central stratagem of Southworth's *Virginia and Magdalene*. To get it right this time, to include slaves, but as a "no thing" labor force, is Southworth's driving ambition in the novel. The shift here is her instantiation of black labor in the South, but as a naturalized discourse of love rather than an economic discourse of mastery and submission. Labor as love materializes in *Virginia and Magdalene* in the domestic women's sphere, where black and white women allegedly share love through the exchange of nature's product, mother's milk. By contrast, the oppression of black men still appears in the novel, but Southworth avoids blaming white men for it. The blame for slave oppression is transferred magically onto Native Americans. In placing the male and female spheres in opposition, Southworth uses the paradigm of New Testament *caritas* women versus Old Testament punitive patriarchs so vividly portrayed in *The Deserted Wife*. But in *Virginia and Magdalene*, the male sphere is divided between a benevolent Old Testament God embodied by white males and an archaic Old Testament God of punishment embodied by the Indian.

Southworth recuperates Hagar for this novel, but through the more complex metaphor of an Indian's granddaughter named Mary Magdalene. Predictably, her foster sister, Mary Virginia, is the beneficiary of the more benevolent white male god named, appropriately enough, Judge Washington. Southworth cannot seem to avoid twinning ethnic southern daughters—one white, the other analogically African—and again the seamlessness of proslavery apologies is disrupted by this dualism. Ultimately, the benevolence of Mary Virginia's white male patriarch proves no less punitive than the patriarchal savagery of Mary Magdalene's Indian grandfather. Again, Southworth's compelling urge toward feminist resistance "taints" the myth of southern white male benevolence. Her narrative strategy in *Virginia and Magdalene* is ultimately flawed because she returns compulsively to the truth of white and black women's gender oppression. And there is an additional truth here haunting Southworth that she cannot wish away: that the white South oppressed and terrorized black slaves. For Southworth, Hagar marks the return of both repressions. Although no character is literally named Hagar in *Virginia and Magdalene,* Hagar first appears in the prayer of the outcast daughter, Margaret Hawk, who thanks God for saving her child from the inclement weather: "Thou hast heard my prayer! Even mine, unworthy as I am! Thou hast heard my prayer!" (2) This repeats a well-known message in Genesis (16:11) that God has heard Hagar in her affliction, and as such it conflates Hagar with Margaret Hawk. Hagar reappears in *Virginia and Magdalene* as both the outcast mother, Margaret Hawk, and Margaret's own "illegitimate" and soon-to-be-orphaned daughter named, fatefully, Mary Magdalene. Southworth marks both women with the Hagar/Mary Magdalene/ethnically black characterization to be found in *The Deserted Wife*.

Here, Southworth uses Hagar's ambiguous ethnicity to hybridize black and white women (through the transmission of mother's milk) without offending white sensibilities. The Hawk family and the aristocratic white southern Washington family become fatefully intertwined when Adam Hawk's wife, Peggy, nurses both her own daughter, Margaret, and the orphaned Mary Virginia, who later becomes Washington's daughter-in-law. It is Adam Hawk who notes that Mary Virginia would have died if Peggy had not shared her milk with her. In Peggy's mind, this makes Peggy "like [Mary Virginia's] second mother in an humble way, for I raised her" (6). Although Peggy's humility is literally ascribed to her lower caste, she (and her humility) narratively mimic the well-known mammy figure, since it was black women who usually nursed aristocratic white children in the antebellum South, and it was the "mammy" who was idealized as loving white children as if they were her own.[1]

Southworth encodes Peggy's "loaning" of biological functions to a superior-caste white woman within the domestic and New Testament discourse of motherly sentiment: "Whoso receiveth one of these little ones in My name, receiveth Me" (Matthew 18:5). As is customary in domestic fiction, Southworth opposes the powerful and evangelical sphere of women's domestic activities to the debased world of capitalistic exchange. But in the antebellum South, domestic discourse covers over the coercive element of slave labor. Maintaining that blacks were part of the extended plantation family was a familiar proslavery argument that masked the underlying economic oppression. As Delores Williams notes, black women's labor roles, including breast-feeding white children, were "coerced surrogacy roles."[2] Southworth retranslates black women's breast-feeding of white children from the discourse of labor into the discourse of freely given natural and maternal love. Breast-feeding was far easier than field labor to translate into amative discourse.[3]

Southworth proceeds to insist that southern white women give equally with black women in the collaborative love exchange of mother's milk and nursing. Her insistence that white mothers nurse black children runs counter to one's sense of probability about the antebellum South, where "nursing was particularly exempted from the white woman's sense of her duties as a mother"—especially from her limited sense of motherly duties toward black children.[4] Because of her shrewd political mind and her knowledge of abolitionist thinking, Southworth may have been concerned that the fictional representation of black women's surrogacy would challenge the Edenic Old South rationale that blacks were enfolded within a benevolent and noncoercive familial structure. Southworth responds by having her white heroine nurse a symbolically black child.

Mary Magdalene is the granddaughter of a white woman and the daughter of a lower-caste white woman and a "secret" high-caste white father. In the politics of exclusion, Magdalene's lower-caste status prevents her from assuming the higher status of her father in the same way that mixed-race "black" children in the antebellum South were excluded from white status through the bloodline of black mothers. Mary Magdalene is also the granddaughter of Adam Hawk, with "latent Indian blood" (38), although Southworth creates murky innuendo as opposed to an explicit reference to the Native American origin of Hawk family blood. This is in line with her mythmaking as opposed to a real concern for the specifics of mimetics. When ideologically convenient for white writers, Native Americans and African Americans were used interchangeably in nineteenth-century American fiction.[5] In Southworth's case, the ideological use of Adam Hawk dictates that he must be Indian, but, for the purposes of her myth, his granddaughter fluctuates between overt Native and covert African American ethnicity. Mary Magdalene's blackness is encoded in the comment that she is "ugly . . . so thin, and black-looking," while Mary Virginia's daughter Ginnie is "so white, and soft, and pretty, and good" (24). Of course, Mary Magdalene's ethnicity had already been suggested by Southworth's inscription of her mother as the biblical Hagar.

Southworth twins both Margaret Hawk and Mary Virginia, and Mary Magdalene and Ginnie as black-white sisters biologically connected through mother's milk. Just as Peggy gave her birthing milk to her daughter Margaret and the orphaned Mary Virginia, so does the adult Mary Virginia give her milk to her newborn daughter, Ginnie, and the recently orphaned and lower-caste Magdalene: "I take . . . Margaret's baby—my sister's baby to my own bosom, and think that God has given me twins!" (21).

Southworth's racial hybridization of black and white women within a discourse of familial love is seriously compromised by its status as a means toward the end of denying status to black labor *as* labor. The denial of black women's labor is behind Southworth's reversal of the position of black and white women in the antebellum household. The white woman's place in upholding the piety of an apology for southern slavery is illustrated by Southworth's idealized presentation of Mary Virginia and then her daughter as the maternal center of the antebellum plantation. The degree to which these two white women take part in nursing and housekeeping, respectively, is not representative of the color distribution for these activities in the antebellum household.

Not only does Mary Virginia take in the orphaned Mary Magdalene; she also adopts an outcast boy, prompting her father-in-law to observe "her talent for colonizing—we shall send you to the West some day" (24–25). Perhaps unaware of the increasingly pejorative connotation of the word "colonizing" in the nineteenth century, Southworth nevertheless shrewdly coopts this political word for the domestic sphere, where the aggressive implications of "taking over" yield to the benevolent implications of "taking in."

Mary Virginia consistently takes care of her children. She "of all things . . . loved best to be *alone* with her children"—away from the dismissed (implicitly failed) black nursemaid, Coral, for whom Mary's babies "became too heavy a burden" (25). An even more powerful proof of her primary role comes earlier in the text, when Mary Virginia takes in the outcast orphan Mary Magdalene to nurse along with her own daughter, despite the nurse's warning that she is too frail to nurse both babies. Mary disputes the point that fair-skinned women are necessarily feeble and responds that the baby will die if not taken "to her bosom." The nurse objects, "Ah, dear lady, but this strange child!—such a thing was never heard of!" "Oh yes, good nurse!" exclaims Mary, "it has been heard of, and done—Margaret's mother divided her cradle and her milk with *me*!" (24).

Black women's household labor is relegated to a "no thing" status in Southworth's presentation of Mary Virginia's daughter Ginnie as the consummate housekeeper; thus it is white southern women, not black women, who actually run the southern plantation: "Virginia began her new career with the zeal and ardor that characterized all the feelings, sayings and doings of our beautiful red-haired girl. What a housekeeper she would be indeed! what bread, what butter, what cheese she would make! what tongues and hams she would cure! What domestic carpets, counterpanes, and quilts, she would manufacture! What webs of linen, cotton, and woollen cloth she would weave! What socks and stockings she would knit!—*or rather*—in what a very superior manner she would have these things done" (61).

As Fox-Genovese notes, white southern plantation women actually thought of themselves as performing the activities of their black women slaves, much as "the typical planter . . . would note that he had 'ploughed [his] field.'" She adds that "historians have not commonly taken those assertions at face value and have recognized that a man with twenty or so slaves resorted to metaphor in claiming to perform his own labor. Those same historians have, however, been less quick to recognize the metaphor as invoked by southern women, although it bears heavily on any attempt to understand the relations between mistress and slaves in the household."[6] Southworth's narrative acknowledges the white women's limitations with her "or, rather," but mitigates this candor with her lengthy catalogue of household activities that seem to belong originally to her white plantation heroine. By the conjunction between "superior" and "have things done," she suggests that managerial tasks are indeed the real work and that black women's labor on the southern plantation is consequently a "no thing."

The message gets even more complex when Southworth shows the "benign" labor of domestic love mistranslated into the discourse of capitalism through her text's patriarchal voices. The strategic battle between love and economic discourse is waged early in the text over the question of mother's milk. At the beginning of the novel when Mary Virginia—and Margaret—are about to give birth, Margaret's father, Adam Hawk, is still furious that his wife, Peggy, was not paid for nursing Mary Virginia, and he forbids his wife to go to take care of her. Hawk also chides his wife for "refusing to take a dollar, poor as you were!" When Peggy counters that there can be "no sale of nature's tenderness," Hawk notes, "People sell everything—stock in trade, labor—that is nothing—but, their affections, their intellect, honesty, health, truth—soul and body they sell for money, and call it 'business,'—so you see yours is a very stupid feeling" (7).

No matter what the women in the Hawk and Washington families say about the nature of this transaction as love discourse, and despite the fact that the narrator takes a negative view of Hawk's philosophical cynicism, Hawk is not wrong; at least, the men in this novel do view mother's milk as an economic commodity, including Mary Virginia's father, who recognizes the need for economic remuneration for the exchange of mother's milk. After Peggy shared her milk, Mary Virginia's father, Colonel Carey, "loaded [Hawk] with benefits, recommending [him] to Judge Washington as a proper man to manage his estate." Then, "when the Judge moved into the new mansion house, upon the marriage of his son with Mary—then, for the love he bore his daughter-in-law, our foster child, he gave [him] this fine old farm-house to live in, with nearly all the furniture, just as he himself had occupied it for all his life" (7). Carey, Washington, and Hawk see a transaction based on caste and money, while Hawk's wife insists on maternal love, freely given, on democratic impulse. While Southworth clearly intends us to privilege the woman's view, her own motive for inscribing black female labor as love discourse inadvertently gives preference to Hawk's resentment of the privileged class and the liberties they can take.

Hawk's dissenting voice is a resistance to southern colonial expansionism masking itself as domestic benevolence. As a problematic "white" man (of Native American descent) separated from the slaveowning class by caste and not by color, Hawk is not automatically enfolded within the white plantation owner's familial network, as is the African slave. Hawk interprets his wife (and her nurturing fluids) as his own natural resource which becomes, to borrow a phrase from postcolonial theory, "deterritorialized" by the plantation class as no longer "naturally" Hawk's and "re-territorialized" by the plantation class as a capitalistic commodity that can be "purchased." According to Robert Young, colonialism is "the rule by force of a people by an external power." Despite Southworth's dialectical defeat of Hawk's cynical reading through the discourse of her white heroines' domestic generosities, Hawk's insistence on reading women's emotional transactions economically is a voice that resists the "alibi" of colonial imperialism. For Hawk reads the "lending" of his wife as a kind of territorial violence. Young writes that "colonization begins and perpetuates itself through acts of violence, and calls forth an answering violence from the colonized. . . . Capitalism is the destroyer of signification, the reducer of everything to a . . . system of equivalences, to commodification through the power of money. This allows a certain degree of historical specificity: for colonialism operated through a forced symbiosis between territorialization as, quite literally, plantation, and the demands for labour which involved the commodification of bodies and their exchange through . . . trade."[7]

Hawk's labeling of, yet cynicism about, economic trade—his feeling that job compensation, a house, are not enough to compensate for the lending of his wife (due to his low caste position)—threatens to deconstruct the antebellum domestic discourse that masks the capitalistic exchange of slaves with a supposedly familial discourse.

Ironically, through Hawk's complaint, Southworth materializes southern minority labor, one of her goals in making the ideology of her text seem more "real." To avoid the peril of exposing myth as myth, as she does in the conclusion to *The Deserted Wife*, Southworth elects not to erase the labor of black men and women in the fields, which does not fall so easily under the spell of domestic transformative discourse. Giving a voice to that complaint through an Indian Adam, Southworth deflects focus from white men onto minority others as the cause for the oppression of antebellum slavery. She "stages" a symbolic fiction where the originary sin of the South is displaced onto the Native American overseer whose tyranny against the black slaves under his rule is bred, Southworth implies, out of an innately "savage" instinct. One of the more remarkable features of Southworth's Edenic ideology is her plan for keeping the southern white founding fathers "innocent" by complicating her fictional landscape with Indians who now bear the blame for black male violence, which in turn is directed against the white antebellum family. It is as though in her mind's eye Southworth turns toward that legendary founding moment on Virginia soil when John Smith met Pocahontas; she places the blame for the fall of the South on the American Indian. Southworth attributes the fall of her "Adam"—Adam "Hawk"—to his mixed-blood origin. His "latent Indian blood" stirs his "stern, dark and fierce" temperament (38) to the abuse of black slaves.

Virginia and Magdalene provides a covert analogue between Adam Hawk's bitter resentment of the appropriation of his wife's "natural resource" and the stealing and raping of Indian lands. Southworth grafts a revolutionary utopian timeframe onto her setting of antebellum America. She imagines the pre-Jacksonian presidencies of Washington and Jefferson as a time prior to Indian land dispossession.[8] In eliminating Jacksonian America, Southworth symbolically removes the motive for Indian vengeance. Hence, she blames Adam Hawk for his own vengeance, which is what Wai-chee Dimock calls "blaming the victim. . . . The strategy here is to equate phenomenon with locus, to collapse cause and causality into an identical unit, to make the Indian at once the scene and the agent of his own destruction."[9]

The fear of slave insurrection was very real in the antebellum South. This fear is dramatized in Southworth's novel by the sequential assassination of Washington family heirs by an unknown avenger. That avenger, it turns out, is a black man. Placing the blame on the Indian for a series of narrative events that leads from the abuse of black slaves to the extermination of a white family takes the white family out of the loop of blame for any minority oppression and makes the white family the victim of incipient and unwarranted violence.

Southworth shifts the focus away from labor as physical oppression to disguise the fact that unremunerated labor is onerous. Judge Washington is Southworth's intended savior for the translation of any plantation labor into voluntary love discourse. A plantation household run "benevolently" supposedly operates on the domestic principle of an extended "family" that includes field as well as household slaves. As one Georgian described it in 1851: "The Slave Institution at the South increases the tendency to dignify the family. Each planter in fact is a Patriarch—his position compels him to be a ruler in his household. From early youth, his children and servants look up to him as the head, and obedience and subordination become important elements of education. Where so many depend upon one will, society assumes the Hebrew form."[10]

Hence, Southworth's portrait of Judge Washington as benevolent. Washington interprets his slaves' greeting upon his return to the plantation on New Year's Eve as "my patriarchal gathering of the clans." White slave owners typically assumed their slaves' adoration for them[11] and, according to proslavery defenders of this tradition, parceled out gifts and monetary favors on prodigal returns and holidays. This is the scene Southworth depicts to first describe Judge Washington: "Here upon this morning in the vestibule, smiling, stood Judge Washington, and from all parts of the plantation, coming up the hill in their gay holiday attire were seen his people—men, women and children coming to wish their venerated master and his family a Happy New Year, and to receive from his hands some appropriate token of regard" (19).[12]

As noted before, Southworth portrays Judge Washington as an Old Testament God, white and benevolent, counterbalanced by the "dark side" of the Old Testament God, Adam Hawk. To portray this punitive God, she conflates the sterner side of Christianity with Indian savagery: "Adam Hawk had gotten the thirty-nine articles of the [Anglican] church well beaten into that hard head of his, and perhaps from the alloy of that stern, North American Indian blood . . . all *he* saw and felt in his religion was—original sin, total depravity, the wrath of God. . . . He experienced an atrocious rapture such as might fire the fierce soul of a North American savage at the prospect of the scalping, torturing, and burning of an infinite number of foes" (39).

Southworth opposes Adam Hawk's Indian legacy of justice, not mercy, to Washington's "naturally GOOD GROUND for the seed of Gospel truth to fall on." Washington's "natural benevolence and great philanthropy" (39) permit this old patriarch, in Southworth's view, to intuit New Testament redemption: "He wounds to heal. I, too, Adam, as you know—I and mine have been smitten in the dust, but we have been raised again" (20).

Judge Washington as the benevolent Old Testament God thinks of the African slaves on his plantation in romantically racist terms as his children. Adam Hawk, Washington's overseer, however, derogates African American slaves as "niggers" (6). Hawk proposes a very different holiday for the slaves under his supervision: "Come!" he tells them. "It's not twelve o'clock yet, quite! but you may all break off there, and go to see the man hanged!" (41) He wants them to see that "the way of the transgressor is hard!" (42). Hawk is a harsh Old Testament God who calls the slaves' shout of joy at the holiday the "confounded howling and shrieking" that marked "the confusion of Babel" (41). Latent but ultimately all-too-plainly evident in Southworth's text is how she manipulates her imaginative fictional landscape to reinvent southern history. She places the blame for the South's original sin—the abuse of the slave—on the American Indian.

This depiction of Adam Hawk is not a realistic one even in stereotypical terms. Southworth is aiming not at "true" stereotypes but at ones that can be exploited to suit her uses. Hence, Hawk is presented not simply as a vengeful Indian but also as a "white" man of lower caste than Judge Washington. In this context Hawk is also a covetous and cynical capitalist whose insistence on money as the basis of trade threatens the domestic principle upon which the genteel Old South operates. What is unwittingly deconstructed through Washington's appropriation of Hawk's "natural resources" (his wife's milk) is the cash nexus basis that Washington honors in labor exchange. His remuneration for the labor of Hawk's wife threatens to unravel the lie of domestic filial labor, and it exposes Washington's real treatment of slave labor, not as a labor of filial love but as a "no thing" labor tied implicitly to the "no thing" status of the African American laborer.

In her reactivation of Hagar/Mary Magdalene, Southworth returns compulsively to a rebellious presence that fractures the increasingly more dense coherence of her proslavery antebellum myth. Southworth's commitment to feminism and her empathetic yet ambivalent identification with African Americans as mutual victims of white male oppression actually works against the Edenic South myth that she elsewhere tries so hard to defend.

White women were supposedly exempted, through the substitutive labor force of slave women, from the subordinate status of laborer. With slavery, argued slaveowner Thomas Dew, the wife is transformed from a "mere '*beast of burden*'" into "the cheerful and animating center of the family circle," making women "no longer the slave but the equal and idol of man."[13] We have already seen that Southworth's nullification of black labor requires that a mask of domestic love discourse cover over the economic interpretation of domestic work as "labor."

Dew and Southworth show gender trouble underlying the patriarchal southern system in their contradictory interpretations of how white women should behave to provide the alibi for southern domestic discourse. White women suffer oppression more subtly than black women. Mary Virginia, for example, must gain leave from her father-in-law to visit her dying foster mother (21). Judge Washington also dictates how much emotion his daughter-in-law should exhibit during the pain of her childbirth, when she should go back into society to find another husband after widowhood, and whom his granddaughter should marry. Hagar, on the other hand, is Southworth's rebellious southern daughter who exposes the gender oppression "hidden" in the loving law of white husbands/fathers. While Southworth has her white Madonna-like granddaughter Ginnie embrace household duties to emphasize that white southern women rather than black women actually run the southern plantation, the rebellious granddaughter, Mary Magdalene, rejects her equal housekeeping "privileges" and "aver[s] that she was sure she should never reach eminence by any of these roads" (61). Her foster-sister, Ginnie, rightly interprets Magdalene's refusal as a rebuff against the love value of housekeeping. Magdalene is not a "true" southern daughter in her scorn for household duties, and her refusal to be a housewife challenges the notion that servitude is voluntary.

Magdalene also bears the "taint" of women's sexuality, which was rendered illegitimate by the white southern patriarchy; in doing so, she bears her white twin sister's unconscious desire to be sexual, a desire hidden within her role as the Virginal Mary. Not coincidentally, the names of all the heroines in Southworth's second Hagar novel are derivatives of Mary: Mary Virginia and Mary Magdalene, the two granddaughters; Mary Virginia and Margaret Hawk, their mothers; and Peggy Hawk, Margaret's grandmother. This is a mariological paradigm imagined, appropriately, by a woman writer whose Roman Catholic ancestors settled in southern states with names that evoke the Virgin Mary—Maryland and Virginia—as does Southworth's name, E.D.E.N.[14] Virgin Mary iconography actually informs the implicit ideal of antebellum white female chastity/purity imagined by an aristocratic southern population that contained many Catholics and Episcopalians. But Southworth adds "Hawk" as a surname and "Mary Magdalene" to her list of Marys. As in *The Deserted Wife*, she hybridizes symbolically white/pure and ethnically other/fallen women.

Southworth aligns her "pure" Marys with Judge Washington, the Old Testament God of white benevolence, and her "unchaste" Marys with the punitive Adam Hawk. Hawk fantasizes his exiled daughter as "shameless," "dressed up in rouge and satin and jewels, now revelling off the old year among companions only less degraded than herself!" Hawk transfers his guilty desires onto his daughter through the alibi of external biblical authority: "No more of her! . . . I wish I *knew* that she was dead! . . . Even as Abraham would have offered up his spotless son—even as Jeptha sacrificed his virgin daughter—so I would immolate my fallen child! would purify her as by fire!" (8).[15] Hawk's fanatic and sexually charged fantasies and condemnation of his outcast daughter are alibied off on his Old Testament vested authority.

Sexual rebellion—the secret marriage of the southern daughter to an ambiguous other—becomes the broader battle between the religiously fanatic Adam Hawk and his unrepentant granddaughter, Mary Magdalene. Her active rebellion and lust for vengeance are mirror images of Hawk's: "Adam Hawk did not stop to consider that his first slave, his *wife*, had been of another race—that as for his *child*, traits of character are not reproduced in the second, but in the third generation, and that in his grandchild his infant SELF was opposed to him" (46).

Mary Magdalene's infant self as a vengeful Adam Hawk-like Native American is a narrative disavowal of women's rebellion as a positive action. In addition, Southworth's narrative opposition between patriarchal and matriarchal religion (as a resistant forgiveness) actively reinforces the patriarchal inscription of women's sexuality as sinful, since the text's white Marys actively forgive sexual sins, thereby implying that women's sexuality requires forgiveness. Peggy Hawk characterizes her foster child, Mary Virginia, as the Virgin Mary Intercessor who can intervene for Margaret against her father's Old Testament fanaticism: "Mary, too, wept when she [Margaret] was lost; but Mary believes her still—so the sinless feels for the sinful. . . . The good ever pity and wish to recover and redeem the erring" (8).

The elder Mary Virginia's role as the Blessed Virgin Mary is confirmed by several of the plot machinations that Southworth employs in *Virginia and Magdalene*. Although Mary Virginia gives birth to a child named Mary Virginia (Ginnie) "for her patron saint, the spotless Virgin," this "child-mother" (26) is widowed before the birth, which endows the heroine with the quasi-status of virgin birth. More tellingly, a virgin birth for Mary Virginia is suggested by her earlier adoption of a dead beggar-woman's young baby, whom Mary Virginia names Joseph after her dead husband. This saintly child, Joseph, has premonitory visions and intuits his mother's thoughts. In Southworth's religious amalgamation, Joseph is both Christ's father and Christ, although Southworth slyly shifts the focus from his saintliness to that of his sister, the "Virgin Mary." Her potential saintliness becomes clear when Joseph reassures his mother that her preference for her biological child is a holy choice: "If you love the baby that *God sends you straight from Himself* better than me, it will be because it will be a gooder child than I am, and then I will be like the little John in the Holy Family" (18) (italics mine).

With her emphasis on mariology, Southworth replaces Christ with the Virgin Mary as the holy child in her southern family. In other words, Southworth replaces a God-centered universe with worship of a passive white mariological system of governance—one whose major function in the symbolic Edenic South is not to rebel against injustice but to implicitly forgive white men as well as "othered" women. In this scheme, Mary Magdalene's sexuality is condemned simply by its need to be forgiven.

The pallidly unconvincing nature of Southworth's chaste Virgin Marys suggests her feminist resistance to her own mariological paradigm of redemptive forgiveness, obedience, and chastity that will usher in the New Eden of the South. Southworth clearly admires and identifies with Hagar, her southern rebellious daughter. Her Magdalene rebels in any number of ways, including defiance of her stern grandfather, Adam Hawk, rejection of safe haven from the Washingtons, pursuit of her passion in a secret marriage that leads her to Europe (at which point she is abandoned), and the assumption of self-reliance and Hagar-like careers. Mary Magdalene becomes a Paris playwright, a teacher in the American Southeast, and finally a famous tragic actress before she is chastened by her own vengeful behavior. Southworth invents her rebellious southern daughter (Hagar) through the conduit of mixed ethnicity—something not white in the heroine that enables her rebellion—in order to breathe life into the air that is stifling for women in this supposedly Edenic, male-dominated southern world.

As Elizabeth Moss notes, antebellum southern women writers did not seek any freedoms for women outside the permissible parameters of patriarchal southern marriage.[16] Southworth invariably turns to ethnic "othered" archetypes to enrich the evacuated center of southern female identity. The turn to an "other" Indian heroine deflects strategically from the Africanized Hagar that caused so much ideological tension in *The Deserted Wife* because of the real-life connection between Hagar and slavery's abuses. Here, Mary Magdalene is ethnicized as American Indian with the archetypal features of a goddess instead of a savage, sexualized Indian. This Indian splitting is parallel to Hagar splitting in *The Deserted Wife*. Magdalene's foster sister praises her as "My Indian princess! my Semiramis! my Joan D'Arc" (70). Formal dress achieves in Magdalene the same Hagar-like apotheosis: "Indeed, Lena [Magdalene], you are superb, empress-like! goddess-like!" (78). In true Hagar form, Mary Magdalene also experiences the sublime: "When out of sight of land, the vast panorama of the unbounded waters aroused all the power . . . of Magdalene's strong and ardent enthusiasm; and this stimulated passion for the sublime and terrific" (94).

Hagar heroines in both *The Deserted Wife* and *Mary Magdalene* achieve their individuality by assuming a male role. Hagar cuts off her hair and dresses like a man after her abandonment (148), taking on male privilege, and Magdalene boldly departs from the protection of the Washington household and journeys alone to become a governess on a Natchez plantation. Unlike fictional English governesses, she is not forced economically to take such a position and she does so over the Washington family's protests: "Magdalene determined to relieve them [the Washingtons] of her company, and herself of her insupportable ennui, by going out into the world alone and upon her own responsibility" (86).

Ultimately, in *Mary and Magdalene,* feminism is lost because power is not portrayed as an asset for southern women. In *The Deserted Wife,* Hagar's operatic career is deemed admirable, as is her ability to revivify her marriage through taking on the traditional male role of economic provider. Hagar's empowerment is closely tied to her archetypally feminine creative gifts as well as to the conventionally masculinized property of self-reliance. Implicitly, in *The Deserted Wife,* the apotheosized new woman has the power to raise the South. In *Virginia and Magdalene,* however, Magdalene's artistic ventures are treated skeptically and perfunctorily, as minimal consolations to her. Southworth polarizes the power of men as a negative force; their compulsion to punish is depicted as the shadow specter of their power. Unfortunately, it is only in these patriarchal terms that she can imagine a source for this Hagar's power. Empowered and powerful, Magdalene experiences the (manly) compulsion toward revenge against her deserting husband that eclipses any attempt at self-growth or career success: "Her soul had passed through a tremendous crisis, a terrible experience. She had, as it were, suffered death; and a new resurrection, more awful than death!—a 'resurrection to damnation!.' . . . One fell purpose filled her life—Revenge! . . . arousing all her deep, stern, unforgiving, unrelenting Indian nature" (103).

Magdalene's "masculinized" independence and her desire for revenge are linked to "that latent Indian nature which forbade her to be quiet any where for any length of time" (91)—"the Indian blood! the untamed nature! the restless energies! the vagrant disposition!" (86). Magdalene's Indian blood explains what was regarded as her unwomanly passion: "She felt that her own strong, energetic, and half-savage spirit would revel alike amid the wild warfare of winds and waves, and amid the powerful emotions of terror, grief and despair they would excite in men" (94).

Southworth's two-way street in depicting Magdalene's Indian ethnicity is prefigured by the familiarity of the Indian in pre–Civil War frontier romances by such authors as James Fenimore Cooper, James Hall, Catharine Maria Sedgwick, and Lydia Maria Child. They employ stereotypes, including what Louise K. Barnett calls "The Bad Indian," which is relevant to the revenge motive and savagery that Southworth applies to Adam and Magdalene Hawk. Defined as "implacable enemies of the whites," according to Barnett, and as "perpetrators of a monotonously repeated pattern of aggression against them," the Indians were condemned by New England colonialists as "salvage people . . . cruell, barbarous, and most trecherous, being most furious in their rage, and merciles wher they overcome; not being content only to kill, and take away life, but delight to tormente men in ye most bloodie manner that may be."[17]

But there is also the more positive, complicating archaic myth of Indians as "Noble Savages." Magdalene is not only impelled by savage moods but is an "Indian princess" (47) endowed with pride and mystical creative possibilities through her Indian ethnicity. This noble savage imagery accords with the pre-fictive image of Indians held by early Virginians, in contrast with early Puritans. Barnett explains that "Virginia's government regarded Indians as worthy opponents rather than demons. However popular the gothic Indian engendered by the Puritan chroniclers, another image of the Indian, which would establish itself in nineteenth-century thought, originated in the Virginia tradition. In the writings of Captain John Smith and his men, Powhatan was habitually and seriously referred to as 'the great King' or 'Emperor.'"[18]

This difference between the historical northern and southern views of the Indian helps to explain why Southworth can project her own ambivalence about a woman's self-empowering anger onto a more complex depiction of her heroine Magdalene's Indian ethnicity. Southworth sees her heroine's passion and energy as both self-generative and ultimately catastrophic to the southern patriarchal plantation system.

Finally, however, Indian ethnicity is no more than a coded layering for the black Hagar that Southworth creates in Mary Magdalene. Her mother, Margaret, is what Jungian critic Marion Woodman identifies as the "poor little match girl outside the window looking in at the Holy Family on Christmas Eve." Woodman uncannily approximates Southworth's description of Margaret Hawk on a "New Year's Eve Night [where] from many a warm and comfortable home came out the festive sounds, glanced out the festive lights athwart the frozen snow and into the fierce and howling night . . . [where] through the fierce, black cold, toiled on this young, slight, thinly clad girl. . . . toward the lighted window. . . . She will go there and look in and see them. . . . She turned with difficulty her eyes upon her father's face. It was sad and stern, and harsher than ever" (4–5).

It is from this position of rejection that Woodman argues the white woman will find her empowering archetype, the "Black Madonna," the unconscious "dark" self that holds anger but creativity as well. For Woodman, as for Southworth, acquaintance with that "dark self" is the condition of woman's sexual and creative fulfillment. Coincidentally—or *not* coincidentally—Woodman calls her outcast matchgirl "Hagar, the dark Egyptian, freed bondswoman of Abraham, who is cast into the desert to care for her son, Ishmael."[19] Drawing this connection, indeed, says much about white women dreaming black women in the twentieth century as a significant (unconscious) repetition of the nineteenth-century past: one might ask why this dream of black women as empowering, rejected, and angry recurs for white women. Anachronistic to Southworth's text, Woodman's black Madonna/Hagar provides a proleptic resonance.

In her novel *Broken Pledges*, Southworth attributes "ardent passions and impulsive temperament" exclusively to "the African Negro,"[20] which is a more telling clue that Hagar is more African than Indian. Arguably, Magdalene's dubious status in the elite antebellum southern family also encodes her African American status. Her participation in society courtships is dependent on whether her paternal grandfather, the politically influential General—soon to be Governor—Mountjoy, will recognize her as his granddaughter after originally prohibiting the marriage between his son and her mother.²¹ Her parents "marry," but the marriage is rendered "illegal—null and void" by the grandparents, as the status of a manumitted slave was often rescinded by southern "law" after the death of an owner. Just as Adam Hawk resents the upper-class appropriation of his wife's nurturing services, so does Victor Washington's punishment for marrying a white woman of lower caste expose the coercive force underlying the supposedly benign southern plantation system. It is a system most punitive for African slaves, but one that binds black slaves and the white lower class. Mary Magdalene increasingly identifies with rebellious and criminalized African Americans (not Indians) on a deeply psychological level. Her response separates her from her Native American father's historicized hatred of African Americans and aligns her instead with African American identity.

As we have seen, *Virginia and Magdalene* provides a covert analogue between Adam Hawk's bitter resentment of the appropriation of his wife's "natural resource" and the stealing and raping of Indian lands by both colonial and postrevolutionary white people. In Southworth's novel, Adam Hawk's abusive treatment of African slaves in turn provokes an act of reprisal from a vengeful black man against the white plantation family who put their own black slaves (their "resources") in harm's way by rendering blood-guilt payment to Adam. Washington hires Hawk as overseer over his black slaves to pay for the milk rendered his future daughter-in-law by Hawk's wife. Despite Southworth's continual disclaimer that white men have no part in—or blame for—Indian or African American violence (148), the specter is raised that white men's treatment of ethnic minorities sets the violence in motion. In the case of Magdalene's anger, Adam Hawk's abuse of his granddaughter places the rebellious southern woman in a situation exactly analogous to that of the incipiently rebellious African American slave. Southworth warns implicitly that the rebellion of the southern woman against her white father-husband-grandfather will precipitate the violent uprising of black hands against the antebellum South. This fear of slave insurrection was already present in Southworth's first long novel, *Retribution* (1849), with its subplot on the Haitian slave uprising that warned of similar dire consequences for racial injustice in the American South.²²

In her depiction of minor African American characters in her subplots, Southworth subscribes to the stereotypically romanticized view that antebellum African American slaves are incapable of rebellion because of their "simple goodliness, kindliness, and affectionateness."²³ On the basis of this stereotype, it makes sense that she would turn to

Indian ethnicity to explain the origin of Magdalene's rebelliousness. But in the "real" as opposed to the "historical" timeframe of *Virginia and Magdalene,* Southworth ties in Magdalene's rebelliousness with the African American race. There was reputedly an African ethnic equivalent to Magdalene's mixed-race status: the mulatto. Southworth turns to the mulatto she names Abram Pepper for her portrait of the Carey and Washington families' dark assassin. By drawing this connection between Magdalene and the incipiently rebellious African American mulatto, Southworth makes her central ideological point.

In her reading of rebellion into the mulatto slave character, Southworth anticipates post–Civil War arguments against racial amalgamation by "attributing the worst outrages [of the African American race] to the mulatto." In the post-Reconstruction South, according to George Frederickson, discrediting the mulatto was one way "of reconciling the traditional stereotype of black docility with the image of bold and violent offenders against the color line which was central to the new propaganda" that promoted lynching, among other racist acts. Mulattoes were argued to be degenerates evolving back into slavery or, more ironically, were considered prone through their white blood to exhibit traits of white male aggression.[24] This latter argument was actually made before the war. Given Southworth's own ideological agenda of exempting whites from ethnic traits of violence, she subscribes to the degenerative theory.

Mary Magdalene's first experience of rebellion against her grandfather occurs when she disobeys his order to stay away from the hanging of a black man who had stolen sheep. He is pardoned at the final moment by the "benevolent" white patriarchal system. This is her first experience of identification with an African American. Although she obeys her grandfather and does not go to town to view the hanging, Adam Hawk's only slave—nicknamed Gulliver Goblin (the Lilliputian "haunter" of the South)—takes Magdalene up to the top of a deserted mansion and tells her "the whole loathsome story of an execution he had once witnessed—with all its soul-sickening details—one circumstance of great horror—of how the rope broke and the criminal fell, and was picked up and dragged, mangled and bloody, blinded and maddened, back to the scaffold" (43). Interestingly, Goblin, this "superannuated gardener" who has "mendacious propensities and ... marvellous tales, all of a raw head and bloody bones character" (40), resembles Southworth's Biggs Chiselly ("Uncle Biggs"), whose early tales fed Southworth's literary imagination. Gulliver Goblin determines that he will take Mary Magdalene

(E.D.E.N. Southworth?) up on a high mount to view the world as, he thinks to himself, the Devil took Christ. Magdalene is thereby "tempted" by the black man to imagine her own rebellion and possible violence that would provoke a punishment similar to the black man's: "Yes! she had heard with unshaken nerves and unfading cheek. . . . Now it seemed to her that some spirit of evil had moved upon the waters of her soul. . . . Yes! the one monstrous—the one atrocious evil in the world, was—the legal SCAFFOLD! . . . Often, often in after years, the woman recalled this first terrible presentiment of the child. . . . She felt a sort of maniac impulse to fly to the scene of the loathsome tragedy—she feared falling into the power of some fiend that should impel her to a crime that should place her—THERE!" (44).

Upon Gulliver Goblin's mistaken testimony that Magdalene went into the city—which becomes the "devilish" testimony that will instigate her anger—Adam Hawk "raise[s] the lash" to his granddaughter, although he is interrupted from committing the lashing. Southworth connects this action to Hawk's punishment of the mulatto slave Abram Pepper, "who was of a very insubordinate temper" (148). In response to one of Abram's resistances—and one can't help but notice the biblical analogs of a fallen Adam and a stern old founding father, Abram, who is in one sense "married" to Hagar/Magdalene—Adam Hawk "did a thing that had never before degraded the domestic government of Colonel Carey's household—inflicted the punishment of the lash upon the culprit. When overpowered, the mulatto no longer resisted, but submitted with a dogged resignation. He went to his work—he never used a threat—never spoke a word—dined with the hands as usual—went to work in the afternoon—supped with them—went to bed. No one suspected him of his immediate intention of running away, or of his darker, deeper purpose of vengeance" (148).

Typically cautious in her overt fictional commentary on questions of race and ethnicity, Southworth breaks reserve in expressing the South's horror at the potential for black insurrection and in attributing the source of such rebellion to mixed-race ethnicity. Abram Pepper becomes a fugitive slave waging war "Against A FAMILY—against all who bore the name of CAREY [or Washington ancestry]. It is one of those awful instances of demoniac passion, of hellish malignity that can only boil forever in the lava-like MIXED BLOOD—in the volcanic bosom of a MULATTO!" (148). And the horror is multiplied because the rebellion is so insidious: "Still no one . . . suspected the mulatto—how, indeed, should they? He had used no threats before his flight, and now he was quite forgotten" (149). Rebellious mulattos and abandoned wives are spectral visitants from the collective antebellum unconscious.

Southworth wastes no time in implying that her ethnically mixed, rebellious southern daughter, Mary Magdalene, is akin to the southern mulatta. We recall from *The Deserted Wife* that the rather timorous secondary heroine Sophie Withers conflates the outcast wife and the fugitive slave; in *Virginia and Magdalene*, the implied comparison is not so sympathetic. Magdalene's ideological resemblance to the mulatta challenges the right of the southern daughter to experience her rebellion against the patriarchy because that rebellion poses an implicit threat to the southern family system. If white women rebel, how soon will the docile African American slaves follow their example?

Apropos of the atavistic theory of mixed-race degeneracy, Southworth notes that the fugitive assassin "dodged and disappeared with the agility of a monkey . . . [with a] monkey-like cunning and agility [that] gave him the appearance of a savage or a maniac" (136). Another Washington family member has a vision of this assassin as "a great spotted leopard" (28). Although Magdalene is never likened to a monkey, she is often called "savage" and described as a "kittenamount" (47), a "panther" (47) and, significantly, a "leopardess" (66). Southworth also taps into the Hagar tradition by suggesting that Magdalene is a slave to her passions: the suitor she entices to assassinate her husband notes that "instead of chaining me a slave to your triumphal car, you have armed and invested me with power over your life!" (111).

Southworth's crafting of a heroine who must resort to violence to quell her anger marks a radical departure from her previous *Deserted Wife* text, where the little match girl, Hagar, is allowed to establish her own home. Magdalene's mistaken impression that her suitor has indeed accomplished his dark purpose (killing her husband) causes her "horror and remorse" and precipitates her chastening awareness that she should have used "the mighty power of influence she possessed!—the mighty power of beauty and eloquence— . . . to *redeem* him, and to save herself" (131). Magdalene falls deathly ill from a "great hemorhage" (132); her "handkerchief dropped saturated with the blood that oozed from her lips" (131).

While Southworth drains out her languishing heroine's ethnic blood, Governor Montjoy on his deathbed gives his granddaughter back her inheritance. This bequest provides her husband—who has loved her all along and unsuccessfully pursued a suit with her foster sister—the final inducement to reclaim Magdalene as his wife, clearing up "a slight informality in the license that would—were either of us now disposed to use it for that purpose—render our marriage invalid" (145).

Certainly Southworth prompts her reader's rueful awareness that Magdalene's status rises or falls on the basis of legalities intended to protect the already powerful. Worse yet, men avoid the law by making their promises in secret—under the protection, one might say, of the sacred domestic sphere. Probably the most ubiquitous instance in the antebellum South of manipulating "a slight informality in the license" involved owners promising their slaves manumission but frequently not granting it. If Southworth is to "save" the South—and remember, southern women "save" through forgiveness—then the legal loophole that exempts "outcasts" from full privileges in the domestic fold must be hushed up. Hence, the narrative concludes by giving the blood-purged Magdalene magical gifts of status and money that reinscribe her within the southern family. *Virginia and Magdalene* is Southworth's requiem to the rebellious southern daughter. Early on in the text of *Virginia and Magdalene*, the prodigal southern daughter Ginnie calls Magdalene "her shadow—her other self" (37)—wise words of self-knowledge that Southworth imparts to all southern daughters. In abandoning that shadow self—that rebellious daughter—in order to "save" the South from the insurrectionist whisper of the black other, in assuming as well that women's individuation can be achieved only through a male warrior archetype of violence and vengeance, Southworth returned herself to the fold at great personal cost to her own spiritual journey. I have to believe it was also at the sacrifice of her profound connection with minority oppression in the antebellum South.

5
The Scandal of Race
Stephens's Hagar the Martyr

Hagar novels by authors far less profoundly engaged than E.D.E.N. Southworth with the racial politics of a black feminist Hagar followed on the heels of Southworth's commercial success. One such novel was by Harriet Marion Stephens, an unexceptional actress of the period who exploited—rather than engaged with—the Hagar novel for mixed personal purposes. Stephens wrote *Hagar the Martyr* pseudoautobiographically, using the revenge aspect of the heroine to target theatre socialites who she imagined (probably rightly) had shunned her. One such antagonist was apparently the famous actress and socialite Charlotte Cushman. Stephens invokes the narrative "I" to describe her encounter with the "cold gray eyes of Charlotte Cushman" (273). Stephens also tries to use Hagar to "write" herself into Hagar's position of social prominence through artistic endeavor. Most offensive is her exploitation of Hagar's sexuality and insinuated blackness to sell books through the titillating medium of "scandal" based on the "exposure" of hidden blackness. *Hagar the Martyr* is unintentionally farcical. It is a pseudopornographic "white feminist" text that appropriates black female identity for voyeuristic purposes.

Stephens, billed in some instances as Rosalie Sommers, at some point apparently began to act under her married name, H.M. Stephens, then worked stock in 1851 for the Boston Athenaeum Company, which had the lowest cultural status of the three Boston theatre companies of the time.[1] She may also have been the actress known first as "Misses Sommers" and then as "Miss Sommers" for whom a theatrical benefit occurred at Placide's Varieties Theatre in New Orleans in the 1853–1854 season. This geography would be commensurate with the narrator's self-nomination in *Hagar the Martyr* as a sometime antebellum southerner.[2]

Her low acting status and her perceived role as an outsider suggest why Stephens wanted to use the novel to gain upward social mobility. "Stock" actresses were equated at the time with sexual impropriety, with "what is lax in the sex." The infamous third tier in the American theatre through the 1860s was reserved for the service of prostitutes, who often concluded transactions in the theater itself.[3] Stage actresses, especially those most economically at risk, were excluded from the higher ranks of "civilized" society through the taint of sexual impropriety; although some actually did profit from sexual liaisons, they were often unjustifiably conflated with theater prostitutes.

Notable stage actresses of the time, such as Anna Cora Mowatt, fell back on their bluestocking upbringing to cling to social status. Equally important for Mowatt and other actresses like her was sustained or upward social mobility through writing women's fiction. We are so accustomed to the struggles of women writers of the time to maintain the status of "lady"[4] that it seems curious for nineteenth-century stage actresses to aspire to the career of fiction writer in order to move up the ladder of respectability. They sought to write their way out of the third-tier geography of prostitution into the genteel pages of *Godey's*, which published not only women's fiction but contributions from Emerson, Longfellow, Holmes, and Hawthorne.[5]

Stephens's first and only novel, *Hagar the Martyr*, marks her attempted upward trajectory. It also marks her attempt to rise economically from a poorly paid minor stage actress to a well-paid domestic *doyenne*.[6] The Hagar story was a good commercial bet for Stephens's literary road to success. She had been the heroine of at least seven poems in popular magazines or giftbooks from 1840 to 1855,[7] of poet Alice Carey's lurid novel *Hagar: A Story of ToDay* (1852), and of E.D.E.N. Southworth's highly successful *Deserted Wife* in 1849–1850.

Stephens's Hagar novel is at odds with itself in its stratagem for gaining social respectability because, like Southworth's, it is written in the style of the "highly-wrought" novel,[8] a domestic variant that can be considered sensational in several ways. *Hagar the Martyr* is sensational both as a Victorian novel that constructs "affects or bodily sensations as natural[ly]"[9] female and socially excessive and as a scandalous text in the sense of a "sensational [story] of sexual [correspondingly racial] exposure."[10] In it Stephens "outs" Southworth by exposing the secret of Hagar's mixed-race identity—her "blackness"—as a scandalous fact to be eroticized. Invariably the scandal is sexual in its "outed" racial component: the audience is titillated by the discovery of a "dirty" secret.[11]

Hagar's blackness is constructed sexually because, as Young notes, miscegenation was the antebellum secret. An abolitionist of the time wrote that "miscegenation is already the irreversible fact of Southern society in every thing but the recognition of it. . . .These Southerners have proved that the repulsion to the alliance of the two bloods extends only to so much of it as the parson and magistrate have anything to do with."[12] The fact that black-white coupling takes place "outside the law" renders it sexually racy, "a sign of an absence of control or rationality,"[13] which, since it is outside the pale of patriarchal regulation, elicits both desire and disgust from the audience.[14]

The "secret" of the daughter Hagar's blackness is exposed in the early deathbed scene of her white antebellum "lady" mother, also named Hagar. The scene is a tableau, a staged representation meant to lure reading consumption: a "Buy me, borrow me, stare at me, steal me" lure that Wilkie Collins personifies as a text saying, "On, inattentive stranger, do anything but pass me by!"[15] Although Hagar's father, Alva Martin, is clearly established as the white plantation owner—"the likeness was too great for a mistake in that quarter" (24)—the dying words of Hagar's mother disclose that Hagar may be her namesake but not her daughter: she is instead "the daughter of———" (23). Immediately, the narrative insinuates that the black mistress of Hagar's father, Minnie Clare, is Hagar's mother. When the crowd of attendants whisper about Hagar, "Whose *can* it be?" the narrator responds that "Minnie's burning eyes flashed triumph upon the crowd" (24).

Stephens redirects the excess of emotive affect in sensational fiction that scapegoats the heroine as passionately unlawful onto the African American female. She eroticizes her slave character Minnie—the candidate for Hagar's biological mother—as a "racy" incursion of the sexualized black woman into the realm of white female chastity. This confusion is already implicit in naming the putative white mother "Hagar." As noted earlier, Hagar's sexual role in the Bible was tied to her Africanness, and Hagar was blamed for her own sexual surrogacy through the naturalization of black womanhood as excessively sexual. Sander Gilman notes that nineteenth-century racist anthropologists and gynophobic doctors conflated the notion of prostitution and black womanhood, endowing both prostitutes and black women with extraordinary voluptuousness, with "disease as well as passion."[16] Gilman's revelation is particularly pertinent to a reading of Stephens, who, in her own attempt to disavow her status as actress/prostitute, orchestrates a fictional "alibi" wherein the white stage actress/fiction writer's excessive and unregulated sexuality is "alibied" off onto black womanhood.

Stephens turns the scopophilic gaze of the voyeur on Minnie to titillate, to dramatize the illicit combination of "illegal" blackness and "legal" whiteness portrayed in lush sexuality mixed with refined womanly features:

> And how gorgeous [Minnie] was! Only those who have noted the perfection of beauty to which *the negro blood just merging into whiteness* aspires can imagine for a moment the extraordinary beauty of this *white slave* of Carolina.
>
> The opaque white of her complexion shone out in dazzling clearness, with just the tinge of bloom swaying backward and forward beneath her cheek. . . . Canova[17] never dreamed of a more perfect form. The broad, sloping shoulders—the full, voluptuous bust, making more conspicuous the round, lithe waist, so perfect in its proportions—the round, taper [sic] arm—the hand long and slender—the feet beautiful in their extreme smallness! But the *eyes*! Let one but once glance into their burning depths, and there would be no thought for aught else. Let her once *speak*, and the melody of her voice drowned even the lustre of her eyes! (20–21).

In the rhetoric of white colonial desire for minority others, African beauty is tantalizing yet also repulsive—a racy adventure into the realm of illegal, repressed sexuality that runs terrifying, and thus also provocative, risks. In miscegenistic economy, the mixture of black with white is perceived as a "contamination" of pure whiteness, "a venomous and dangerous ulcer, that threatens to disperse its malignity far and wide, until every family catches infection from it."[18] Racial theorists, of course, argued that contamination from naturally inferior black blood would weaken Anglo American and Anglo European white civilization.

Stephens exploits this fantasy and fear by suggesting that Minnie's coupling with Hagar's father has caused the death of her white "mother." We are told that the white woman has turned her face to the wall because of her husband's sexual betrayal. Figuratively, Stephens exploits a deeper fear in white colonial fantasy by suggesting that the white woman's disease may have been transmitted from her promiscuous husband, perhaps as syphilis—a common fear of the time.[19] Sander Gilman notes that in the nineteenth century black skin color was speculatively connected with congenital leprosy, which was believed to cause syphilis.[20] The mythological link between black womanhood and prostitution also tied black female sexuality to feared disease. Stephens imprints the sadistic fantasy of mastery and domination as well as its feared punitive results on Minnie's words: "'Don't blame *me*, master—*my* master,' murmured poor Minnie, laying her soft hand upon the husband's shoulder; 'you know I would have died at any time to have saved her a moment's pain. I couldn't help it!'" (24). These words may suggest the spousal neglect caused by the "master's" relations with Minnie or the threat of syphilitic "contamination" that the more vigorous Minnie miraculously survives, or both. For the purposes of Stephens's sensationalism, however, what is usually repressed in antebellum southern sexual economy—the relations between the black slave woman and the white master—is now exposed, not to deconstruct ideal notions of patriarchy but to sensationalize the exposure of the tabooed "hidden."

The offensiveness of Stephens's exploitation of black womanhood is apparent from the way she eroticizes relations between a slave woman and her white "master": "master—*my* master," Minnie murmurs suggestively. By projecting erotic desire onto the plantation slave woman, who is perpetually the victim of white male power and sexual violence, the narrative replicates the pornographer's fantasy of imprinting his own desire on the body of the objectified or victimized woman. The eroticizing of Minnie endorses the nineteenth-century racist stereotype of the black woman as a desiring "Jezebel."[21] Also, through the power imbalance, it suggests the usual pornographic dynamics of imagining the woman's masochistic submission to the slave master's "domination." Susanne Kappeler has emphasized how the representation of pornography contains the same psycho-physiological dynamics as the actual commission, and how pornography, whether propagated by a male or a female artist, is directed toward the male: "Men look at women. Women watch themselves being looked at.... The surveyor of woman in herself is male: the surveyed female. Thus she turns herself into an object—and most particularly an object of vision: a sight."[22] By encouraging male fantasy that imprisons women as objects of tabooed sexuality, Stephens imperils all women's freedom. But in her use of the antebellum code of white female chastity versus black female licentiousness, Stephens attempts to deflect attention from accusations against white women's sexual propriety.

The taint of scandal in Stephens's own life is suggested by her use of the prototypical Hagar traits of empowerment to exact revenge on the social world that she feels has slighted her (Stephens in fact not only interjects her personal resentment against Charlotte Cushman, but she has her Hagar heroine protest that women authors are driven to suicide by male literary critics—aspiring authors, presumably, much like H. Marion Stephens herself [194–95]). Stephens's Hagar text is marked by a perniciously racist Hagar-splitting in the heroine—between goddess traits that Stephens confiscates for her whiteness and the sexual traits that she splits off onto Hagar's reputed blackness. This blackness is exposed twice in the novel with scandalous salaciousness and is eventually sloughed off as a fictional hoax.

Just as Southworth ambivalently transfers sexual and emotional passion from a racialized black female onto her southern white heroine, so Stephens is both afraid of and exhilarated by the liberating emotional affect of her "black" heroine for the empowerment of white female identity. Stephens's fantasy of avenging social ostracism by becoming a writer is commensurate with the Hagar paradigm. Many of the common features of the prototype are present, including the typical associations with Hagar's name. After Hagar is orphaned, she is sent off to boarding school. "What a funny name!" chants one of her boarding school friends. "*Hagar*! It makes one think of the outcast Hagar of the wilderness. Wonder if she is any relation?" (25).

Stephens not only employs the name definition common to Hagar fiction, she also establishes the mother-daughter connection of abandonment and orphanhood that one finds again and again in the Hagar novella of T.T. Purvis (*Hagar, The Singing Maiden*), and the novels of Alice Carey (*Hagar: A Story of Today*), Mary Johnston (*Hagar*), Southworth, and others. Stephens suggests the matrilineal legacy in naming the mother and daughter Hagar, and in the description of the mother's death she echoes the goddess-like attributes that Southworth gives Hagar: "Hagar—the saint, the improvisatrice—the martyr woman! Hagar, the superb, the haughty, the glorious queen of poesy and of love" (19).

We recognize immediately the wild sublimity of Southworth's former Hagar in the first appearance of the soon-to-be-orphaned Hagar Martin, "a strange, wild, beautiful creature [who] flung herself half over the sill into the room" (21) where her supposed mother is dying. And we recognize as well the similar attribution of a "strong, wild, large-brained infancy" because of the extended invalidity of Hagar's mother (27) that had isolated the child from the world of female domesticity. Like Southworth's Hagar, Stephens's is a hunter who, with "rod in hand, or gun upon her shoulder, . . . would wander till the sun went down upon the mountains" (29). She is also, as in *The Deserted Wife,* likened to an eagle (28). Stephens follows Southworth's lead in suggesting an exotic blood connection: "There was a wild, dark tinge of blood in the nature of Hagar that sent her heedlessly into every excitement calculated to stir and quicken the blood. Equestrian exercise [one of the hallmarks of the Hagar character] was her delight and pride. She could sit the most fiery horse with the grace and ease of a thorough-bred jockey . . . the beautiful Arabian [another hallmark of the Hagar character] understanding her lightest word, and paying the most implicit obedience" (39).

Passion is prominent in the Hagar character; it is the source of her creativity and self-reliance and also of the destructive propensities that cause her trouble in society. This is certainly true in Stephens's novel. Hagar's tempestuous personality is established in the Prologue, a narrative prolepsis that anticipates a later point when Hagar's fiancé, Walter, leaves her because her scheming friend Anna has erroneously charged her with infidelity: "What was it to her that the lightning swept in like a flood of flame through the heavy mass of drapery. . . . What was it to her that the rolling thunder pealed over her head, as if all the armies of heaven were in passionate warfare? The tempest without accorded well with the tempest within. . . . She could bear wildness and desolation, for she was desolate and wild *in* that desolation" (8). In Stephens's novel, as in Southworth's, passion is the creative force that allows Hagar to triumph over any sexual scandal threatening her with ostracism.

Stephens's investment in her heroine on the level of fantasized projection is reflected in her emphasis on the social benefits of Hagar's writing: "Hagar . . . was the centre of a circle celebrated for its wit, its independence, and its intellect. Her home was the resort of the gifted and noble" (123). The social slights that Stephens apparently felt as a result of her stage activities are reflected in one of her subplots staged as a Restoration-style comedy derived from Anna Cora Mowatt's stage play *Fashion.* An intrusive narrator (a thinly-veiled Stephens) sympathizes with social slights to the rustic heroine of her subplot by noting, as previously mentioned, her own rejection by the New England actress/society matron Charlotte Cushman (272–73). Cushman's slight would have been a devastating blow to H. Stephens because Cushman was one of the few actresses who became well connected socially. She was, for example, friends with James T. Field and his wife, with Hawthorne's sister-in-law and Boston activist Elizabeth Peabody, and with Louisa May Alcott, who idealized Cushman in her novel *Jo's Boys.*[23]

In addition to feeling constrained by the slights of other women who were similarly ambitious, Stephens was furious with white male critics who blocked women's social mobility and power by condemning female passion in the sensational novel, more particularly in the novels of actress-writers. The hurled invective she empowers herself to deliver through the voice of Hagar Martin is worth quoting in full:

> I never meet with one of this "stab-in-the-dark" class of men without wondering for what good end God Almighty formed them. For my part, I am inclined to think they are the *hell* of this world—a sort of breathing retribution for the sins of omission or commission with which human frailty is burdened. Perhaps some one of my readers may ask, "But why devote a chapter to their benefit?" I will tell you. I *know* a clique of this kind who will say, "The author is writing from her own heart." And if I am, what then? I have seen so much of the heartlessness of society, of its assumption of virtues which it does not possess, of its attempts to *seem* rather than to *be,* that I have grown reckless and fearless of the critical bravo's stiletto; that I have determined to paint out real scenes and real characters; at the same time premising that my associations have been with a class of people [actresses, one assumes] no more given to error than are those of the "bread and butter" writers whose works abound with angels. My war is not with the unfortunate, but with the *masked pretender* . . . against hypocrites and dissemblers. . . . While necessity bids me write, common honesty and common humanity shall dictate the material, despite the venom of would-be critical and whipper-snapper censors. (123)

In one of the novel's most pathetic passages, Hagar's servant, Meg, attempts to console her mistress for her fear of being "cast . . . off" from society: "Come, cheer up, honey. . . . Cheer up; the worst can but come to the worst. You can write all around them, and when you are dead they will print your book, and get a monument for you, and be sorry that they hunted the life out of you; so they will; that will be a treat, won't it, pet?" (167).

The anger Stephens feels toward her white male critical audience is a very real gauge of male response to women's range of emotional experience and moves for power in the novel of sensation. Her Hagar novel was in fact singled out in the "Editor's Table" of *Graham's Magazine* in February 1855 as the epitome of the worst of "this lady literature." This was a magazine publishing James Russell Lowell, Edgar Allan Poe, Park Benjamin, William Cullen Bryant, Richard Henry Dana, and Henry Wadsworth Longfellow. For several excruciating pages Stephens's book is lambasted, its "intensely written" text quoted at length, until the reviewer exclaims, "Why, we ask mildly, why will ladies sit down and write in such a style as that? Where is the need of exhibiting such womanly weakness in the matter of telling a story and describing the agitated feelings?"[24]

Stephens's *Hagar* is a jumbled whirlwind of contradictory strategies aimed at attacking, diffusing, and seducing a reader whom Stephens hypothetically constructs as both white and male. At the heart of her strategy, as noted above, is sexual scandal, regarded as the most extreme boundary of woman's emotion in the sensational novel. Cvetkovich observes that "for the critics, one of the most distressing aspects of the sensation novel's focus on sexuality was its depiction of women who transgress social conventions."[25] The presentation of sexuality was, in other words, a transgression of the regulatory functions of a patriarchal society that repressed women by repressing their sexuality.

The threat of women's sexuality is apparent in the self-protective fear that her fiancé, Walter, expresses when Hagar is provoked into anger by his flirtations: "And yet we might be so happy if you could—if I was *sure* you could—restrain that fearful temper. Try, Hagar, for my sake, for both our sakes—won't you?" Hagar's anger is not only inappropriate to the code of the ideal future wife but also questions the white male's privilege to encode a double standard of sexual conduct. Walter refuses to stop flirting with Hagar's nemesis, Anna, saying, "I cannot, Hagar—at least not now. After what has just happened, people would say you forced me to give her up. . . . A man's heart is naturally too proud to indulge the supposition of its being ruled" (227–28). The text wavers between judging Walter a "true-hearted, honorable" (156) voice of reason and a weak, hypocritical dilettante. His "somewhat vacillating nature" and "vain-glorious pride" lead him to "rattle you off a string of maxims as long as the moral law about the inconstancy and untruth of women," while being a "'fast liver,' who crowd[s] ten years of common existence into one" (170). Hagar nevertheless "must yield obedience to his dictates: [she] must learn to take his little peculiarities as a matter of course" (223).

Despite her ambivalent engendering of Hagar's anger as an empowering force for women, Stephens is trapped in the vise of male judgment; she is mystified by patriarchal power and attends to its demands through the betrayal of her heroine. We have already seen how Stephens ingratiates white male readers through her initial staging of a scandalous tableau that eroticizes women—more to the point, black women. Scandal continues to be the method by which she engenders emotion as female, eroticized for a constructed white male audience, and constrained by the regulatory forces that accompany scandal. Cohen notes that "scandal teaches punitive lessons, often deliberately intended to induce conformity in its audience . . . [although] its thrilling terrors always pose the danger of inciting disobedience to the norms they advertise."[26]

From the beginning, when her mother is revealed to be not her mother, Hagar falls into one sexual scandal after another, and each time a dominant feature of the scandal is her black blood, "the wild, dark tinge of blood in the nature of Hagar that sent her heedlessly into every excitement calculated to stir and quicken the blood" (39). When her supposed mother dies and it is suggested that Hagar is mixed-race, she experiences a primary repression. She goes off to boarding school with no conscious sense that she has been "tainted" by black blood. After she leaves school and returns home, Stephens mimes tragic mulatto fiction to exploit the potentially scandalous secret of black identity—scandalous from the racist perception of blackness as sin, or crime. After Hagar's return home from boarding school and the death of her father, she is faced with a ruthless suitor who brands her black and threatens to enslave her. The near-white heroine, sent East for education, who has her mixed-race identity disclosed to her by a villain when she returns home to the South to find her family in ruins is the central plot of tragic mulatto fiction. Stephens's white villain, Laird, is a widower who perversely tries to blackmail Hagar into marrying him after he is rejected by Hagar's widowed stepmother. The sadistic eroticism latent in Southworth's former fiction, where the white man forces his will on the Hagar heroine, is now scandalously exposed for what it truly is—the racial dynamics of the "Old South"—for Laird stakes his claim on Hagar by informing her that she is a mulatta.

Again, as in the incident with Minnie, the scandal is displaced from white male sin to black female sexuality. Through Laird's words, Stephens turns a scopophilic gaze with the precision of the racial geneticist on the black woman as eroticized object.

> Lift up the drooping fringes of those proud eyes, and see there the rim of opaque blackness, indigenous *alone* to the slave. Examine those long, taper [sic] fingers, whose heaviest task as

yet has been to toy with a book or a fan; or press back the clasp of lovers' palms, and mark the indentation of mingled color which circles the nails; then raise that mass of curly jet, and trace there the short crisp wave of hair that separates the negro from the white; then, if that suffice not, go to your mirror, girl. Take feature after feature of that superb face. Examine them individually—the luscious lips, the high cheek bone, the broad, low forehead, the unshapely nose—all bright, gorgeous, and fascinating *together,* but apart and distinct, undeniably African. (95)

Stephens's Hagar is rendered vulnerable through the death of her father, which is caused by Laird's kidnapping of her stepmother. Upon revelation of her blackness, Hagar experiences what Judith Berzon calls the tragic mulatto's "crisis": she is "bewildered . . . gather[ing] up the drooping rings of her black hair," in self-loathing, and saying "I was so proud of it. . . . A *slave*! O, ignominy! O degradation!" From the perspective of white racism, explains Berzon, "discovering that one is literally kin to a darkly 'mysterious' race of people whose origins are in the 'primeval jungle' is traumatic."[27]

Stephens's construction of a racialized sexual scene of mastery is designed for the voyeuristic pleasure of a white male audience. On the other hand, her vested interest in Hagar Martin as a surrogate voice for her own feminist resistance directs her interruption of the pornographic scene. Foreshadowing her alibi of whiteness, Stephens sets the ground here for Hagar splitting, where whatever must be disavowed to avoid white male displeasure is projected onto Hagar's putative blackness. In *Location of Culture,* Homi Bhabha speaks of "splitting" as the break inside the self of an illusionary internal coherence, brought about by the experience of what has been thought "other" within the self. Bhabha's work addresses the potential deconstruction of the authoritative self that has been constructed by the negation, repression, or dehumanization of the "other" as a projection of the denied self. Splitting of imperialist identity brings a healthy correction to the tyrannous dream of self-plenitude that constitutes wholeness of self through colonial domination. For Stephens, on the contrary, Hagar splitting is the disavowal of her own feared weakness—that is, of what she knows to be considered weakness in the dominant cultural code. Hagar can resist white male domination only by "splitting off" her blackness: "I'll be no *slave*—no wife that's worse than slave! There's no drop of slave blood in my veins! I am as white as you are, as free as you are, and I will not be enslaved" (100).

Stephens's fantasy that blackness is the sign of female captivity is of course the reverse of her own fantasized trajectory of using Hagar's blackness for white women's empowerment; that said, dreams or myths contain the vacillating and selective elements that serve the driving desire of the dreamer. Suddenly, it is southern white women who are courageous and Hagar's "slave-mother," Minnie, who is defined as the coward when Minnie and Hagar attempt their fugitive escape from Laird. Minnie recoils at impending capture: "'My Lord, what *shall* we do?' moaned Minnie, ready to fall to the ground for fear. 'You know how they punish runaways. O, I wish I had never started.'" We seem intended to admire Hagar's stunning lack of respect for the woman who is allegedly her mother: "*Woman!* Coward! If the worst comes to the worst, we can but die!" Minnie responds that she does not want to die and wishes she were "safely at home." "'*Craven!*' hiss[es] Hagar" (102–3).

In presenting Minnie as a seductive mulatta character willingly involved in sexual relations with her "master" and with a cowardly resistance to effecting her own escape, Stephens perpetuates the racism that the tragic mulatto genre was intended to defeat. She uses the form superficially for its commercial and sensationalist value. Karen Sanchez-Eppler notes that the depiction of the slave in miscegenist tales published in the Boston Female Anti-Slavery Society's annual giftbook *The Liberty Bell* (1839–1858) was "thought to have its own market value," in part because "the buyers of these representations of slavery [were] fascinated by the abuses they ostensibly oppose[d]." If freedom for the slave was offered in such tales, according to Sanchez-Eppler, it was through the mechanism of obliterating blackness, as in Lydia Maria Child's tale "Mary French and Susan Easton." In this story a child is kidnapped, stained black, and sold into slavery, but she saves herself through her own tears, which wash her white.[28] In Stephens's *Hagar,* we see again the exploitation of the sensationalist value of hidden blackness, and the expunging of blackness from the dominant heroine Hagar Martin. In both instances also, it is a crucial point that woman's range of emotion is split strategically between sentiment and something that is "other," and that other is assigned to blackness; notably, in Stephens's novel, that other is sexuality.

After this nonrecognition scene exposing Hagar's blackness, the thrilling terror of sexual miscegenation that Stephens introduces with the "taint" on Hagar's bloodline immediately goes underground, reemerging when Hagar, having escaped Laird, ends up out of her senses—out of her constructed "whiteness"—in a brothel, where she has an illicit affair with a minister that produces a baby who dies after birth. Although race is not constructed overtly as a causative factor in Hagar's sexual blunder, it is certainly there, haunting us, in Hagar's "insanity."

According to Sander Gilman's study of the pictorial imagery of race prejudice, the ubiquitous figure of the black servant in European art of the eighteenth and nineteenth centuries was used "to sexualize the society in which he or she is found" and, in addition, usually to mark "the presence of illicit sexual activity."[29] Although in Stephens's story Hagar Martin's "temporary insanity" allegedly develops from her discovery that her true love, Walter, has married (the villain shows her a newspaper article to this effect), the text merges her blackness with her sexual indiscretion. In a later passage, for example, she is accused of having a heart "burnt and blackened by wantonnness" (333). "Insanity" becomes the ploy of our next Hagar writer, Charlotte Moon Clark, to enact the split between white Hagars and black Hagars, just as in Southworth's *Deserted Wife* the specter of the white man's insane runaway wife is confused with the figure of the fugitive slave. "Insanity" provides a kind of failsafe for white women's "otherness"; they are out of their mind—in other words, not white—when possessed by deep emotion.

The death of the baby suggests the antimiscegenist theory that a child of black/white sexuality will be diseased, that miscegenation will produce a degenerate race and finally death. Slave mothers are rendered responsible for the loss of their children by their very blackness and hence by their sexual passion, which overrides the normal regulatory functions of "natural" parenting. Blackness becomes chaos. As the furthest extreme of women's emotion, it overrides the regulative "natural" functions of society: babies die, wives are diseased, husbands are "killed" by women's anger: women are out of control.

The woman writer's choice to impose a duality upon women's emotional versus sexual selfhood can derive from an attempt to rescue some part of a woman's range of emotions by punishing the patriarchal system. As Cohen notes, scandal regulates because authority responds by enacting punishment on the sexual transgressor. In the woman's world, the element of Christian atonement in the Hagar/Virgin Mary/Mary Magdalene constellation discussed in the previous chapter proves an ongoing method of "saving" wayward women in the domestic text through the mariological paradigm of forgiveness. It brands women's sexual passion as a sin to be forgiven, yet "saves" a wayward heroine through the surrogate enactment of both punishment and a forgiveness not available within the external code of white patriarchy. Women's dream of self-punishment can indeed be gruesome, as the death of

Hagar's baby indicates, but even at its most gruesome this punishment is preferred to the irrational terror of anticipating patriarchal punishment. Alice Carey's *Hagar* (1852) follows the formula of atonement to a T; Stephens uses Carey as a guide for her own heroine's atonement.

Under atonement, a woman's emotion is anesthetized from passion through the code of sentimentality. Guilt and strong remorse replace positive energy as a means of retaining woman's sexuality. But sexuality is retained negatively as a force of self-destruction. Perhaps Stephens was drawn to Carey's Hagar through the latter's poetry, which was frequently published in the 1850s in *Gleason's Pictorial and Drawing-Room Companion,* in which Stephens herself published. In addition one should not ignore the pornographic pleasures, for a male reader/voyeur, of a sadomasochistic enactment of female sexual atonement. Stephens would have relished the heightened sensationalism that went along with the grave moral tone of Carey's *Hagar* for its potential to shock, horrify, and dazzle—for, in other words, its commercial value.

Unlike Southworth's *Deserted Wife,* Carey's *Hagar* follows an alternate trajectory for the Hagar heroine. Remorse replaces victory through Carey's plot features—the lurid death of Hagar's infant and Hagar's obsession with atonement. Elsie asks to be called Hagar after her lover, the "eloquent" (174) one-time preacher Nathan Warburton, abandons her and steals their child. The continued literary use of a particular proper name in scandalous events is what Cohen calls a "homology between proper names and sexual discourses . . . one of the crucial junctures of indeterminacy that enables the erotic and the literary mutually to generate each other."[30] Cohen's "juncture of indeterminacy" expresses the tendency of scandalous proper names to reproduce and regenerate scandal. As Baym points out, Hagar was a synonym for the fallen woman in the nineteenth-century woman's novel. The name Hagar recurrently suggested a sexual discourse.[31] In like manner, Carey has her character rename herself Hagar at the point where the literary text generates its sexual discourse in part through the use of this particular proper name.

After a period of years, Carey's Hagar searches her now-famous lover's study to discover that "in a case of black and polished wood was a coffin, decayed, as if it had been buried many years; the lid was removed, and in it was a skeleton, which instinctively I recognized as my child; and from the accumulated dust, red beads glittered in the light of the close lamp" (291). The murder of Hagar's baby is an anticipatory self-punishment that attempts to deflect the more terrible punishment Carey assumes her heroine would receive at the hands of white male society. Carey's Hagar discovers her dead baby in a casket in a safe in her lover's study: self-punishment is an anticipatory masochism aimed at hiding one's sexual sin from the punitive gaze of society. In addition, although nowhere in the text does Carey suggest Hagar's blackness, her name connoted blackness in the public consciousness. The stealing and murdering of her baby by its father while Hagar is asleep would be understood as a colonial miming of the slave process in which children were wrenched away from their black slave mothers. If order is perceived as conscious self-control, then sleep is a state of unconsciousness that mimics chaos. Hence Hagar's sleeping becomes a synonym for her lack of control, which blocks her function as a protective mother. This lack of control also represents symbolically her out-of-whiteness, her uncontrolled passion. All are lapses from the conscious containment of her emotion.

Stephens retains the death of Hagar's child as a punitive source of sorrow in *Hagar the Martyr*. Only in her fiction and in Carey's does Hagar's child die, and in both that death initiates Hagar's self-punitive atonement. "O that I had died with thee, my child!," moans Stephens's Hagar. "O that I had died with thee! ... No hope! No light!.... My child! My child!" (161). In Carey, Hagar becomes "an outcast from the world, seeking, in continual prayer and penitence, to atone my sin, or to stay back a little the vengeance of Heaven" (210). Carey turns atonement around, rending pleasurable emotion out of the very jaws of self-torture. "It was," observes the narrator, "a melancholy life she surveyed, and with all its suffering, all its sin, the retrospect brought a feeling kindred with joy—the sense of submission and expiation, under which martyrs have sung their divinest triumphs" (213). Though Stephens appropriates "martyr" for her Hagar title, she implies that her Hagar does not really want to be martyred; she wants to live in the world, accepted and even approved by society.

By marking her novel as southern, in particular in the antebellum subplot around a minor heroine, Effie Rose, Stephens is able to call upon antebellum myth to reposition white men as benevolent regulators.[32] In the Effie Rose subplot, Stephens stages the survival of her southern white Hagar heroine by putting all white women's emotion under the regulatory force of plantation ideology—a mentality she endorses because of the general benevolence of plantation slavery life that she perceives:

> Luckily for *me*, my experiences of slave life have been among the humane and the benevolent. I have passed many years of

my life investigating, as far as practicable, the peculiar institutions of a slave country. I went south with all my northern prejudices warm within my heart. The first sight of a *slave* was to me a sensation of itself alone—a something no more to be *re*produced in description than to be the second time experienced. I made my home for years on a plantation where slaves were part of the family; not in point of actual association, perhaps, but as far as needs, desire, and humane treatment were concerned. No wonder, then, that I look with dislike upon those who, by a vigorous pen, strive to waken all the bad impulses both of master and slave, and wedge in the life already in bonds of servitude by stricter vigilance and a greater severity of discipline. (76–77)

In this passage, Stephens evinces her own fascination/repulsion with black ethnicity. She places herself within the aversive male position of voyeuristically perceiving black slaves as both present and indescribable. Black slave identity cannot and should not be *re*produced, and yet home is made with such people. They are "part of the family," yet not "in point of actual association," because their sheer unrepresentationality renders them "no thing." But, by virtue of the patriarchy's benevolent treatment of repulsive people best left unrepresented, Stephens is able to embrace all women, not just black, within the allegedly mild disciplinary measures of white male regulation.

Accordingly, Stephens subjects white women's potentially repulsive emotions to social regulation in her subplot about the southern belle Effie Rose and her "knight-errant" beau, Charley Lee, with a "thousand negroes at [his] service" (40, 42). Effie Rose and Charley are neighbors of Hagar during her youth in South Carolina, but they are worked into the text to idealize southern plantation homes such as "WILLOWDALE! with its antiquity, its quietude, and its gorgeousness; with its great hills, its drooping willows, its solemn dates. *Willowdale!* The very name ripples lovingly from the pen and I love the stern stillness of its surroundings, for the rich haze of memory lingering amid its shadows. *Willowdale!*" (72).

To her slaves, plantation "missis" Effie Rose is an "angel of light. All the honest, faithful feelings of their nature were called out by the invariable kindness of their 'young missis.' They were always sure of her ear and her sympathy; and woe to the taskmaster who had abused his authority!" (75–76). Interestingly, despite her angelic character, Stephens turns the motherless Effie Rose into a surrogate Hagar, in whom "all the wildness, the recklessness, the inconsiderateness and the eccentricity of the colonel, her father, had been reproduced" (73). Hagar-like as well, Effie "sat a horse as if she had been part and parcel of the same flesh" (73).

The confiscation of Hagar to describe a white southern belle trivializes the serious use of this archetype for female empowerment and for discourse on racial injustices that are parodied here in the farcical use of terms of enslavement. Effie Rose, who finds Charley "just her style of a man," discovers that her father has prearranged their marriage: "That was enough for Effie. She was to be made a barter of, sold, traded away.... The spice of romance which made more piquant the rich flame of her disposition was likely to mar all the preconceived notions and plans of her father for future aggrandizement and elevation" (75). Effie resists "being made a barter of," her father explains, because "she's romantic as a toad, and be hanged to her" (82). The opposition between "Passion" and "Reality" in the subtitle of Stephens's novel suggests the ultimate denigration of woman's passion in favor of the higher realm of white male reason—what allegedly reasonable men call real in this novel. Women's passion for freedom from male dominance is perceived by the proslavery patriarchs as romanticized whimsy, which the men in Effie's life indulge by working around for her own good. Stephens's sinister fooling with the language of slavery trivializes her heroine's resistance to male will as an ill-perceived mistake based on an absurd notion of freedom. Effie—all Effies—all black women slaves—do not want to be free; they just think they do.[33]

In the resolution of the subplot, Effie's father, Colonel Rose, devises a conspiracy to outwit girls, "with their girl notions, and their highfaluten romances" (346). He makes Charley Lee an exile and condemns him as "a reckless, foolish, miserable gamester!" (349), so that Effie of course elopes with him, much to her father's delight. Unlike Southworth, who points out what is sinister about disguising economic transaction as familial relation in the antebellum South, Stephens treats Colonel Rose's hidden motive—"to bring the two farms together—I mean the two children together" (348)—with humorous indulgence.

Stephens reserves this denouement of Effie Rose's story for her final chapter—her final word—before the epilogue. By turning Effie Rose into a Hagar who is not black, and by simultaneously turning the white woman into a slave who is not a slave, Stephens effects cancellations more potent than her previous declaration that the supposedly mulatta heroine Hagar is actually white. She has been creating a split in the novel between what is "good" and real—"Reality"—and what is passionate and foolhardy—"Romance." It does not take long to realize that by the end of the novel Stephens has implicitly canceled out her entire preceding melodrama about the archetypally passionate and potent Hagar, along with Hagar's blackness, by placing it in the discarded realm of romance. Stephens constructs a novel in which the idealized antebellum South of benevolent relations is deemed "real," while a racist South that abuses women, especially black women, is romantic mythology. A novel that begins with the dramatic unveiling of *who Hagar really is* as a woman of mixed race and as a marker of the racist antebellum South concludes with a full-force denial of Hagar's very existence.

In her concluding scenes, Stephens reactivates the specter of her Hagar heroine as black to cancel out even more effectively her heroine's "taint" of blackness. But this return of black womanness is motivated at least in part by the compulsive return of the white woman writer's female anger, which must be alibied as black. Even though she brackets woman's emotion in the Effie Rose subplot as "romance" versus "reality," Stephens never fully purges her driving anger against the patriarchal code that has depleted her own social status and robbed her of sexual freedom. Hagar Martin does not "atone"; she is wilfully determined to live on, and fully—to become a successful author and seek prominent marriage—after the "sin" in her past.

But this "emancipation" of her heroine is inconclusive because Stephens is unwilling to stage an honest confrontation between patriarchal values that determine women's "sin" and a heroine who would sincerely resist such values. Stephens's heroine accepts her past "sin" as sin without challenge: it is "a hidden stain; a stain that has eaten into my soul; that has cankered my best impulses; that has risen up before me at all times, in all places, under all circumstances, till I loathe myself for the crime you [her former lover] won me to perpetrate" (161). At the same time, there is that reactionary anger at the male verdict that proves overwhelming to self: Hagar is only a "martyr girl" (114) insofar as she is a victim of other people, not a responsible agent. "To struggle as she had struggled for redemption, to atone in bitterness of spirit as she had tried to atone, and then to have the hands of *men* busy in seeking her downfall, O, it was too terrible!" (154).

But this anger so ambivalently engendered rests invariably, in Stephens's reading, on the shoulders of the black woman. The white woman is always "saved" from her own anger and "rescued" into the arms of an accepting white society by the complete expurgation of her blackness, which Stephens effects through a *deus ex machina* public declaration at the end that Hagar is totally white. The two layers of Hagar's hidden self—her secret sin, her secret blackness—converge in the novel's final pages when the villain, Laird, masquerading as a southern planter, resurfaces at a party in Boston to declare Hagar "my slave . . . my property." There is no doubt in the text which secret is the more sinister, promiscuity or mulatto identity, since Hagar's past affair is dismissed by the crowd, but "horror stricken indeed seemed the friends of Hagar" (340) on the latter pronouncement. A massive sigh of relief from the crowd, and, in particular, from her fiancé Walter follows the discovery that Hagar's actual mother was her father's sister and that Hagar was adopted by her uncle. This final scene follows the novel's opening prolepsis where Walter doubts Hagar's fidelity. The excitement of "exonerating" Hagar from blackness renders the promiscuity rumor negligible in the eyes of Walter and the public. In the last disturbing pages of her novel, Stephens's overriding strategy for dreaming blackness becomes all too clear. She alibis white female resistance by racializing black women as sexualized "others" whose very blackness so exceeds sexual license that white female sexuality, by comparison, becomes virtually "no thing."

6
Hagar Splitting
Clark's Modern Hagar

Preceding chapters have noted the interdependence of female power and woman's full range of emotions in the composite image of the archetypal Hagar: her emotion, indistinct from her sexual passion, catalyzes her artistry, which makes her goddess-like in her triumph over social oppression. In Southworth's fiction, it is the hidden aspects of the undifferentiated archetype that allow the author to appropriate empowerment for her white antebellum southern heroine. She can imagine white feminist resistance only through archetypal traits of an African goddess and creator, but she can employ this imaginative paradigm only by obscuring the African ethnicity that informs it. Not yet completely siphoned off, Hagar's blackness is an essential element in Southworth's white heroine, a candidate for the concept of hybridized identity as suggested by Homi Bhabha. One can infer from Bhabha's theory that the "shadow" of "othered" identity in this instance is constitutive of southern white women's identity. Southworth cannot help but acknowledge the real conditions of the black slave woman of her time through her *process* of using Hagar, despite her ultimate reduction of Hagar to an unambiguously white southern heroine in the service of proslavery myth.

Passion (attached archetypally to the African Hagar) effects the survival of indomitable fictional Hagars. Contrary to the conventional sentimentalist text that praises the passionless, virtuous woman, these texts offer radical endorsement of independent American women whose epic passion inspires both the tragedy and the triumph of Hagar in her mythologized form. Even if fictional heroines suffer shame for their passion, they transform that emotion into energy that results in Wagnerian atonement, as in Alice Carey's *Hagar*. Usually passion is obtained through the heroine's blackness, through racist assumptions that stereotype black women's sexuality; but in the more positive sense of the archetype, passion arises from the composite imaging of a black goddess/heroine whose sexuality is simply taken in cultural stride as part of powerful womanhood. In Southworth's texts, Hagar's African American identity was covertly suggested as black *and* white. In Stephens's *Hagar,* this twinning, although superficial, retained such a connection. In these cases, black and white coexist in an unresolved tension that is potentially creative: black and white, two mirrors reflecting, two faces of Janus, two sisters, a woman self-twinned. This tension results in great part from the encasement within one body of this racial duality.

Ironically, as the nineteenth century progresses, writers expose Hagar's hidden blackness not to liberate, or openly acknowledge, real black women or the indebtedness of white women to their imagination of self-empowerment through contacts with black slave women. Instead, as evidenced in Stephens, exposing Hagar's blackness becomes a strategic ploy to effect a split between black sexualized ethnicity and the imagined benefits reaped from it. White feminists progressively disavow the interrelatedness between black and white women's identity by dividing the heroine between good white Hagars and bad black Hagars who become so marginalized that they serve as "fools" or end up insane. The post-Reconstruction novel of Charlotte Moon Clark—pseudonym, Charles Clay—*The Modern Hagar: A Drama* (1882) exposes Hagar's blackness so completely as to mystify the fact that she was ever racially complex. In complete contrast to Homi Bhabha's conception of "splitting" as the democratics of self-fracture, Hagar splitting has already sutured black women's identity. Southworth's texts deny black women's identity but through a process of disavowal that admits there is an existence requiring disavowal. That is, to have to disavow an identity is to admit its presence in the first place—ideological failure, since myth requires the assertion of prior, not secondary, origin.

By contrast, Clark splits her white and black Hagars before her text begins. As Bhabha notes, "An important feature of colonial discourse is its dependence on 'fixity' in the ideological construction of otherness"[1]; fixity depends on the fiction of myth's ahistoricity. In Clark's text, Hagar has always been inherently either the black sexual victim or the white empowered goddess; the cultural construction of "race" is affixed to the natural order. In fact, the exposure of Hagar's blackness is essential if the myth of white cultural supremacy is to claim authoritative presence for itself. Roland Barthes explains that "*myth hides nothing;* its function is to distort, not to make disappear."[2] Exposure fixes the minority "other" in a place of rejection.

Just as Stephens deconstructs the hidden in Southworth's text to expose Hagar's blackness, so Clark deconstructs the hidden blackness in the pictorial representation of Hagar as white in nineteenth-century America. But Clark does more: she exposes the hidden secret in antebellum marriages, Hagar's biblical role as sexual surrogate to Abraham. Early in Clark's novel, Kate Cartaret marries a New York millionaire, Simon Hartley, and moves to his "large, old-fashioned house built on a high, wooded knoll that overlooked the Hudson" (I:59). Clark weaves in the gothic secret of the black sexualized Hagar. This is quite literally a haunted house; at least, Kate's mulatta maid, Rose, relates the sighting of a ghost the preceding night, and when Kate discovers that she has been denied access to the locked rooms behind heavy drapery in her husband's library, she muses to herself, "Bluebeard's closet!" (I:60)

Hartley is indeed the ultimate gothic villain in the drama of ideal white southern womanhood. The evidence behind his locked rooms reveals the psychological depths of repressed thoughts and deeds, often sexual, typical in American gothicism and specifically appropriate for the antebellum southern tale. For Kate as a recently married southern white woman, it is the "bitter knowledge of good and evil." Her forced entrance into these secret rooms provides evidence of her husband's infidelity with a black slave woman, in this case a mulatta slave named Lucy whom Kate insists on calling "Hagar": "It was not the mere uncovering of the feet of clay, the flaw in the divinity of the god, but the proof that the idol [her husband] was brutally and sensually human. It was a profound calamity, for it extinguished the sacred fire on the altar of marriage; it was infinitely sorrowful, for it struck at the existence of an infinite love; it was the end of faith, of reverence" (I:73). Hagar and her child represent Kate's husband's past, which is the denied secret of southern womanhood. Mary Chesnut remarked that "every lady tells you who is the father of all the mulatto children in everybody's household, but those in her own she seems to think drop from the clouds, or pretends to think."[3]

Clark openly exposes the black slave woman as the genuine Hagar for the first time in white American culture. By contrast, the spectral wife in Southworth's *Deserted Wife*, who testifies to the abusiveness of her bigamous husband, is a white woman although she is tied indirectly to the black runaway slave for whom onlookers mistake her. In Clark's fiction, however, the "ghost" Lucy (I:68) is a quadroon slave woman whom Clark's heroine ritualistically renames Hagar, a spectral image still haunting the grounds of Hartley's mansion on the Hudson. Lucy scares Rose "into thinking 'twas a ghost. She's a heap paler 'an she used to be' . . . 'an' a heap more like a lady than a quarteroon" (I:77) Clark's quadroon Hagar is a troubling psychological double for the southern white woman. She could pass as white and she is a "lady"—a term applied, according to Elizabeth Fox-Genovese, very exclusively to distinguish white upper-class southern females from those who were African American or white lower-caste, identified as "women."[4] Her white appearance and elevated status would seem to undermine threateningly the antebellum argument that black slaves are justifiably slaves because they are racially distinct and less human than whites.

But the reverse is true. Before Clark, the persistent representations of Hagar in nineteenth-century America seem to emerge from a "repetition-compulsion" in the American historical consciousness. That is, the culture's fascination with Hagar, and her obscured representation as suggestively black yet literally white, seems to have arisen in Southworth and in American pictorial representation from the compulsion of antebellum white unconsciousness both to "admit sin"—for the plight of blacks, in particular of black women—and vociferously to deny it. To deny sin and guilt was to deny African American identity. It could not have been much of a leap to connect the biblical slave mother Hagar with the antebellum black woman slave in all these texts. And thus the lavish sympathy rendered Hagar in antebellum fiction and poetry might be understood as a sort of vicarious experiencing, albeit exploitative, of the grief of the African American slave or as a vicarious experience of white America's guilt.

Clark's exposure of a black sexualized Hagar, however, fixates black womanhood as sexualized other. Since Hagar is so consistently objectified in literature for her representational value, Clark's deconstruction of the "white" Hagar through art is appropriately symbolic. Her heroine, Kate Hartley, discovers Hagar's African American identity in her husband's art gallery. Her mulatta slave, Rose, manages to procure the forbidden keys to Hartley's private apartments; again, in a symbolic sense, a black woman gives the white woman the "keys" to her own repressed knowledge. Kate then unlocks the outer chamber of her husband's library, where she walks with great enjoyment and innocence "from engraving to engraving." But in an inner chamber she discovers in "a portfolio . . . fallen from an easel" the "scattered contents of engravings and sketches" that Rose has spilled.

Kate is riveted by a prominent oil painting which she describes as having "the hackneyed [subject] of 'Hagar in the Desert.'" Noting that it has been greatly revised, Kate instantly identifies the woman in the picture (though she has not seen her in person) as her "rival" (I:70), Lucy. Kate's instantaneous response that Lucy is Hagar, and her reconstruction of a less hackneyed Hagar who is her husband's black mistress, "exposes" black female identity in a distorted sexual role where black is split from white and black women are ostracized through the mark of sexual shame.

Given the fixated sexuality of this representation, Clark's pictorial disclosure of the real rather than the conventionally hackneyed Hagar as the mixed-race white/black American Lucy serves to "shame" African American womanhood into social submission. In *The Modern Hagar,* Clark splits the image of black from white women and deflects the focus from her modern black Hagar by funneling her more positive attributes into one of her white women characters, Rue Leszinksky, Kate's cousin once removed, who has a more direct line to the Cartaret fortune than Kate and shares equal billing in the novel with Kate. Rue is a carry-over from Clark's earlier novel *Baby Rue* (1881). The early incidents and later adventures of Rue Leszinksky are largely sustained in the atmosphere of Clark's sequel novel, which (as the title indicates) is a book about Hagar. But Rue, not Hagar (Lucy), gets the positive Hagar attributes.

Like the typical Hagar heroine, Rue Leszinksky is an orphan in the wilderness—this time the western wilderness—with the predictably absent father who has left her largely undisciplined in the tradition of Hagar fathers. Rue/Hagar is a "witching little despot" with "a wild, untrained grace" (I:22) and an "imperious temper" (I:229) who "had been taught to ride in her babyhood" and can "swim ... shoot ... fence" (I:357). She is a "little princess" who "might have been a child of Julius Caesar" (I:172). As with other Hagar heroines who implicitly take on masculine properties, "Rue was rapidly acquiring the manner of a boy accustomed to rule by the slightest expression of will, and to whom instant obedience was given" (I:358).

Consistently, the warrior-like power and passion of this heroine derive from the exoticized element in her blood rather than from her white ethnicity. Since Clark has already diminished her portrait of the mixed-race quadroon, whom she exposes as the real Hagar heroine of American paintings, she creates a new mixed-race heroine in Rue, who gains her goddess/warrior qualities from her Polish blood (I:37). By sleight-of-hand, Clark siphons off the power-aligned attributes of Hagar from her Lucy and invests them in a surrogate mixed-race heroine who is, though Eastern European and thus not immune to xenophobic prejudices, indisputably and most significantly white.

Clark's story is channeled through three southern or pseudo-southern white women: the frontier heroine Rue Leszinksky, the proud southern bride Kate Cartaret Hartley, and the socially political resident of Cincinnati, Mrs. Carisbrooke, through whom Clark manages to present her pro-southern mythology of antebellum politics. Lucy's plight is merely a footnote in the lives of Rue, Kate, and Mrs. Carisbrooke. As in many Reconstruction novels, war is presented through the eyes of white men and women, northern and southern. This viewpoint is usually extended only marginally to the African Americans over whom the war was ostensibly fought.[5] But since Clark calls her novel *A Modern Hagar,* Lucy's story—as Lucy is renamed "Hagar"—is implicitly central to the tale of these three white women. We can catch the historical moment; we can trace the remnants of the hidden Lucy/Hagar, who appears and reappears, literally haunting the textual background as the dispossessed embodiment of African American womanhood cast off by white feminists after the Civil War. These feminists were white women who declared their autonomy from abolitionist rhetoric and from their own black sisters in a separate search for their own independence.[6]

Clark divides black from white womanhood—and correspondingly the white South from the sin of black slavery—through an elaborate dissemination of southern space to other locales in the United States. This allows the drama of abused black womanhood to be more easily displaced, while white southern women can be the clear heroines with no trace of villainy. Taking Hagar out of the South helps to disseminate and marginalize her blackness in those nonsouthern regions where the abuses of slavery are more muffled. Black Hagars geographically displaced become pale shades of their white vampire sisters; the latter claim for themselves the vitality of this heroine in American as well as foreign spaces—the West, New York, Cincinnati, Washington, Europe—where black victimhood is quite literally fantasized away. The West, for example, becomes the place where Rue can champion American Indians while remaining true to her Virginia legacy by treating slaves patriarchally. In the section of her novel set in the West, Clark's focus on the northern dispossession of Indians during colonial times becomes the means by which the American "Fall" is transferred to New England. In this displacement, Rue's sympathy for the Indian becomes a strategic deflection from her endorsement of southern slavery.

Putting Rue in 1850 in a borderland between Kansas and "Indian" territory, with no slavery, only Indian problems, is a particularly fantastic reinvention of history to suggest the supposedly mild diplomacy of southern land acquisition in pre–Civil War America. By contrast, Clark demonizes the policy of land aggression in the northern relocation of Indians that began in colonial times. She suppresses her own historical time in order to fantasize a utopian South in the American West. Clark's American West necessarily eludes the question of slavery in order to retain its utopian features. In reality, the increasing annexation of western lands during the nineteenth century provoked a constant revisiting of the slavery question that was defrayed only temporarily by a succession of congressional compromises. Debate finally crystallized in 1853 over the free or slave status of the territories of Kansas and Nebraska, territories vital to the construction of a railroad to the West Coast. Stephen Douglas urged a bill based on "popular sovereignty" that allowed the citizens of a territory to determine whether the territory went pro- or antislavery. The Kansas-Nebraska Act had disastrous results. By mid-1856 there were pro- and antislavery territorial governments in "Bloody" Kansas, abolitionist John Brown had killed proslave supporters in that state in the "Pottawatamie Massacre," and intimidation and violence ruled on both sides. When Congress finally resolved the stalemate between pro- and antislavery legislators in Kansas in 1858, after a bitter battle, Kansas was declared a free state. For the first time "there was no more territory to divide between the contending factions. Someone had to lose. It was the South that lost, and they knew it."[7] For Clark in the face of such loss, another dividend of imaginary southern dissemination was the fantastical colonization of the entire United States—not just a reclaimed West—as the South.

Clark's *Modern Hagar* ignores northerners' claims on the West and disseminates southern land by situating the beginning of the story "in the Indian territory." Here it "was Christmas eve. The day had been one of those warm days that sometimes linger into December in the Southern States" (I:7). Clark situates the home of the Leszinksky family at "Bouie Hill" at the foot of Fort Gibson, Oklahoma, which was, in the 1850s, part of the unorganized territory largely occupied by the Indian nations of Creeks, Choctaws, Chickasaws, Seminoles, and Cherokees. Although Pawnees (Kansas) and Seminoles (Oklahoma) are equally part of this tale situated on the borders of chartered and unchartered territory, Clark avoids situating the Leszinkskys squarely in the volatile racial region of geographical and racial contestation—Kansas. Kansas is mentioned later during the proslavery Cincinnati convention, but Rue—Virginia itself— must be insulated from the contamination of the South's racial question. Here instead, Clark creates an exclusionary Southwest for her idealized

Leszinkskys. In this Southwest, Native Americans, not African Americans, are the victims of national, not southern, prejudicial policy.

Clark's "mythstory" thus obliterates slavery as a primal southern sin. In her Southwest context, the author alludes to selective historical elements of a noble pre-Revolutionary Virginia to contrast with an aggressive and avaricious colonial New England which will be seen, in the southwest, to have committed the original American sin of abusing Indians. There was historical precedent for assuming that Royalist antipathy to Indians was minimal—even when it came to miscegenation, as with Pocahontas and Rolfe. Despite the shared exclusion of African Americans and Native Americans from citizenship rights in Virginia, James Ballagh concludes that early on Indian "slavery was viewed of an occasional nature," while slavery was fixated on "the one alien race, the negro."[8]

In the mythology surrounding the "Matter of Virginia,"[9] Indian slavery was destabilized, easily displaced or distorted, in contrast to the fixed enslavement of African Americans. Clark reinforces the link between Oklahoma's border with Kansas as an outpost for dispossessed Indians and for "Old South" descendants by tying Rue/Hagar's ancestry to the "Matter of Virginia." As evidenced in Southworth's fiction, this was one of the most potent "mythstories" because it could be employed to wish away slavery and reestablish an earlier tradition of a noble pre-Revolutionary and Jeffersonian Virginia where African American slavery could be imagined as pre-antebellum, pre-exploitative. Antebellum Virginia writers invoked the colonial past "as a means of deriving usable values from history, and of putting those values beyond the reach of critical demystification."[10] The Smith-Pocahontas story, first fictionalized in 1805 in *The First Settlers of Virginia* by Englishman John Davis, was part of a mythified colonial past that deflected focus from a proslavery present to a supposed time when northerners, not southerners, perpetrated violence against a minority.[11]

Rue relates paternally to the notable "Old South" Virginia Masons and to the Virginia Cartarets through her deceased mother, Margaret Carteret Leszinksky, which makes her the most direct heir to the Cartaret fortune. The Cartarets *are* the "Matter of Virginia": "Some of these Virginians had higher patents of nobility, better title to consideration, to respect, than numerous slaves and broad acres. [In other words, slavery is almost a side-issue in the "Matter of Virginia."] Notable among such stood the Cartarets. First, they were a historic race. . . . The Cartarets were part and parcel of the history of England. . . . [As Royalists] They had carried an unstained name through centuries of trial. . . . The day after Cornwallis's surrender they returned to their plantations on the James River, where they led the quietly useful lives of country gentlemen, diversified by occasional winters in Richmond and Washington" (I:102).

Clark uses this federalist Virginia connection to tie Rue to intuitive sympathetic identification with the Indians: "It [the abuse of the Pawnee chief Lo-loch-to-hoo-la by white Indian traders] was Rue's first lesson in the wrongs of the Indian. It enlightened her much more fully than one could easily believe possible at so early an age to so unripe an understanding. . . . 'You shall not starve, my chief! You *shall* live with us. You shall eat at my table, I tell you!' And the voice rang loud and firm. '*My* table! I hate the people who were bad to you. I love you next to papa. . . . You will come with me, my chief. O my chief! you will always stay with me'"(I:57). This is addressed to Rue's surrogate father, the Pawnee chief who "found the child and saved her from the tomahawks of his people" (I:9) in the Witchita hills. She identifies with the Pawnees, who had been "driven from their lands" by "the Great Father of the white men" to "starve in the wilderness" (I:56).

One of Clark's more ingenious simplifications is her mythification of Kit Carson, whose history as a ferocious Indian fighter and agent renders his relations with Indians at best ambiguous. Clark predictably glosses over the inherent violence and cruelty in Carson's relationships with Indians and invents a personal relation between Carson and the Seminoles. Clark's novel begins with Rue/Hagar lodged at "Bouie's Hill" with Kit Carson's wife, the alleged daughter of the legendary Seminole chief Coacooche who "when Carson was nigh unto death, . . . found him and nursed him with the gentleness of a woman" (I:33). In reality, Carson married at a trappers' lodge in 1835 in Utah and fathered a baby girl with an Arapaho Indian who eventually died in 1838.[12]

By making Carson's wife Seminole rather than Arapaho, Clark purposely connects Rue/Hagar and the South with the Pawnees, notably with Chief Coacooche, who was legendary among the exiled Seminoles for his attempts to protect fugitive slaves who had joined the Seminole tribe in Florida. Although the Jefferson administration had consistently demanded that Seminoles return to their owners harbored slaves as well as the "Black Indians" indigenous to their population, during the Seminole wars the Jackson administration actually recruited Creek Indians to capture Seminole "Negroes belonging to the citizens of the United States"[13] who were resisting exile from Florida. In Clark's text, Coacooche visits

Bouie's Hill for the purpose of "protect[ing] the interests of his allies, the Black Indians" (I:29).

Clark's fictional Kit Carson praises his father-in-law as a "patriot . . . a prince . . . an untamable lover of natural liberty . . . with heroic qualities and bold achievements that would have graced a civilized warrior. . . . He lived a wanderer and a fugitive in his native land, and went down . . . without a pitying eye to weep his fall or a friendly hand to record his struggle" (I:35). Clark appropriates these words from Washington Irving's essay "Philip of Pokanoket" to link Coacooche to the colonial past. Irving paints Philip as the original victim of colonial New England's appropriation of Indian lands: "He saw the whole race of his countrymen melting before them from the face of the earth; their territories slipping from their hands, and their tribes becoming feeble, scattered, and dependent. . . . [with] the intrusion of the Europeans."[14]

Ironically, Clark connects Indian loss of land to the southern fear of losing slave territory in western lands. The fantastical linkage between this (which included vociferous attempts to reclaim Seminole blacks as stolen contraband) and the Seminole fight to retain land that would protect blacks from slavery is an expedient measure to make the North the original abuser of American minorities. Clark's defense of the Seminoles—even of their abolition of slavery!—is part of her more complex intention to pit antebellum southern agrarian ideology against northern capitalism, whose land lust, she intimates, created the plight of the Indians.

Clark's conflation of southern and Indian identity is strategically promoted through naming Rue's homestead in Old Virginia "Mount Hope." As Clark knew from Washington Irving, Mount Hope was the British name for the ancient tribal seat of Pokanoket.[15] The southern-Indian sympathies of the white frontier Rue/Hagar strategically displace the more reasonable site for Rue's southern angst, her problematic connection closer to home with black slave oppression. Southern abuse of slaves is intentionally muted not only by the geographical displacement of the South to a frontier that actually included other regional identities but also by the portrayal of loyal slaves in Fort Bouie.

The older slaves (named, ironically, Abram and Sara) carry the household gods of Old South tradition with them to Fort Bouie. Clark makes African Americans the fictional biblical patriarchs who essentialize their own victimization through what to present-day readers seems an embarrassing introjection of white values. In the tradition of antebellum proslavery novels, Clark makes slaves the spokespersons for her proslavery view and for the racism against Indians that the white southern Rue so virtuously lacks.

When Rue's father remarries "a quarter-bred French Injun" after Margaret's death, it is the black slave Abram who delivers the biblical "jeremiad" that calls forth the imagined horror of ancestral Masons "buried in ole Firginny" over "the fallen glory of his master's house" in "de New Jerusalem" (I:25–26). Like Southworth, Clark reclaims for the Old South a millennial mission traditionally associated with New England and the Puritans, although the uncharted West is now the "New Jerusalem" wilderness that opposes the Paradise of "ole Firginny." Clark uses the postbellum racist strategy most popularly employed by Thomas Nelson Page to express "Before the War" proslavery nostalgia through the stereotypically loyal old black servant and "patriarch," Abram, which is the original Old Testament name. Hence proslavery Virginia is smuggled onto the frontier through a strategic evasion of white blame for its presence.

Despite her programmatic use of Native Americans to indict northern racism, Clark strikes a false note. By the 1880s few practical efforts could be made to save the disappearing Indians. Clark's staging of the ultimate massacre of her Indian characters at Bouie's Hill suggests her real lack of interest in a minority that posed no lingering threat to white identity. In the massacre Carson's Indian wife, one son, and Rue's Pawnee chief—Lo-loch-to-hoo-la, who had earlier saved her life while his own family was massacred by whites—are murdered by drunken white marauders intent on killing the chief despite Rue's effort to rescue them through her brave flight to nearby Fort Gibson for reinforcements. Rue's lamenting "O my chief my chief!" (I:189) upon his death is an eerie echo of Walt Whitman's lament to Lincoln, "Captain, my Captain." Northern assassination of the Indians—historically traced in the novel—symbolically replaces Lincoln's assassination as the focal point of injustice. Rue, as the mixed-race white Hagar with the positive dimensions of pride, will, and self-reliance, occupies Lincoln's place as the potential emancipator of the Indians. In constant danger of assassination by sinister forces wishing to steal her southern heritage, she is potentially a castoff in the wilderness in danger of being dispossessed by northern plots. Hence are the northern grievances against the South symbolically reversed in Clark's post-Reconstruction novel. The white Rue as Hagar rather than the black Lucy as the Hagar mentioned earlier is made to occupy the dual Hagar roles of victim and survivor described by Delores Williams as endemic to American black women's identity. Not only are Indians conveniently exterminated in Clark's epic frontier novel after they have served her ideological purpose of vindicating the South, but Lucy will also have to be dispossessed of her archetypal value so that a white southern Hagar can appropriate her role.

The Kansas frontier is one of three symbolic geopolitical southern spaces in Clark's *Modern Hagar*. It is notable, for example, that the black Lucy/Hagar does not exist in the imaginative contours of Clark's Southwest. Also, in this frontier space Indians replace African Americans as the source of relation for the southern white Rue/Hagar. This is the most imaginative, mythological space in Clark's novel, the place where, as in the conclusion of Southworth's *Deserted Wife*, black presence is disavowed as a relational source for southern white identity through fictive recursion to an Edenic colonial Virginia "before the Fall." The compression of the Southwest as the site of Indian struggle rather than the "bleeding Kansas" ground of slavery evades the historical reality of the time in favor of a mythological origin that distorts black presence and aligns the South with the plight of the politically oppressed Indian.

Rue is a pasteboard Hagar in this program of regressive denials; her flat representation deprives her of the relational complexity she would have from sisterly twinning with African American identity. This geopolitical use of space manages "blackness" through strategic erasure. In Clark's southernized New York and her southernized Ohio, different strategies and ethnic Hagar identities reemerge. A black Hagar is present in both these political spaces, for example, while the white Rue/Hagar gradually loses her prominence, tainted by a trace of blackness through her repositioning in the Ohio plotline. Clark's Ohio plot follows proslavery novels written by such fellow southerners as Mary Eastman and Caroline Hentz. In these texts slavery is reinstated as a "real" southern issue, but its tragedy is neutralized by the patriarchal code of southern benevolence.

Clark moves her white Rue/Hagar to Ohio to engage her with slavery as a benevolent tradition. She situates Rue in an ironic inversion of the imaginary situation faced by runaway slave women in the North in the novels of Eastman and Hentz. Both Eastman and Hentz write conventional scenes in which women slaves are seduced to flee from slavery by northern antislavery orators whose affection for blacks and promises of job opportunities prove false; the women beg to return to the comforts of slavery.[16] Clark uses Rue in a scene usually reserved for antebellum African American characters. She is sent "East" to Oxford, Ohio, to an aunt and an uncle who is "a Calvinist, an Abolitionist, and a fanatic, but honest and sincere" (II:237). In her ironic inversion, Clark deprivileges blackness by suggesting that white women can resist such rhetoric and by reinforcing the notion that black people are protected by southern slavery. Rue says to her uncle, "My father told me you would teach me how to care for and protect my black people. . . . He said if the people of the North and South knew each other's thoughts and troubles it would teach them to be more charitable. . . . But you have slandered my father in your prayers. You hate us, and you do not really love our black people. If you did you would not pray for evil to come upon us, for they love us. My father prays for them and for me, that I may do them good"(I:322–23). Ironically, Clark transfers the passionate rebellion of the black woman to her white heroine in order to disempower black women—to derail the abolitionist argument that a black heroine would undoubtedly use to free herself. Even though the African Hagar heroine is typically the direct opposite of Hentz's and Eastman's helpless black women who require the "protection" of slavery, Clark's double-edged strategy to expose Hagar as both black and stereotypically reliant on her white slave master is an attempt to diffuse the radicality of the Hagar myth that had imputed so much strength to black women.

It might seem surprising to some that Ohio could be considered a real seat of politics for the South during pre–Civil War times. A pro-southern reading of the Cincinnati convention is provided by Mrs. Carisbrooke, the southern spokeswoman for the Ohio section. A shrewd and politically savvy hostess married to a prominent doctor, she is (like her husband) "a Southerner [a Virginian] by birth and a Northerner by residence" (I:209). Charlotte Clark's narrator—a transparent veil for Clark herself—finds in Mrs. Carisbrooke a mouthpiece for overt southern racism, a sentiment invisible in the frontier section and disguised by sentimentality in the novel's New York section.

In Clark's ongoing "mythstory" that shifts blame for minority abuse onto northerners, her narrator actually argues through the setting of a pro-southern Cincinnati conference that the North bears the blame for slavery's worst abuses because of its capitalistic exploitation of southern lands that southerners had targeted for emancipation during postrevolutionary times. After the Revolutionary War, Virginia and Connecticut were forced to cede broadly allocated lands from their original land grant so that all states felt equitably treated and inclined to sign the Articles of Confederation. New states formed from the Northwest Territory included Ohio (1803), Indiana (1816), and Illinois (1818). Clark incorporates a prerevolutionary southern Ohio in her recollection that Cincinnati is "the commercial centre of the territory which Virginia had given to the federal government" (I:145). Clark symbolically redeems Virginia from its historical taint of slavery because northerners took the land that Virginia had ceded for a free soil territory, and northerners, not southerners, reintroduced slaves there to raise northern cotton. It was Ohio whose production of surplus food also compelled the federal government to remove "Indians from the Gulf States and the Mississippi Valley, that cotton might be grown to enrich the [New Northwest, especially Cincinnati] trader[s], who furnished food to feed the laborers" (I:146–152). "It is only fair to say," the narrator surmises, "that the sin of slavery [and Indian displacement] does not wholly rest at the door of the South—certainly not upon the lintel of Virginia" (I:152). Suddenly the sympathy displayed by frontier southerners for dispossessed Indians gains a context: Indian removal in Clark's vision marks the end of the Jeffersonian agrarian/anticapitalist idealism that had created the "mild and clannish serfdom which domestic servitude had become in Virginia" (I:147) as opposed to the northern capitalistic greed that had replaced it. Hence the political arguments fomenting in Cincinnati provide the perfect rationale for the antebellum proslavery novel, where slavery oppression is reencoded as "mild and clannish serfdom."

Although Clark geopoliticizes antebellum Ohio, especially Cincinnati, as southern, the conflicting presence of an abolitionist who preaches to Rue in Oxford, Ohio, explains Clark's need to produce selectively real historical specifics to ground her own text in an authoritative presence. Since slavery and plantation life were extinct in post-Reconstruction America, resurrecting Civil War politics might seem useless as a resistance to Reconstruction political power. There were high political stakes, however, contingent on reinterpretation of the Civil War conflict. After Reconstruction, white southerners sought northern political support to end what seemed to many a reign of black political activism in the South. Southern victory culminated in the Supreme Court decision in *Plessy vs. Fergusson* (1896), which legalized segregation. Revisionist pre–Civil War history helped set the ground for the demise of northern support for black political power in turn-of-the-century America.

The racism in the Ohio section and Clark's ideological use of historical specifics result in part from her own increased personal investment in a pro-southern antebellum Oxford. Charlotte Clark was herself a Virginian, a child in the Moon family that was descended from British royalty and migrated to Oxford, Ohio, in 1834 to live across from the

Miami University campus. Among her beaux was the soon-to-be-famous Union general Ambrose Burnside, who secured Charlotte's promise of marriage only to be jilted at the altar when she answered the marriage vows, "No siree, Bob, I won't." An apparently patient Burnside and a flirtatious Lottie continued to correspond amicably until her marriage to Ohio Court of Common Pleas judge James Clark, who said "I do" with his gun gently prodded into Lottie's side at the altar lest she again have second thoughts.

Clark's sister Virginia committed several celebrated acts on behalf of the Confederacy. Offended by the sentiments of her northern classmates, she shot every star out of the United States flag at Oxford Female College,[17] and she also promised to wed sixteen Confederate soldiers on the grounds that "I thought if they died, they would die happy, and if they didn't, I didn't give a damn." One of Charlotte's most dangerous courier missions was a trip to Confederate headquarters in Canada, from which she brought back a message to Jefferson Davis "asking upon what terms the South would unite with the Northwest against New England and the Federal government."[18]

Lottie married a member of the Copperhead proslavery political organization, and together they became part of an influential group of proslavery midwestern sympathizers led by the former Ohio congressman Clement Vallandigham.[19] Staging Oxford and Cincinnati, Ohio, as southern spaces, Clark expresses her own personal experience of history as a Confederate spy who believed that the Midwest was literally the South. Throughout Kentucky, Missouri, Iowa, Illinois, Indiana, and Ohio in the early 1860s, an economic depression brought on by a Union blockade of the Mississippi River, which closed the southern market to goods from the Midwest, caused many midwesterners to feel that "the Lincoln administration had sold its soul to New York capitalists and New England manufacturers." Many felt the North was compelling the Midwest to pay for an unwanted war and to "do most of the fighting as well." In addition, a high proportion of foreign immigrants in the Midwest were anti-abolitionists because they feared freed slaves would replace them as cheap labor.[20] There were also many southern immigrants in the Midwest who, like Clark's Mrs. Carisbrooke and Clark herself, brought their proslavery sentiments with them.

In Illinois alone, newspapers, including the Joliet *Signal,* Carthage *Republican,* Macomb *Eagle,* Quincy *Herald,* Cairo *Gazette,* and Lewistown *Fulton Ledger* advocated a separate Northwest confederacy in sympathy with the South in the prewar 1860s.[21] In the beginnings of

Lincoln's administration, pro-southern sympathies caused the defection of some members of his cabinet,[22] and Washington was a major headquarters of the Copperhead movement.[23]

Clark's personal investment in a historical facsimile of a pro-southern Ohio is registered in her attention to specific historical incidents, such as the Sumner affair (which occurred in 1856) and the Cincinnati convention's indictment of New England abolitionist minister Henry Ward Beecher for his gunrunning (I:168).[24] Clark campaigns to canonize pro-southern history with her use of such specifics in the Ohio section. Her investment in historical specifics and in Copperhead fervor expose the racist values that the former Confederate spy can barely disguise.

Mrs. Carisbrooke is Clark's spokesperson. Her mild diplomacy and disgust at fractured southern politics at the Cincinnati convention—her neutral blend of southern and northern allegiances—rapidly dissolve into strong southern racism. In the code of the pro-southern antebellum text, her semblance of fairness masks the overtly partisan view of the real southern author, Charlotte Clark.[25]

The reintroduction of southern racism, which is masked so completely in Clark's frontier mythology, is vividly apparent in Mrs. Carisbrooke's views on Kit Carson and Indians. She is most quintessentially Virginian in representing a certain disquieting voice of "Old Virginia" prejudice, despite the revisionist views of newer models for southern women approved by the narrator, Rue Leszinksky, and Kate Hartley, in their alternative imaginary geopolitical spaces. Mrs. Carisbrooke's resistance to having Kit Carson as her son-in-law, with "his half-breed heir-apparent" (I:299) resembles the earlier-mentioned "jeremiad" against Leszinsky's marrying a "quarter-bred French injun," a jeremiad spoken by the "patriarchal" "Old Virginia" slave Abram, who protects the tradition and reputation of his Old Virginia "Master." Mrs. Carisbrooke calls Carson "a carroty-headed sachem of the Illinois swamps!" (I:331).[26]

Clark intensifies racism when she condemns Carson's part-Indian son, who is, Mrs. Carisbrooke says, "a bar-sinister which I dare not cross" because of his maternal relation as great grandson to King Philip. As "the protector and friend of a mixed tribe called the Black Indians" (I:313), King Philip did not "import the slaves from heathenish Africa, as good Christians should, but . . . captured them from white owners" (I:313–14).

This vituperative view of the Seminoles is deliberately constructed by altering the facts of Carson's historical life. Kit Carson did marry again, but not to a southern ingenue such as Mrs. Carisbrooke's Molly. He married a Mexican woman named Jacinta who became his lifelong companion. Clark also changes Carson's birthplace from Missouri to Illinois. In doing so, she explains away why Carson fought for the Union in the Civil War. Since Clark has Carson marry a southerner, his Union affiliation can be rationalized as a reluctant honoring of his "home" state of Illinois. Clark's Ohio section deconstructs her antiracist frontier mythology, confirming the suspicion that the real value of Indians is, or will soon be, that they are safely dead. Their worth lies solely in their recuperative value as a symbol in order to engender a benevolent South opposed to northern oppression.

Mrs. Carisbrooke's obsession with slaves as southern property fuels her anger at the Seminoles and her own obsession with the black Hagars who now enter Clark's fictional scene. Who better than the shrewd and racist Mrs. Carisbrooke to expose Hagar's blackness as a means of appropriating her vitality and demeaning black women as improperly sexual? Mrs. Carisbrooke attributes to the "whitened" version of the Hagar character, Rue, "homeric heroism" and "princely faults" of passion that mark her as marginally exotic in terms of her faulty passion. But Rue is a side issue for Mrs. Carisbrooke. At the Cincinnati convention parties, she becomes obsessed with exposing and denigrating Lucy's (Hagar's) daughter, Mai (who has been inducted into the social world by Hartley's sister Julia), as African American.

Mai's secret lineage is her quadroon mother, Lucy, and her ruthless white father, Simon Hartley. Mai, in the tragic mulatto form that Clark obviously exploits, does not know she is mixed-race; she believes herself an orphaned distant relation under the guardianship of Simon's sister Julia. But Mrs. Carisbrooke "knows" Mai through her unerring racial typology, for at her first sight of Mai she has "the strangest recollection. . . . As she looked at the full, sensuous beauty of the girl, through some subtle likeness that worked the transformation the pale, worn face, the shrunken, fragile form, of the quadroon Lucy seemed to stand before her. She was so startled at the thought that she looked quickly around, as if in fear of some one reading her thought" (I:341).

Interestingly, Mrs. Carisbrooke knows the girl through intimacy with Lucy (who had been her nurse). This awareness never penetrates her conscious mind, but from her unconscious comes the intuitive recognition, at once so familiar, as if the most intimate awareness a southern white woman would have is of the black female domestic servant who is relegated to the background but to whom the white woman is unconsciously sistered. Seldom do white Hagar writers dream kindly of the black woman, however. Mrs. Carisbrooke replays the Sarah/Hagar dualism in its most sinister form, imagining Mai as "an insult to Kate, this presentation of a relative whom Mrs. Cartaret [Hartley's sister Julia] should have ignored." This is white Sarah's jealousy of African Hagar, for we find that "unconsciously she was provoked and jealous of the beauty which so eclipsed [her daughter] Molly's" (I:345).

For Mrs. Carisbrooke, exposure is revenge, as she encourages her political friend and slaveowner from Arkansas, Mr. Roane, to indulge in his theory that Mai shows a "visible admixture of African blood" (I:345). Roane's detection provokes "a secret triumph in her thought, which it was hard to keep from expression, that, despite the girl's beauty, something betrayed the octoroon to eyes so keen and so experienced as those of the Arkansian slave-owner" (I:346).

"Betray" is a key to the psychological game played by Mrs. Carisbrooke, who encourages Roane by asking for his proofs. "Betray" is also a good word for how the author implies that race can be detected. Mrs. Carisbrooke reasons that if she can goad Roane into convincing the other listeners, she can betray Mai by typing her as part African and thus diffuse Mai's power over the social circle. The fact that it is not Mai's color but her power that Mrs. Carisbrooke resents is an implicit giveaway that color is not an inherent sign of inferiority. Mrs. Carisbrooke must invoke the stigma of color to destroy Mai's power, but it is her beauty, not her color, that is Mrs. Carisbrooke's problem. Skin color is simply an alibi.

Among Roane's "proofs" are the lack of blue reflecting in the surrounding ivory of Mai's eyes; the color (undisclosed) and the wave of "the silky hair" (I:348); the discoloration at the base of nails (which cannot be detected here because Mai wears gloves); and "the infallible test," the "point of the nose" which, even if arched Roman or Greek, will have "no perceptible division of the cartilage of the nostrils at the outer point of the nose." That all are participating in a mean-spirited and offensively voyeuristic game is mutually acknowledged when "the 'nosologists' look guiltily at each other as the 'Beauty' [Mai] appeared with Molly in the open doorway. But Mrs. Carisbrooke had privately determined that a certain scientific looking into things is not only permissible but laudable" (I:349).

Mrs. Carisbrooke incites a sexually prurient act of discourse for the sake of shaming and demeaning her daughter's rival. She cannot resist going further, conjecturing that Mai's subsequent actions are "the outcome of some Voudoo witch who worked her evil through hidden and deadly mysteries ages ago where the Nile spring bubbles into life" (II:220). She further labels Mai "a goddess. Evolved from a witch, has she a human soul?" (II:221) Separating Africa from the Christian myth of Creation, Mrs. Carisbrooke imagines an African genesis with a black woman witch rather than a white male God.

The witch figure who is evil in taking away life as well as giving it appears early in primitive cultures as the "Terrible Mother" dimension of the "Eternal Feminine" in such figures as "Ishtar, Isis, Artemis, and innumerable goddesses of the underworld and the dead." In her complexity she is also "the caldron of incarnation, birth, and rebirth." In Jungian thought, the negative witch status originates because "in her the declining matriarchate is already devaluated by the patriarchal principle, and the mythical reality she represents is personalized, that is, reduced to a mere personal level and so negativized."[27] The projection of Hagar as the witch will be discussed further in the following chapter. Here, Mrs. Carisbrooke (Sarah), brought up in antebellum white culture, fantasizes the negativized aspect of the witch to demean what she perceives as a powerful African American female rival.

In Clark's New York section, on the other hand, this antebellum plot of political diplomacy that deflates black presence through pornographic exposure is replaced by the Hagar novel of female emotion that permits the psychological relation between white women and black women. All Clark's plots are strategic managements of the southern sin of slavery, but the southern stage is reconstructed three times to include ahistorical myth, the politically "real" circumstances of pre–Civil War southern politics rendered bland in an antebellum proslavery context, and the psychological plot of engagement between southern white and black women that is invariably addressed in Hagar novels.

Clark's Kate Hartley is perhaps her new southern woman, a revisionary model of the biblical Sarah. Where resentment for her black Hagar rival was ascendant in Mrs. Carisbrooke's "Sarah," (I:215), Kate's resentment dissolves when she can imagine love for herself. This occurs during an encounter with the husband of her late cousin Margaret, Rue's father, when Colonel Leszinsky finds a resemblance between Kate's "cold, proud, beautiful face" and that of his angelic late wife. "Ah!," he relates, "I see a likeness now," to which Kate inwardly responds, "There was no intention of compliment. She knew there was not. Yet of all the fine things ever said to her of her beauty nothing had ever so touched her. For the first time in all the long years since the hardening process had begun, her heart went out in sympathy to the sentiment of love" (I:280–81).

The thought of Margaret recalls Lucy to Kate, since Lucy was originally Margaret's maid. Once Kate feels love, she immediately questions "how she could have been so pitiless to Lucy—how she could have cared. . . . She knew already that she had never loved her husband. Now she became conscious of love's worth" (I:282). Through Kate, Clark shows how the white southern Sarah's fury with Hagar comes from her feeling of not being loved herself and from her denial of responsibility for that lack. Kate's impulse is to rescue Hagar from exile, only to discover that her husband has separated child from mother and sold Lucy to a Baltimore trader. Lucy escapes and finds haven with the Carisbrookes, who do not recognize her, since she is "half insane from the loss of her child and her betrayal into slavery" (I:264); she has become a "hollow-eyed, spectrally-thin, ill-clad woman stagger[ing] up the walk and [falling] senseless[ly] on the steps" (I:247). But she is recognizable to the reader as the exposed black Hagar, marginalized as insane, determined so by white doctors such as Dr. Carisbrooke because of her abnormal love for children: "an apparently incurable mental trouble—not exactly insanity, but a harmless mania . . . an abnormal and passionately intense devotion to children, especially young girls" (I:247).

Lucy's natural love for her daughter is rescripted by white society as insanity. She is implicitly a "no thing," a "no mother," with no rights to love, labeled and made insane by a society that would bar her from feeling. The effect in the text is to inscribe her insanity as the natural effect of her blackness. Lucy saves up her money and leaves periodically to haunt the footsteps of her beloved lost daughter Mai, returning with a "fixed despondency" that, when questioned, "brought on violent hysteria" (I:248) perceived by Dr. Carisbrooke as a part of her insanity. We are given one insight into Lucy's own degree of decimated motherly agony when she sees "the suffering child" Rue left after the departure of her father and the death of Lo-loch-to-hoo-la "to the ministration of that spirit of motherhood [Mrs. Carisbrooke!] which has strayed out of Paradise to dwell in the hearts of the daughters of Eve" (I:223). But it is predictably Lucy, not Mrs. Carisbrooke, who better cares for her. We are granted one privileged moment with Lucy's true feelings: "Tearless, aching eyes gazed a moment at the lady and the child, who were unconscious of the watcher. Then, crouching down, the quadroon whom Mrs. Carisbrooke called 'Lucy' crept through the door of the adjoining room, and, throwing herself upon her face, begged of the Eternal Giver, not life, but death and forgetfulness" (I:224).

No wonder Kate discloses in a letter to her friend Mrs. Carisbrooke that Hagar "has been a sore spot in my conscience for years" (II:215). In her earlier conference with Leszinksky, she confesses that she and her maid had discovered Lucy's manumission papers six years previously in a satchel in her husband's study, but that Kate let Hartley sell Lucy anyway. Kate regrets her early insistence that her husband sell both Lucy and Mai as a condition of her return to his mansion, but she feels shame even more for the gladness she experienced when Lucy was punished by Hartley's separating "that mother from her child" (I:290).

Kate has a redemptive relation to Hagar's child because Mai resembles Kate's stillborn baby. She tells Mai, "'Forgive my rudeness. Your eyes are my excuse. They are very like—like eyes that were dear to me long ago.' There was a questioning look in the girl's beautiful eyes; but they closed softly as Kate, *knowing this was Hagar's child,* stooped and kissed the blue-veined lids" (I:342). For Clark, this miraculous endearment implies "that the divine spirit of motherhood has been crowned Queen of Heaven"; it takes just that much, Clark ingenuously acknowledges, for a white southern woman to overcome her aversion to a mulatta stepchild. "But for the eyes so like her child's," it is later pointed out, Kate would have been "courteous" for the father's happiness and "for the wrong she believed she had brought upon Lucy." Instead "Mai would always be personally dear to her. Kate could never go back of that first greeting. She would now always see in Mai the sister of her child" (II:32–33).

This deference to her husband remains despite the fact that Kate has rebelled against the code of southern womanhood carefully articulated in the novel. She has refused to hide from her father her grievance against her husband and has ultimately effected a "divorce . . . all the more complete because human law had never pronounced it" (II:32). In reflecting upon the code for antebellum married southern women, Kate's father, Judge Cartaret, resentfully apprehends that his daughter is about to break the code by revealing the "hidden skeleton in the house" (I:106): "That particular portion of earth which, with its inhabitants, constituted the world to Judge Cartaret was sternly intolerant if a woman made any outcry of discontent, any sound to shock the ears" (I:111). Hence there arises, for the southern white woman, the ubiquitous nineteenth-century feminist use of the metaphor of slavery: "No! she must bide under the shelter of her husband's roof with the sad company of her lost love-dreams. For his son's sake, for her sake, he dare not assist her to freedom from this most horrible slavery, this serfdom of the soul, that suffers through the senses" (I:113).

Kate breaches the wall of this convention: "I suffer, papa—I suffer so cruelly I can no longer endure this life I am compelled to lead. If you go without hearing me I know I shall be driven to something desperate. Will you help me, papa? Will you listen?" (I:121). Suddenly Clark reveals the truth behind the southern white woman's appropriation of Hagar: Sarah *is* Hagar, in terms of the patriarchy, for this is the echo of God's words to Hagar that He has heard her.

As the "new woman" of the South, Kate unlocks the key to her husband's hidden chambers through her willingness to pursue her own unconscious and exposes the "secret of the South"—the collusion between the southern husband and wife to repress the knowledge of the mulatta mistress and the husband's miscegenistic offspring. Kate's disengagement with Hartley, her "Abraham" (she lives apart from him and acknowledges Hagar) would seem, in Teubal's reading of the biblical story, to reestablish remnants of the original relation between Hagar and Sarah. Teubal suggests that their friendship predates the estrangement effected through patriarchal labeling of female sexuality as improper. The moment Kate denounces her husband and refuses to absolve him of responsibility, she can begin to find room for Hagar in her "conscience. . . . If there is ever anything that I may be permitted to do for her, the doing it will be a pleasure and a favor to me. Had I been gentler in speech and temper that first summer of my stay at Oakhill, if anger had not blinded all sense of justice, that poor mother's life might not have been altogether one of suffering" (II:215).

But the question of Hagar's own status in her rape or seduction by a white man is turned back to Mrs. Carisbrooke, the more malicious Sarah of the traditional patriarchal Bible text. In arguing Lucy's case for recognition by her resisting daughter, Mai, Mrs. Carisbrooke explains, "She [Lucy] has been a slave, but she is a loving woman. Her faults came from poison in the blood, from the degradation of one race [implicitly her white father, the gambler, Hoyt] and the sin of another" [implicitly the blood of the African] (II:211). Mrs. Carisbrooke's plea is shrouded by her implication that somehow Mai's mother has sinned. Since Lucy is such a scion of motherly virtue to all ailing children in Mrs. Carisbrooke's view, the only sin that could be meant is the assumption of Lucy's sexual complicity in her procreative act with Simon Hartley—despite our knowledge that she was wrenched away from her devoted and loving relationship with her husband Oscar, a character mentioned so late in the text that Lucy seems to be the source, and not the victim, of her predicament. The potential reunion between white and black sisterhood in the cause of feminist freedom from male sexual violence and other forms of domination is rent asunder by the implicit attachment of sexual impropriety to the black slave woman Lucy.[28]

The sexual passion often attributed to the goddess archetype of Hagar, though potentially empowering for the white southern woman, carries volatile implications for stereotyping of black women when associated with the white Hagar's foreign blood (her covert blackness). Whatever inroads Clark intends to make in redeeming her new white southern heroine from past minority abuses are incidental to her larger goal of empowering the white southern woman to disentangle herself from the bonds of an abusive marriage. It is an interesting sidenote that in empowering Kate through Hagar allusions to free herself, Clark abandons one of the archetypal characteristics of the more complex Hagar heroine—sexual passion or sexual engagement.

By the time of the more radical socialist politics of Mary Johnston's 1913 *Hagar*, which is reminiscent of an H.G. Wells utopian novel such as *Ann Veronica* (1909) that explores questions of intellect in the context of an individual's roving passions, we discover that a white Hagar finds freedom through the exercise of her intellect, suffragism, prolabor political activities, and literary endeavors. Such freedom also requires sexual abstinence when the heroine is faced with her soulmate and destined lover, who, by a twist of fate, happens to be married to a fellow reformer. Betraying this woman, whom Hagar admires, would be like betraying a sister. Sexual chastity is the final death of the archetypal Hagar; this is the reaction of the new southern Hagar to the conventional southern male, Ralph: "You are more remotely ancestral than almost any man I know!" (308). Life instead is "a metaphysical adventure—a love-quest if you will. There is a passion of the mind, there is the questing soul, there is the desire that will have union with nothing less than the whole" (292). The white southern woman gains her independence through her own sexual chastity, no longer joined in her feminist quest by the black sister upon whom she has projected the label of illicit sexuality.[29]

A premonition of this conclusion is Clark's pejorative depiction of Lucy's daughter, Mai, as a vestigial Hagar "goddess" (II:161, 172, 207, 208) who has "one [Hagar-like] great gift: she is one of earth's rarest singers" (II: 44, 11–12, 222). Despite all the narrative time spent on

Kate's charitable conversion to an acceptance of Mai, the narrator presents such a shallow creature in Mai that Kate's conversion is almost gratuitous; it would seem absurd except that Mai's nature is incidental to Clark's reformation of her white southern woman. The narrative neglect of black women reaches this new level of sophistication in which the abuse experienced by the Hagar character becomes a "station of the cross" toward the white woman's self-expiation—her movement onward, in other words, away from the black woman toward her own freedom.[30]

Clark demeans Mai as sexually improper; she calls her a "witch." In Freud's terms, this would be the crone figure who embodies "the autonomy of [woman's] desire."[31] Mai quarrels with her "discreet chaperone" and promotes a retired governess to the status of companion, "a sheep-dog" who "would be sufficient for an emancipated young married woman, but it is hardly the thing for a young girl who drives in the Bois in the centre of a cavalcade of admirers" (II:161). According to Mrs. Carisbrooke, Mai Hilton is "a heartless coquette" (II:202).

In her own words to a friend, Mai invites a negative comparison to the white Rue/Hagar, who defends her mother, "telling *me* [Mai] that I was an *ungrateful, despicable creature;* that I knew Lucy was a harmless woman, who had lost her only child; that Lucy *could* not be my mother, for I was not '*true or faithful* enough to be the *child of so good a woman.*' I have never liked the *nasty, proud thing* since" (II:490).

Mai's dilemma is that of the tragic mulatta faced with the discovery of her own hidden African American ethnicity, but Clark presents a character so shallow that she avoids the existential consequences of her identity altogether. Instead Mai marries a European duke willing to "look away" and share his title in exchange for her money. In presenting Rue's defense of Lucy, Clark takes no note of the fact that Rue owns five hundred slaves and that possession of "Mammy" Sara (II:238, 296–97, 366) is a nonissue for Clark. Clark stages a scene in which black woman turns against black woman, with the requisite intervention of the superior white woman to save one black woman from the disgust of another.[32]

Revenge is also a vestigial Hagar characteristic proposed as Mai's motive for bilking her father out of his millions to pay for the "dot" to purchase the duke, revenge for his damage to the mother that she herself loathes, and for the taint of caste that he has imposed upon his daughter (II:211–12). Clark takes her own revenge by having Mai and her husband disappear from the pages in an unhappy, quarrelsome state.

The staged disappearance of minorities from post–Civil War America is the ultimate, and perhaps desired, result of Clark's *Modern Hagar: A Drama*. When Mrs. Carisbrooke speculates in "the wildest visionary" mode that if there were "sex-equality" then white men would be coerced to treat their wives morally, which "would make the modern Hagar impossible" (II:318), she does not so much imagine that black women would be the beneficiaries of more constrained white men but rather that black women would not have to be imagined at all. If white husbands were morally upright, the black Hagars would simply disappear from the southern scene. The yoke of intimacy between the southern white woman and the southern black woman would be loosened, and the white woman, expiated through her remorse for the past, could turn to a future in which black women would not exist in her mind.

Minority disappearances are effected in the unfolding melodrama that concludes the novel. First there is Oscar, the African American slave whose wife (Lucy) was stolen away even before they had had children. In light of his childlessness, it is interesting that the narrator says of Oscar's reluctance to tell his story that "words would have been impotent, even if he could have told of his marriage with Lucy." Potentially a strong character of resistance in this novel, Oscar is robbed of his opportunity for action, rendered impotent by the great loyalty he holds for "Marse Stan" Leszinksky: "Why, my mammy nussed him when she nussed me. Why, he'd—yes, sah—*die* to keep me from bein' put upon and wronged" (I:105). Leszinksky, of course, does not avenge the robbery of Oscar's wife. When Molly Carson tells Oscar's story to Kate late in the novel, she explains that "Oscar's devotion to his master and to his master's child was absolute; so there were later and almost stronger reasons for his hate than his own wrongs or Lucy's" (II:371). This is a tale of a black man rendered impotent by the benevolent "Old Virginia" plantation system that enfolds him. In rendering Oscar impotent, Clark removes him as a threat to the proslavery system.

Oscar is part of the triumvirate of protectors who saved the infant Rue from Indian massacre, a trio that also includes "Big Chief" Lo-loch-to-hoo-la and the crippled, rough-hewn frontier soldier and hunter Bob Stearns. When Bob and Oscar discover that Hartley caused the train derailment that they believe has finally killed Rue Leszinsky—so that Hartley can inherit Rue's money through his wife—they track him to a cabin where Oscar declares "I'm a-gwine to kill him, Marse Bob. . . . He's done me harm 'nough. And 'ithout talk' o' me, thar's Lucy's 'count with him waitin.' Marse Carson b'lieves and I b'lieve he had somethin' to do with that broke rail on the track thar whar Miss Rue was killed"

(II:342). What they find in the house is a dazed Rue with a pistol in her hand and Hartley on the floor "shot through the head" (II:348).

Rue has not killed Hartley. Conveniently, Lucy has wandered to the house and opened the door, compelled by a delusion of Mai calling "Mother! mother!" In proof of the symbolic interchangeability of Mai and Rue as Hagar daughters, Lucy had actually discovered Rue in the house in a state of half-consciousness while "Hartley stood by the bed, looking at the sleeping girl." Perhaps the best line in the book is the Faulknerian stoicism that follows: "She [Lucy] says the look in his face made her kill him" (II:377). The power invested in this image of Lucy as Hagar "survivor" is quickly dampened by the fact that she is dying, and with her last breath she throws up her hands and calls "Oscar!" This triumphant dying testament to her love and to the defeat of her rapist is mitigated entirely by the intervention of Doctor Carisbrooke: "It was the cry of conscience. The ties of the flesh are not so strong as the law of the spirit. Affection may die, but conscience is immortal" (II:379). This conversion of Hagar's demise from the victorious to the pitiful under the cover of conventional piety reveals Clark's apparent determination to impose a moral stigma on the black Hagar—to hold her to blame for the forced sexual acts over which she triumphs in the end. Oscar and Hagar are denied their love and mutual loyalty. At the same time Kate is left with the expiatory consolation that "for pity's sake Lucy has forgiven me" (II:381), since Kate had been "in the wrong." "Through love" Lucy "was obedient to evil. . . . But God pitied her. He gave her a child and touched her with the divine spirit of motherhood, which has cleansed her of sin" (II:381). The Hagar meaning of "fallen woman" pertains to Lucy but is kept clear of the Anglo American characters, in particular Kate and the white Rue/Hagar.

The martyred role that Bob takes on as Hartley's killer evolves from the irony of events that keep Oscar and Bob misinformed about the true identity of the murderer. Rue is hidden away in the hills, also in ignorance of this plotted conspiracy to protect her. In the final scene of *The Modern Hagar,* Carson rides into town to deliver a last-minute reprieve from the governor to stop Bob's hanging. On his way he meets an unwitting Oscar, who is guarding Rue's residence and has been unaware of Bob's trial and forthcoming execution. They have to beat the clock, but the horse runs out of steam and so Oscar, with a "wild look of fright," declares that the horse "can't do it, Marse Carson, but I mus.' You know how I used to run." And, "with his head erect and his arms close up the negro sprang forward in his race with death" (II:399–400).

> The reprieve is too late as Oscar stumbled blindly forward; the blood gushed in a bright red torrent from his mouth. As some one took the paper from the outstretched hand he fell at the foot of the gallows—across the lifeless body of the man they had cut down as the people shouted, "A reprieve!"
>
> Two of the faithfullest hearts that have beat in the century were still. . . .
>
> The heart of the child-like Christian [Bob] was crushed by the crime of the nineteenth century. . . .
>
> A caged bird in the jail-window began singing in low, broken runs, and then thrilled the hot, slumbrous air with a burst of melody. The crowd stirred uneasily; the dumb lips were unclosed: "Father, forgive them; they know not what they do." (II:401–2)

What Clark means to say in this monumentally overdetermined conclusion is unclear. Perhaps the hanging of Bob is actually supposed to be considered *the* crime of the nineteenth century. More likely, the death of Lo-loch-to-hóo-la, Oscar, and Bob and the plight of the modern Hagar may be meant to stand together as the great crimes against minority humanity in America that can only be forgiven by the intervention of the Christlike victims with a merciful God. Nevertheless, the treatment of the antebellum plantation system in *The Modern Hagar* is too freighted with approval and ambiguity to make this final support for minorities and indictment against white America very credible. Intentionally or not, Clark removes "the crime of the nineteenth century" from the inspection of post-Reconstruction America. Her project is to render the "modern Hagar" impossible by making her unimaginable. Clark can do that only by undermining the power of the African American Hagar that she finally exposes for just that purpose. She robs Hagar of her voice, in other words, and deflects authorial focus instead to southern white women and their newfound freedoms and moral catharsis. The irony is that this catharsis is imagined to be possible by converting the Indian fighter and the black man into Christlike figures who purportedly die for the white woman's sins.

Clark's final vision is the ushering in of a new century at the expense of American minorities that have been necessarily eliminated for the sake of Anglo American redemption.

7
Prodigal Daughters
Hopkins's HAGAR'S DAUGHTER and Black Female Identity

At the eleventh woman's rights convention in 1866, African American writer and activist Frances Watkins Ellen Harper characterized the different, and potentially divisive, concerns of black and white feminists: "You white women speak here of rights. I speak of wrongs. I, as a colored woman, have had in this country an education which has made me feel as if I were in the situation of Ishmael, my hand against every man, and every man's hand against me."[1] Later, to make the same point about the divergent paths of late nineteenth-century African and Anglo American feminism, an African American writer shifted the ground symbolically to Hagar.

In *Hagar's Daughter: A Story of Southern Caste Prejudice*, serialized in the *Colored American Magazine* from March 1901 through March 1902, African American author Pauline Elizabeth Hopkins incorporated several popular fictional elements—the novel of detection, tragic mulatto fiction, and the element of minstrelsy—as promotional features.[2] But the grounding element of Hopkins's fiction is its status as a Hagar story. *Hagar's Daughter* is a direct response to the undermining of black female identity in nineteenth-century white women's Hagar texts. It reclaims Hagar for the empowerment of black women that forms a part of African American tradition.[3] Earlier Hagar novels by white women provide a destabilizing lapse from the certitude that Hagar belongs to an African American tradition. Reading Hopkins serves as a cipher for reading backwards into a distorted system of Hagar codes in which Hagar's blackness becomes increasingly invisible.

I read *Hagar's Daughter* first among the Hagar novels discussed here. Discovering that there was a preceding tradition of such novels written by white women, I prepared myself for the bizarre finding that Southworth's, Clark's, and Stephens's Hagars would form an insular Anglo American canon lacking an awareness of the parallel tradition of Hagar as a mixed-race symbol of African American identity. Instead, I found that Hagar is a radically hybridized symbol for white women dreaming black: African American ethnicity, albeit coded, empowered the white heroines in nineteenth-century American texts to rebel against the patriarchal mores of their time. At the same time, the racialized strategies of bad faith splitting and subsequent reification of women's illegal sexuality onto a split-off African Hagar denied the temporary twinning between white women and black women that was engaged in white Hagar texts.

Southern white Hagar writers embraced the scope of women's emotion—in particular, sexual passion—through a vicarious taking on of Hagar's sexualized blackness, albeit temporarily. But along with passion, female power in general seemed part of the black Hagar goddess archetype for white southern women who conceived of African American slave women as especially powerful. Phyllis Marynick Palmer observes that even now "it is black women rather than white who popularly symbolize courageous, industrious womanhood."[4] Historian E. Franklin Frazier helps us to understand why, more than we have suspected, these white Hagar authors incorporated the factual historicity of black slave women. He observes that "as a worker and free agent, except where the master's will was concerned, [black women] developed a spirit of independence and a keen sense of personal rights."[5] While white women may have turned to Hagar as a model of independence genuinely grounded in reality, they were wrong to extend that power to a black woman's sexual control over a "master."

In *Hagar's Daughter,* Pauline Hopkins demystifies the African woman as a superhero who, because of her supernatural powers, bears the blame if her own womanly strength does not allow her to transcend social stigma. Hopkins actively resists the racial stereotyping of a black Hagar as inappropriately sexualized. And, cannily, rather than reclaiming the archetype for black women alone, Hopkins brilliantly reinforces the hybridization of a black/white Hagar through textual strategies. In doing so, she makes a political statement, reappropriating and exposing the hybridized status of Hagar heroines in past fiction by whites, invoking the necessarily twinned sisterhood between black and white women in America and insisting that black and white women will not survive if they remain separated in their otherwise futile resistance to patriarchal forces. In *Hagar's Daughter,* Hopkins proclaims that only through the mutual recognition of Hagar hybridity can American *fin de siècle* women disarm the reader constructed in Stephens's *Hagar:* a white or black male reader who confines women within a stultifying domestic role and fantasizes women in a pornographic scene that exploits and abuses them.

Hopkins made a lifelong exploration of the various ways in which black women could politically empower themselves. In *Hagar's Daughter* and in *The Colored American Magazine,* Hopkins openly fought reactionary attempts by the patriarchal press and more conservative women to narrow the scope of black women's ambition to the traditional role of mother and housewife as a means for securing the Victorian endorsement of African Americans. Although unlisted on the journal's masthead, Hopkins was the literary and probably more general editor of the *Colored American* from its beginnings until 1904,[6] a period that corresponds to the multiplicity of voices addressing black womanhood in the magazine's woman's fiction.

During Hopkins's tenure on the *Colored American,* fictional models celebrated expanded dimensions of black womanhood. Woman's self-identity, her sisterhood with other black women, her intellectual capabilities, and her common-sense ability to see through male deception in the marriage quest dignified women who did not subordinate themselves to men. Portraits include that of an intelligent college senior who overcomes her jealousy of a more attractive friend to protect her friend's virtue. Another story depicts women overcoming their initial competitive jealousies to expose their minister as the potential seducer of their daughters. These stories emphasize bonding between women to achieve empowerment and higher education, rather than prescribing male protection as the black woman's aid. A particularly powerful story is "Aunt 'Ria's Ten Dollars" by Georgia F. Stewart, in which a black woman enlists the promised help of the lawyer son of her former white mistress so she can buy land to rescue her husband, who is being exploited as a sharecropper. Also appearing at this time was Gertrude Mossell's "Mizeriah Johnson: Her Arisings and Shinings." Mizeriah overcomes her parents' negative mirroring of her rebellious independence of manner to "rise and shine," expressing in church and outside of it her creativity and natural ebullience. When community disapproval is provoked by her "ceaseless desire to 'rise and shine,'" Mizeriah is vindicated by the parishioners' young pastor, who, enchanted by her independence, marries her (4:3, 232).[7]

Hopkins's firing from the *Colored American* by black male management was likely related to these empowering tales of women. Gertrude

Mossell, author of "Mizeriah's Risings and Shinings," was a black suffragist and feminist widely known during her time for her syndicated newspaper columns and advocacy of women entering professions such as medicine and journalism. Rosalyn Terborg-Penn notes that Mossell "dismissed the notion that a woman had to choose either to have a family or a career."[8] Since Hopkins was the literary editor, it seems likely that she sought this contributor whose stance on black women's role outside of marriage did not agree with that of the majority of the staff. Most scholars attribute Hopkins's "resignation" in 1904, after businessman Frederick Moore bought the financially troubled magazine for Booker T. Washington and moved it from Boston to New York, to her agitationist politics, which opposed Washington's policy of assimilation.[9] But is it coincidental that after Hopkins's departure, dialogical voices of female empowerment in the *Colored American* ceased? Poet and fellow contributor William Stanley Braithwaite called Hopkins "temperamental" and complained that her inflated regard for herself "as a national figure" while on the magazine caused her to feel "free to impose her views and opinions." Braithwaite often sided against Hopkins on editorial decisions made by R.S. Elliott, coincidentally the only white staff member on the magazine. Donald Joyce notes that after Hopkins left, "the editorial focus of the *Colored American Magazine* changed from the arts and literature to business, politics, and education."[10] Not only did literature diminish, but the woman's role as mother became a consuming emphasis in later issues.

Amid the voices of other female contributors calling for black female empowerment, Hopkins's *Hagar* voiced resistance to entrapment within the narrowing confines of a coercive male construction of female identity. To consider the motherhood role as entrapment seems a more likely focus for white women's turn-of-the-century texts, such as Kate Chopin's *The Awakening* and Edith Wharton's *Summer,* which often revealed motherhood as antagonistic to white women's freedom. As Claudia Tate has demonstrated, typically motherhood and the domain of the nuclear family in *fin-de-siècle* texts by black women signified freedom from the oppression of slavery and the assertion of the kinship bonds that had been severed by the separation of children from their mothers and wives from their husbands under the antebellum code of slaves as property. As Tate argues, black women's texts politicized the domestic sphere as the cradle for racial uplift.[11] Hopkins was not insensitive to motherhood as a sacred role for black women. One of her critics points out that her *Contending Forces* demonstrates a "worship of a domesticity which sanctified motherhood."[12]

In *Hagar's Daughter,* Hopkins responded to the particularly stultifying way in which men presented motherhood for black women in the pages of the *Colored American Magazine*. Messages about women's roles told women of their innate intellectual subservience and the impropriety of their feeling sexual desire. Women must "liv[e] up to the moral law with a Puritan rigidity," declares one male essayist in his 1905 February "Educated Colored Men and White Women." They must as well achieve sufficient "intellectual attainments" to gain respect but should realize their "inferior[ity] in intellectual capacity to men" so that "any deference which the educated colored man pays to the feminine opinion beyond certain limits, arises more from a practice of knightly courtesy than belief in that particular party's judgment." As Paula Giddings notes, "Following the Civil War, men attempted to vindicate their manhood largely through asserting their authority over women." This need to subordinate women for the empowerment of men is evident in another male writer's complaint in "Why the Men Don't Marry." Black women's entrance into business has "so reduced man's means to a livelihood that, he finds the task of supporting a family a more difficult one."[13]

Despite Tate's resurrection of the motherhood role as female empowerment for black women in *fin de siècle* domestic texts, essays in the later years of the *Colored American* exploited home as a means of keeping in check black women's social and political efforts. The late *Colored American*'s puritanical judgments on women's sexuality and didactic messages about women's subordinacy restrict "H-O-M-E" to moral influence rather than the site of men's and women's political and collaborative advocacy. In the late *CAM,* the mid-century Victorian "angel in the house" is repeated in the "true mother,"[14] whose nurturing role and sexual chastity are paired with overt presentations of her lack of "erotic" desire—notably sexual but also political.

In *Hagar's Daughter,* Hopkins exploits the Hagar paradigm found in the white domestic novel, not only to reclaim Hagar for African Americans but also to model a womanhood that might go beyond the role of mother. Like other Hagar writers before her, Hopkins deconstructs the male-engendered sacred code of motherhood with its guarantee of male protection for women, through the plot element of Hagar's abandonment. Hagar is also a synonym for women who rebel against patriarchal forces in their quest for creative self-engenderment and who challenge proscriptive taboos on their sexuality. In other words, Hopkins's use of the complex Hagar paradigm is a gauntlet thrown down; anyone familiar with the Hagar paradigm—black or white—would have been hard-pressed *not* to see her as representing a resistance to women's narrower role within patriarchal construction.

Hopkins's knowledge of how Hagar had been deployed as a voice of resistance in white women's fiction is revealed in textual affiliations between her Hagar and those of preceding white women writers. Her home is the antebellum Maryland of E.D.E.N. Southworth's heroines, and, like several Hagars before her, this Hagar's journey ends up in Washington, D.C. That Hopkins knew the particular form of feminist resistance encoded in former white Hagar fiction is also apparent in her own articulation of the independent nature of her heroine. Hopkins's Hagar, in true Hagar form—think of Southworth's Mary Magdalene—chafes against the southern ideal of woman's domesticity: "She longed to mix and mingle with the gay world; she had a feeling that her own talents, if developed, would end in something far different from the calm routine, the housekeeping and churchgoing which stretched before her" (33). As a more superficial point, Hopkins's Hagar also has the equestrian skills seen in the other Hagar heroines (46).

Interestingly, Hopkins's redeployment of Hagar as a desiring subject whose role exceeds the boundaries of chaste and self-sacrificial motherhood is anticipated in an essay on and illustration of Hagar in the *Colored American Magazine* the month before Hopkins began serializing *Hagar's Daughter*. The essay appeared in February 1901, accompanied by a painting of Hagar with a more mature version of Ishmael by French painter Hugues Merle, who was known for his religious painting of "Jephthah's Daughter"[15] but probably more for his 1861 portrait of Nathaniel Hawthorne's Hester Prynne, which hangs in Baltimore's Walters Art Gallery.[16]

Merle's painting challenges previous American representations of Hagar. It portrays her for the first time as unambiguously Egyptian. Dark of skin with an elongated face and thin, elongated nose, Merle's Hagar suggests an Egyptian ethnicity. Note also the depiction of Ishmael as a full-grown adult, which arguably deemphasizes Hagar's limiting role as a nurturing mother who has implicitly transcended her sexual being.

Charles Winslow Hall wrote the accompanying essay on "Hagar and Ishmael" that appeared in his running series on "Fascinating Bible Stories" in the *CAM*. Hall was likely the first nineteenth-century American periodicalist to aver openly that Hagar was African: Ishmael was "the son of a Caucasian father and African mother." Significantly, this first prose interjection of Hagar and Ishmael into implicitly antebellum

Figure 8. This first-time illustration of an ethnicized Hagar is from a painting by Hugues Merle, more famous for his painting of *The Scarlet Letter*'s Hester Prynne. It appears as the frontispiece in the February 1901 volume of the *Colored American Magazine*.

plantation history appears in the first general-interest *fin de siècle* African American periodical.

Unlike the condemnatory prose indictments of Hagar as an overpassionate, failing mother that Mary DeJong cites as prevalent in Anglo American Victorian prose, Hall's piece describes Hagar's motives from a positive view that seems to override gender considerations in favor of Hagar's emblematic significance as a biblical model of African American empowerment. Ironically, Hall's fascination with Hagar's role as a *willing* concubine for Abraham is a harbinger of the problem that Hopkins will have in presenting a passionate black Hagar. Although Hall evades it, the perception that black women desired their sexual relations with white antebellum masters caused black women slaves to be blamed for what was often their own rape, and fostered the social ostracism of black slave women as innately promiscuous.

As previously discussed, the equation of an African Hagar with sexual desire fed right into the racist construction of black women as "over-sexed" in Victorian America. Paula Giddings notes that even African American men, such as the important early abolitionist and author William Wells Brown, questioned whether African American slave women had not willingly entered into relations with the "Master."[17] The male assumption of white women's essential chastity, as opposed to black women's unlicensed desire, was the informing premise for the *CAM* article quoted above on the relations between "Educated Colored Men and White Women." Giddings quotes a reporter from the *Independent* in 1902: "I sometimes hear of a virtuous Negro woman, but the idea is absolutely inconceivable to me. . . . I cannot imagine such a creature as a virtuous Negro woman." According to nineteenth-century activist Fannie Barrier Williams, "Too many colored men entertain very careless, if not contemptible opinions of the colored girls. . . . We have all too many colored men who hold the degrading opinions of ignorant white men, that all colored girls are alike."[18]

Hall skirts this issue by aligning Hagar's erotic desire with her independence. His Hagar is "a tall, stately, graceful woman. . . filled with the desire of love and offspring, of wealth and prestige, which no condition [of subordinacy] in life or sense of dependence can ever eradicate or stifle." Hagar as desiring woman is admirable to Hall. He identifies her as the prototype of Cleopatra, since Hagar "played and risked all for love of the grandest man of a land in which Egypt had already found her most gallant enemies." While Hall does not discredit Hagar's position as desiring woman, Sar-ai's role as abusive enforcer—Hall uses the archaic biblical name—is portrayed as the direct cause of Hagar's dilemma: Sar-ai, this "impatient, disappointed, jealous, unhappy woman who had not spared to sacrifice a husband's devotion and a woman's chastity to her unbridled desires." For Hall, Sar-ai is the white antebellum slave mistress who not only delivers up the black slave woman to her husband as a sexual surrogate but does so, interestingly enough, as a vicarious acting out of her own "unbridled desires."[19]

Hall can have his cake and eat it too in this revisionist endorsement—so common in Hagar fiction—of a passionate and desiring Hagar whose loss of chastity is not, however, the result of her own desire but of her enforced surrogacy by a wicked Western woman who conspires to rape her. In *Hagar's Daughter,* Hopkins must be more cautious. She feels forced to cancel out black woman's desire as the dangerous weapon used by racists to marginalize black women for their alleged sexual promiscuity. But Hopkins, like Hall, sees the potential for women to claim a subjectivized status through their own assertive desire. Rebellion against the patriarchy is compelled by the mechanism of desire in the Hagar character's psyche.

Hopkins in fact overtly refers to one of the more confrontational and passionate poems in the Hagar canon near the beginning of *Hagar's Daughter.* Hopkins's heroine is the first openly mixed-race African American heroine to follow Charlotte Moon Clark's, but there are significant revisions. For example, although Hopkins's Hagar goes temporarily mad upon discovering her mixed-race identity, she experiences the temporary madness typical of the Hagar heroine rather than the all-consuming madness Clark assigns to her overtly mulatta character Lucy/Hagar in *The Modern Hagar,* which serves effectively to kill her. In *Hagar's Daughter,* the instrument of Hagar's exposure is the immoral St. Clair, the covetous younger brother of Hagar's wealthy plantation husband, Ellis Enson. St. Clair links up with a reprehensible slave dealer, Walker, who claims to know that Ellis's apparently white southern bride is unwittingly of mixed-race identity.

Walker's facts appear incontrovertible; upon hearing them, and overcome by her own faint remembrances, Hagar swoons and then is taken to her parlor, where she secludes herself in an agony of fear and self-loathing. Typical of the nearly-white heroines in *fin de siècle* fiction by black women, this Hagar shares some racial prejudice with the antebellum white southern woman: "Her mother a slave! She wondered that the very thought did not strike her dead. With shrinking horror she contemplated the black abyss into which the day's events had hurled her. . . .

Was she, indeed, a descendant of naked black savages of the horrible African jungles?" (57).

By casting her heroine into "a slough of despondency" that the implied author cannot possibly endorse, Hopkins arrives at a critical moment through this depiction of Hagar's self-loathing. Although some of Hopkins's white audience may have responded sympathetically to this white racial narcissism, Hagar's likening of African American descendants to "naked black savages of the horrible African jungles" hardly renders her Hagar appealing to the many readers who must have felt contemptuous of Hagar's racism.

It is at this point that Hopkins diffuses her heroine's racial narcissism by deftly removing her from one level of identification to another. Hagar moves to a point of identifying herself with the biblical and extra-biblical and literary tradition that gives her courage, resilience, and transcendent pride in African American identity. "Horrible fatality that had named her Hagar," the heroine finally concludes after her mental derogations. In this she resembles numerous other Hagars in the canon who, by this one expression, link themselves to a powerful archetypal paradigm of female survival and pride in themselves. Appropriately, Hopkins allows Hagar to remember empowering lines: "Somewhere she had read lines that came back to her vividly now," the final stanza of a poem published by Eliza Poitevent Nicholson in the November 1893 issue of *Cosmopolitan*. In this poem, Hagar fights back against Abraham's rejection by hurling invectives and curses from her homeland of Egypt. Her immense pride and the intense Egyptian nationalism that empowers her are vividly revealed in the final stanza, which Hopkins's Hagar remembers, word for word, and mentally repeats:

> Farewell! I go, but Egypt's mighty gods
> Will go with me, and my avengers be.
> And in whatever distant land your god,
> Your cruel god of Israel, is known,
> There, too, the wrongs that you have done this day
> To Hagar and your first-born, Ishmael,
> Shall waken and uncoil themselves, and hiss
> Like adders at the name of Abraham.[20]

This passionate and rebellious response is suggestive of the Hagar heroine in contrast to the tragic mulatta whose tale is rooted in William Wells Brown's *Clotel* (1853). Typically, the near-white heroine of Brown's tale, upon discovering her blackness, faces the disaster of enslavement, which is averted only by suicide.²¹ Indeed, Hopkins follows this line of the tragic mulatto plot when the villainous St. Clair enslaves Hagar and her child and takes them to Washington to be auctioned. Brown's famous scene showing his heroine at the bridge is replicated as Hopkins's Hagar flees at dusk with her child and is caught on the Potomac bridge, as memorialized in Alexander Skeete's fine illustration: "Then she raised her tearful, imploring eyes to heaven as if seeking for mercy and compassion, and with one bound sprang over the railing of the bridge, and sank beneath the waters of the Potomac river" (75).²²

If the tragic heroine is rescued from the hands of slavery, as in Frances Ellen Watkins Harper's *fin de siècle* novel *Iola Leroy* (1892), she becomes typically docile and survives the crisis of her new racial encoding through an altruistic channeling of her white education into racial uplift. As a given, she *does not pass,* and romantic passion is channelled into her altruistic mission.

Hopkins avoids the simplistic victimization of her Hagar heroine by swerving away from the tragic mulatto tradition into the path of resistance inscribed in the popular Hagar canon. Hopkins's Hagar jumps off the bridge with her baby and they both disappear. This erasure resists the display of black Hagar as a self-consuming artifact. When Hopkins's Hagar resurfaces in Washington, D.C., twenty years later, she has changed her name to Estelle—a star—and emerges as a heroine who has transcended her crisis. In line with the Hagar archetype, as distinguished from the tragic mulatta figure, this Hagar's temporary absence involves a survivalist migration to the American West, where she has met and married a "self-made," "ungrammatical" California mining entrepreneur who had worked on a Mississippi steamboat, joined the Union army during the war, and now was a senator. Hopkins's imagination of the West as multicultural and tolerant of ethnic diversity is reminiscent of Clark's use of the West as a democratic Utopia, although Hopkins edits out Clark's exclusion of American blacks from this Utopia. Hopkins's character, Bowen, has Indian ethnicity—"the hair and skin of an Indian"— metaphorically spliced onto "the man of the world, experienced in business and having that courage, when aroused, which is common in genial men of deadly disposition" (80). He is a real western man, with a profound indifference to geographical place—"the North Pole, Egypt, Africa—all were one to him" (81), indicating his multicultural tolerance. Hopkins tends to invent some Caucasian "escape hatch" for African Americans from the terrors of white racism.²³ In *Hagar's Daughter,* as in Clark's significantly modified version, the West symbolizes racial tolerance.

Figure 9. The well-known African American artist Alexander Skeete illustrated all of Pauline Hopkins's novels in the *Colored American Magazine*. This scene of Hagar jumping from a bridge appeared as the frontispiece in the May 1901 issue. Notice how Hagar appears to ascend rather than fall.

Hagar's resurfacing as white in a racially intolerant Washington, D.C., as Estelle ([white?] star), would be severely condemned by the moral code of the tragic mulatto tale, which insists that the worst sin the hero or heroine could commit would be to "pass." Hagar's passing—and the narrative neutrality about it—are twin signs of betrayal within the terms of tragic mulatto fiction. Hopkins's knowledge of past Hagar fiction by white women writers allows her to endorse Hagar's passing as a sign of African American empowerment. In the white Hagar tradition, white women gain their empowerment by "passing" as black—that is, by appropriating imagined African American female identity as a means of fighting the antebellum patriarchy. Hopkins tropes this tradition by making her black heroine "white." The passing of a black woman as white to survive in a racist world displaces the passing of a white woman as black to survive in a patriarchal one. Hopkins resists colonial appropriation by Hagar "miming."

Mimicry, according to Homi Bhabha, is "the sign of a double articulation; a complex strategy of reform, regulation and discipline, which 'appropriates' the Other as it visualizes power. Mimicry is also the sign of the inappropriate, however, a difference or recalcitrance which . . . poses an immanent threat to both 'normalized' knowledges and disciplinary powers." To continue, Bhabha notes that "it is from this area between mimicry and mockery, where the reforming, civilizing mission is threatened by the displacing gaze of its disciplinary double, that . . . instances of colonial imitation come."[24] In Hagar fiction written by white proslavery southern feminists, authors engender white heroines who pass for African American to acquire a mythologized empowerment. These white writers have already deconstructed the racism of their own colonial antebellum discourse by assigning power to black ethnicity. But these writers reinstate proslavery colonial discourse by strategically disavowing the blackness of their white heroines at the ultimate moment.

If read in the context of the tragic mulatto genre, Hopkins's passing heroine is in grave danger of betraying her race. Understood as a response to previous white Hagar fiction, however, Hopkins's use of passing actively resists racism. In the context of Bhabha's theory, Hopkins engenders a passing heroine to mimic and thus displace the strategy of white Hagar texts. The white heroine who passes for black and is revealed to be white in racist Hagar fiction is transformed, in *Hagar's Daughter*, into the white/covertly black heroine who passes as white and is then revealed as actually black. Hopkins's passing Hagar accomplishes what Bhabha calls the "displacing gaze of the disciplining double." Hopkins appropriates the power of the colonial Other—its whiteness—and secures its power, thus displacing it. Her Hagar's strategy of passing is a mode of survival in racist Washington that deconstructs the play of white discourse that addresses passing on an imaginary level. Hopkins's passing text—in which Hagar is finally revealed as black—contests past Hagar fictions that finally erase black identity because of white women's obsessive need to *really* be white. The *"almost the same, but not quite"* valance of a white/black/white/black Hagar as opposed to a white/black/white Hagar displaces racial discourse by destabilizing it "into an uncertainty which fixes the colonial subject as a 'partial' presence."[25]

Pauline Hopkins's resistant mimicry of the white Hagar tradition in fiction parallels Edmonia Lewis's resistant mimicry of the white Hagar tradition in American art. Lewis's white Hagar statue (1875?) is traditionally read as coded black by art scholars. For example, notes in the curator's files at the National Museum of American Art, where Lewis's Hagar is exhibited, suggest that "while Hagar's face is decided [*sic*] not African, Lewis and her contemporaries did associate Egypt with the African American. Thus, Hagar can be viewed as a generalized portrayal of the strength of black women."[26]

Lewis, orphaned early, was born in Albany, New York, the daughter of a Chippewa Indian mother and a free black father. She was adopted by abolitionists and sent in 1858 to the first college to admit women on a nonsegregated basis, Oberlin College in Ohio. She left the school for Boston after being accused, although acquitted, of "poisoning" her roommates with an aphrodisiac she put in her friends' wine as a prank. Around 1865 she was sent by patrons to study in Rome, where she adopted the neoclassical style of her teacher, Hiram Powers.

Lewis's white neoclassical representation of Hagar can be explained by her artistic training, but this training did not prevent her from overtly representing Native American ethnic features in such sculptures as "Old Arrow Maker" (National Museum) and even, arguably, African ethnicity, in her recently recovered "The Death of Cleopatra." The latter is a monumental work, also on exhibit at the National Museum, that departs from tradition because Lewis sculpts the fatal asp.

Although Lewis's white marble Hagar has neoclassical features, African American art scholar David Driskell remarks that her Hagar "is an Old Testament character [used] to represent the will and strength of an oppressed people, symbolizing the stride toward freedom by the black race."[27] Elsa Fine writes that Lewis's "Hagar" "deals with the struggle of the Afro-American in terms of Biblical symbolism."[28] Kirsten Buick, who

Figure 10. "Hagar in the Wilderness" by African American sculptor Edmonia Lewis (1875; marble, 4'4"). National Museum of American Art, Smithsonian Institution, Gift of Delta Sigma Theta, Sorority, Inc.

notes the disparity between Hagar's overt whiteness and her coded blackness, temporizes that the sculpture "is an allegorical statement about the abuses suffered by black women when a black patriarch is not in place to protect them." Buick, who, as former fellow and Lewis specialist at the National Museum, probably wrote the notes in the curator's files, echoes her sentiment there that since "Egypt was coded as black Africa among abolitionists and colonizationists in the nineteenth century Hagar was a particularly pertinent allegory of chattel slavery and the indignities that black women suffered." Buick suggests that Lewis's disguise of blackness may have been intended to engage Anglo American women in the plight of African Americans.[29]

If on the other hand Lewis's white Hagar was recognizably "black" so that her blackness would be "signified" to black Americans but rendered subliminal and disavowed in white America, then it mimics prior and future American pictorial representations of Hagar as white by displacing her whiteness with a difference. One radicalizing difference is the mixed-race ethnicity of the artist, whose cultural mimicry—as Homi Bhabha's theory would suggest—parodies authority through its insinuation of difference into seemingly self-contained authority. Mimicry is "a desire that, through the repetition of *partial presence,* which is the basis of mimicry, articulates those disturbances of cultural, racial and historical differences that menace the narcissistic demand of colonial authority."[30] Lewis's Hagar imitates white representation by diverging into difference: she has clasped hands and the upward gaze common to Hagars and abolitionists' antislavery emblems,[31] but her face is barely uplifted in Lewis's depiction. As well, Lewis's depiction of a standing Hagar counters the most famous representation of black slave womanhood, that by Lewis's mentor, Hiram Powers. His analogical slave statue, the "Greek Slave," kneels and is also unclothed and chained, neither of which is true of Lewis's statue. In addition, although Lewis's statue includes the vessel shown in so many Hagar pictorials, the ubiquitous child is missing, which implies a recovery of Hagar and *her* story in place of Ishmael/Abraham's. Lewis minimizes Hagar's role as supplicant—subordinate—mother to reposition her in a fuller range of womanhood. This restitution talks back to a patriarchal politicization of motherhood as a sacred site that transcends female desire. Lewis's deviation from the Hagar Bible story, her disinvestment in Hagar as mother, resembles the foregrounding of passionate women in Hagar fiction. But the minority mimicry of white Hagars by Pauline Hopkins in *Hagar's Daughter* talks back to white Hagar writers who displace their own sexuality onto blackness.

Previous to Hopkins's text, the sexual Hagar, placed outside the sentimentalized role of domestic mother, is marked as black. As one sees with the work of black feminists Delores Williams and Savina Teubal, if the Genesis text is not resisted, Hagar is conceived as a victim and survivor of enforced sexual surrogacy and of abandonment and exile at the hands of a white man. Even if the story in Genesis is read as a patriarchal incursion into an originative Egyptian tale in which women are virtually twinned, sexual performance still differentiates the women and places one woman over the other.[32] The split between black and white women that we have seen in white women's Hagar fiction results from the social stigmatizing of black women as inherently sexual; as a consequence, Hagar seems recursively bound to perpetuate racial oppression through her sexual component.

In *Hagar's Daughter* Hopkins avoids the easy solution of rendering black women as universally chaste. As a feminist, she could not betray women by depriving them of emotional substance—including sexuality—despite the fact that as a black feminist, Hopkins knew what the portrayal of black women's sexuality could mean politically. Her brilliance in *Hagar's Daughter* lies in her rebellious refusal to examine or judge the *content* of women's sexuality. Instead, she focuses on the *process*[33] by which female sexuality becomes socially enculturated as a sign of degradation. Hopkins offers a critical examination of the psychoanalytical process by which the passion of women—black women, in particular—becomes the negative justification for decolonization.

Stephens's *Hagar* in particular reveals how the excess of emotion that condemns the heroine as unlawfully passionate in Victorian novels is redirected in nineteenth-century America onto African American womanhood. Susanne Kappeler explains that authors who portray women as sexual objects put all readers in an erotically charged position that simulates male mastery.[34] Hopkins seeks to derail male mastery and male racist readers by producing two conflicting narrative levels: she submerges the demeaning white masculine view of black female sexuality within the novel's intradiegetic level of discourse; that is, female sexuality is filtered through white male characters who exist within the story itself. In conflict with this is the voice of the implied author, a "construct inferred and assembled by the reader from all the components of the text." As Rimmon-Kenon points out, "Implied authors are often far superior in intelligence and moral standards to the actual men and women who are real authors" and, for our purposes it must be added, far superior to the white male focalizers through whom women's sexuality in the novel is filtered.[35]

Points of focalization, as distinguished from narration, are located in characters from whose perspective the reader experiences the story. The implied author resists the male focalizations of female sexuality, although she runs the risk of losing her readers in the phantasmagoria of white male focalizations of their sexual fantasies. There are clear signs, however, that Hopkins expects less than enlightened readers. From a more disingenuous position as the extradiegetic narrator who mimes authority, Hopkins in fact appropriates racial/sexual stereotyping from past Hagar fiction to serve as red herrings for the detection of black female identity. These miscues lead to reading misprision and expose to readers their own racial prejudices.

It is easy to distance oneself from the more obvious white male villains in Hopkins's text, such as St. Clair and his sidekick, Walker, who scandalize Hagar as black and thus sexually available and outside the protection of the law. But Hagar's security rests in the protection of her loving white husband, Ellis Enson, who has previously idolized her and who, up to this point as a white male focalizer, has shown a unique ability to resist his personal sexual anxieties for the sake of a more authentic, collaborative relationship with Hagar.

Enson is the character to whom in the second half of the book Hopkins grants the noble profession of a Pinkerton detective. This suggests his ability to "see" more deeply within himself and thus to "see" reality with a clarity lacking in repressive denial. For Hopkins, the ability to detect starts with the self and the self's ability to avoid projecting its inner fears onto a racialized other. Neither women nor men can be narcissistically appropriated and objectified as possessions to complete the self. Enson's self-ownership, so to speak, is clarified by a vignette at the novel's beginning. Voyeuristically gazing at Hagar through the window of the kitchen where she is washing dishes, "with the sleeves of her morning robe turned up to the shoulder" (34), Enson, along with the reader, is checked in his gaze by Hagar's regard in return: "A quick wonder flashed in the eyes that met hers; the color deepened in his face as he saw he was observed" (34).

Enson's ability to realize himself as the object of someone else's gaze, particularly a woman's, indicates his proximity to what feminist and psychoanalytical critic Shari Benstock calls "the unconscious, or that which derives from an experience of 'self' as fragmented, partial, segmented, and different." Benstock notes that "Man enforces a 'unity and identity across time' by 'reconstituting' the ego as a bulwark against disintegration" and pushing "into the darkened realms of the repressed" any experience of himself or the world that is self-alienating and symptomatic of mortality.[36]

Enson resists the appropriative gaze that would turn Hagar into an object instead of a person. His self-consciousness and shame brought about by the displacing gaze of his Eve suggest the allegory of the Fall into sexuality and human mortality. This for Hopkins is clearly a healthy Fall involving the acceptance of human difference. The early seamlessness between the conscious and the unconscious in the courting episodes between Hagar and Enson brings out the sexual desire passing between them: Enson "fell to day-dreaming, and the dreams were tinged with gold, bringing a flush to his face and a thrill to his heart" (36). The dream blends into reality: "'Hagar—my darling,' he said again, . . . 'will you marry me?' She trembled as his lips pressed passionate kisses on hers. The veil was drawn away. She understood—this was the realization of the dreams that had come to her dimly all the tender springtime. Never in all her young life had she felt so happy, so strangely happy. A soft flush mounted in cheek and brow under his caresses" (37–38). In the presence of this suitor who honors her separate identity, Hagar finds herself the object and subject of desiring passion: "Hagar had not dreamed that such passion as this existed in the world. It seemed to take the breath of her inner life and leave her powerless, with no separate existence, no distinct mental utterance" (38). This unity of souls is predicated on the recognition of difference from and respect for the "other." In Freudian terms, this other represents a frightening "potential loss of self through fragmentation," since the presence of otherness suggests that the self is not whole. This fear can in fact prompt a rejection of the other for the sake of a "cathartic recapitulation of a plenitude of being."[37] As Bhabha explains, colonial superiority—or wholeness—requires the denial of the exoticised other.

The danger of rejecting Hagar's otherness occurs when she is first clothed in antebellum idyllic discourse that denies such a difference: Enson sees her as "pure, spiritual, and open as the day," "gowned in spotless white" (44). She was, suggests the narrator, "Eve's perfect daughter" (46). This myth of Eden, which J. Lee Greene shows as the foundational myth of southern plantation ideology, excludes African Americans from the sanctified garden; more often, in proslavery fiction, African Americans are engendered as the subhuman agents who bring about the quintessential Fall.[38] While as a white male focalizer, Enson is able to engage collaboratively with Hagar in their premarital sexual feelings, marriage discourse—Enson thinks of Hagar now as part of the collective of "wife and baby" (44)—enables the transcendence that "purifies" Hagar, remakes her into "Eve" in "spotless white." This discourse of marital transcendence denies the woman her sexual and emotional otherness.

Enson's refocalization of Hagar as black unravels marital discourse for him: "I cannot, I dare not, and the law forbids me to acknowledge as my wife a woman in whose veins courses a drop of the accursed blood of the Negro slave" (59). Our previously enlightened white male focalizer projects onto Hagar the death fear he has been able to manage rationally with a passionate white woman. Hagar is, of course, still the same woman; it is her cultural signification, rendered by race, that is reconstructed in Enson's white sexual economy. In a perverse way, black women help white men in this text to manage their own irrational death fears which are projected onto women's sexuality; intensely caricatured, made extreme, black women's sexuality is "dreamed" by white men as a place of violence, chaos, and death projected outward rather than claimed within the self: "How changed, too, he thought, a blight had even fallen upon her glorious beauty. He who had always upheld the institution [slavery] as a God-given principle of humanity and Christianity, suddenly beheld his idol, stripped of its gilded trappings, in all its filthiness" (59). Even this offensive passage foreshadows Enson's remaining potential for later enlightenment. The chiasmatic crossing between the blight of wife/beauty and the gilded/filth of slavery in Enson's thinking suggests that his projection of "filth" onto his wife is already finding its more proper place—the institution that encodes such faulty judgments. Unfortunately, Enson's disavowal of sexual and racial encoding comes too late to defray the plot by his brother, St. Clair, to kill him and enslave his wife. In the context of Hagar emplotment, Hagar has been abandoned. Her abandonment fits into the pattern of secret Hagar marriages that place the blame for the precipitous illegitimacy of a wife and her offspring on a failed husband or lover who takes advantage of the legal code that works on behalf of the patriarchy, as in *The Deserted Wife, Virginia and Magdalene, Hagar the Martyr,* and *The Modern Hagar.* As previously noted, "Hagar" was a synonym for "fallen woman" in woman's novels.

In Hagar novels, the status "fallen woman" rebounds on the man rather than on the woman, while the author's play with the "fallen woman" status gives the heroines a latitude of life experiences that fall outside the domestic code. Hopkins uses Hagar's status as a pseudo-fallen woman to reveal that this status is always latent in the antebellum African American woman; her promiscuity or lack of it is exposed as irrelevant to the white patriarchal legal code that declares her illegitimate, sexually improper, because blackness has been encoded as the extreme of sexual passion that has no bearing on the real-life conditions of individual subjectivities.

Hopkins's Hagar resurfaces in the nation's capital, where "the darkened realms of the repressed" and "the black abyss" of self-unknowing undergo safe repression through a fantasized projection outward onto "naked black savages of the horrible African jungles" (57). African American characters are reified as what they are not to shore up the self-constituted purity of whiteness. *Hagar's Daughter* is a "migration to Washington" narrative. Lauren Berlant claims that such narratives posit Washington as the source of American national identity, in the Oz-like sense that sojourners follow a quest to Mecca to validate selfhood in a unified political identity. Dystopia results from one's disillusionment with the denials that make the myth seem innocent. To deny the political corruption and ethnic hierarchies at the heart of the nation protects the innocence of the infantilized public, the imaginary little-girl audience, according to Berlant, at the heart of the national myth. Hence Washington can only be affirming to those who embrace national innocence. Yet Hopkins's *Hagar's Daughter* deconstructs the purity and whiteness that masks the full range of American identity.[39]

Hopkins turns Washington, D.C., into a Miltonic Pandemonium in which internal chaos is projected outward onto the national landscape. This later chaos is foreshadowed by Hopkins's earlier description of the 1860 proslavery convention in South Carolina as Hell; the same players are in place, but now in their truly reversed position:

> The winged heralds by command
>   Of sovereign power, with awful ceremony
>   And trumpet sound, proclaimed
>   A solemn council forthwith to be held
>   At Pandemonium, the high capital
>   Of Satan and his peers (8)[40]

Engendering the white southern Eden as Hell is a crucial resistance to white racist myth, an expulsion of the racial stigma on blacks that is required by distorting simplifications of national myth.

The lack of Ishmael in Hagar novels is an equally resistant foregrounding of Hagar—hence of woman's empowerment and survival—in the biblical story. Hagar novels imagine Hagar's daughter, instead of son, as the great warrior and race progenitor, imagine that in the Old

Testament it is not the prodigal son but the prodigal daughter who returns to the fold. This feminist revision funds nineteenth-century American Hagar fiction. Often Hagar takes over Ishmael's orphan role, which subordinates her role as a mother. *Hagar's Daughter* begins similarly, since the baby in Hagar's arms does not survive, to her knowledge, a fact that "frees" Hagar for the subsequent adventures that lead her to Washington. But the book's title—*Hagar's Daughter*—and textual suggestiveness soon hint that her daughter may still be alive so that, for the first time in Hagar fiction, the reunion between prodigal daughter and husband or father is replaced by a reunion between daughter and mother.

This reunion is intensified in Hopkins's novel because positive identification of Hagar's daughter is delayed until the very end. Usually Hagar fictions rely on the identity of the Hagar heroine/daughter being known from the beginning, despite the frequent splintering off of her popular qualities onto a more "appropriate" ethnic other in later fiction. Not only does Hopkins retain the original Hagar mother—who typically dies early, often in childbirth, in this fiction—but she also nominates two alternative heroines as Hagar's daughter, which effectively turns her novel into a "whodunit" and her audience into decoding detectives.

Hopkins lays a trap of textual red herrings about who the daughter is, based on a set of assumptions about her audience's cultural construction. Whether or not Hopkins's readers actually knew the past Hagar stories, she uses the canon as a metonym for the broader racial bias of possible readers. Just as Enson must risk self-fragmentation to earn his skills in detection, so Hopkins's audience is disarmed by the double codes of Pandemonium. Two young women—which of them is Hagar's daughter, hence, another Hagar, and how do we know?—inspire our detective skills. A question also raised in the text is whether women readers can avoid white male construction as focalized by the white male hero introduced in the second half of the text, Cuthbert Sumner. Finally, we need to see how Hopkins encodes hybridization in the interest of racial tolerance through her proliferation of confusing signs for Hagar.

The displacement of the irrational fears of white people onto black people is exaggeratedly hidden in postbellum Washington—the national mecca—since all the major slave exploiters from the early part of the narrative resurface there with new sound-alike names that barely "hide" them. This device denotes the simplifying rhetoric of Washington. These characters' chaos can be unleashed on the world undetected.

The unscrupulous slaver St. Clair Enson now becomes "General

Benson." His brother, who narrowly escaped St. Clair's attempt on his life, is now a Pinkerton detective named "Henson." His Pinkerton career reestablishes the antagonism with his brother; Benson is still in league with Walker, now named "Madison," who has been in "exile abroad" after being foiled in an attempt to assassinate Lincoln, a historical allusion, perhaps, to a Copperhead plot to assassinate Lincoln in Maryland or Virginia on his inaugural route to Washington—a plot that was thwarted by Pinkerton himself, along with his operatives.[41]

The names "Henson" and "Benson" are so comically similar to each other and to their original surname that they surely provide no suspense or drama. It is hardly believable that Hopkins intended to create a mystery for the reader around *these* identities. Her point is that the usual run of white characters in the book are afflicted by self-denial that keeps them blind to the process of detection, which enables villains such as Benson and Madison—racists and financial swindlers of white people—to hide their villainy. Devils can walk the earth and Pandemonium can reign when American whites demonize American blacks instead of recognizing the devil within themselves.

The only individual who truly needs to keep her identity hidden is Hagar, who renames herself "Estelle," suggestive of a more angelic, platonic identity symbolized by the diamond star she receives from her new husband (88). The need for the drastic name change contrasts with the easy shift to "Henson" and "Benson" and exposes America—in particular, the nation's capital—as Hell for a tragic heroine who must go into deep hiding to negotiate her identity and her freedom. As the novel finally proves, white people, stupid in their ability to decode the "darkness" within themselves, are intent on decoding (and expunging) "blackness." As one southern white woman in the novel comments, "We shut our eyes to many things in the South because of our near relationship to many of these despised people. But black blood is everywhere—in society and out, and in our families even; we cannot feel assured that it has not filtered into the most exclusive families. We try to stem the tide but I believe it is a hopeless task" (160).

Hagar's attempt at passing is an effort to hide from racist detection, although, by the logic of racist paranoia let loose in this novel, of course she can't. As St. Clair becomes a sleuth in his unerring attempt to decode Hagar's blackness, we are challenged, as readers, to decode Hagar's daughter.

Through the device of splitting, Hopkins parodies—"mimes"—the preceding white feminist Hagar canon in *Hagar's Daughter*. Her text sets up two young women as candidates for the daughter identity that none of the characters in the novel suspect. Only the audience—the canny Hagar audience—is in possession of contextual knowledge, since Hagar references are spliced onto two female characters that connect allusively with Hopkins's title. These two young women—Aurelia Madison, the supposed daughter of the nefarious slave trader Walker/Madison, and Jewel Bowen, Hagar/Estelle's step-daughter—are given the variant traits that white Hagar writers finally split between a white and a black Hagar. The white Hagar retains self-reliance but represses her passion; the black Hagar bears the mark of tabooed sexuality. This split occurs when Hagar reenters the patriarchal world—that is, is caught in the scopophilic gaze of white male construction that, as with Savina Teubal's reading of the Hagar story in Genesis, splits apart woman from woman, or woman's empowerment from woman's passion.

Hopkins parodies this split by leading her reader down the path of the split Hagars' journeys. Although both Jewel and Aurelia are ostensibly white, one *must* be mixed-race if she is Hagar's *daughter*. In the language of the white racist Hagar canon, Aurelia Madison is the obvious candidate. She is dark, seductive, and sexually promiscuous. Yet confusing this identification is Jewel Bowen, who is white and sexually chaste but shows signs of being the good white Hagar already split off from the archetypal paradigm. This confusion in Hagar identities mimes racist splitting by obscuring its distinctions, but Hopkins also dramatizes Hagar's enchantment—her ritualized splitting—as a process that occurs through white male construction.

Senator Bowen's daughter Jewel hints vestigially at Clark's western white Hagar heroine, Rue. The narrator notes that she (Jewel) is "a Western girl with all the independence that the term implies" (118). Not only does Jewel's independence fit the Hagar paradigm, but Jewel also resembles Rue/Hagar in her love of horses and passion for natural wilderness: "I miss the freedom of the ranch," Jewel confides to a dance partner, "the wild flight at dawn over the prairie in the saddle, and many other things" (119). This mutual codification of the West as the site of Hagar's freedom situates both Jewel and Rue within the good split of Hagar identity. The equestrian allusion clinches Jewel's place in the legacy of southernized white Hagar heroines (Southworth, Clark).

As the white Hagar—Hagar daughters themselves assume at least the symbolic role of Hagar— Jewel is the "Saxon type, dazzling fair, with creamy roseate skin. Her hair was fair, with streaks of copper in it;

her eyes, gray with thick short lashes, at times iridescent. Her nose superbly Grecian. Her lips beautifully firm, but rather serious than smiling" (82). One might recall, however, that in Clark's paranoic code of detection in *The Modern Hagar,* African blood is shown by a lack of coloration "in the surrounding ivory of the eyes" (I:348); this lack of color comes close to Hopkins's description of "iridescent." Focusing on the *lack* of color to determine mixed-race identity is part of the absurdly reductive economy that, ironically enough, reduces black ethnicity to colorlessness or perhaps to white.

The most fantastic irony Hopkins arranges for her reader is that an audience schooled in tragic mulatto fiction would undoubtedly pick up on Jewel's near-white pigmentation as an additional sign that she is Hagar's daughter. This is excruciating irony because Hopkins doubly indicts Jewel as black through a contradiction between generic modes—the Hagar canon and tragic mulatto fiction. The confusion arises with white Hagar texts that if Jewel is the good white Hagar heroine split away from her blackness, then how can she be recognized as the bad black Hagar? The answer is that recognition of her identity is dependent on her disavowed blackness. White Hagar writers radically disavow Hagar's blackness, but they do this first through encoding Hagar's blackness and then splitting their white Hagars away from it.

Hopkins actually uses the central trope in tragic mulatto fiction to decode the racist Hagar canon, since in terms of the tragic mulatto genre it is Jewel's near-whiteness—indeed, the erasure of her blackness—that traditionally marks the tragic mulatta heroine as black! This is a rich confusion for Hopkins's readers. In the minimalist economy of tragic mulatto fiction, Hagar is black if she is white. In the minimalist economy of white racist fiction, Hagar is white because she is hinted to be black; in other words, she must first be tainted black *before* she can recover her whiteness. This rhetorical chiasmus between the Hagar canon and tragic mulatto fiction renders ethnicity totally fluid from the perspective of female identity. The two genres say this: the former, that she is white, so she is black; the latter, that she is white but actually black but actually white. By Hopkins's conflation of the two traditions, women are ineluctably hybridized.

Black/white, white/black Hagar-Jewel is fixed by her apparent whiteness into the split Hagar white character of white male desire. Jewel's white fiancé, Cuthbert Sumner, defines Jewel through her whiteness as his "saint, his good angel; and he loved her truly with all the high love a man of the world can ever know. He trusted her for her womanly goodness and truth" (103). Divesting Hagar/Jewel of her sexuality through the platonic code of idealized white femininity, Sumner engenders white womanness in order to evade his own sexual fears. Jewel protects Sumner's white racial narcissism. Sumner contains his unconscious fear of female sexuality through projecting it onto African American women, and he regresses into narcissistic plenitude by inventing a white woman who transcends sexuality. Sumner experiences black womanhood as uncanny (not of himself). When Henson/Enson discovers late in the novel that Estelle is Hagar and tells Sumner that he loves her, Sumner is provoked to admit, "You make me feel uncanny, Enson, with your visionary ideas," and to remark, "Thank God, I have my wife [Jewel has married him]; there I am safely anchored" [by her unambiguous whiteness] (271).

Robert Young notes "the ambivalent double gesture of repulsion and attraction that seems to lie at the heart of racism." If the colonial subject "define[s] himself specifically through the exclusion of what is marked dirty and low," this "disgust . . . return[s] as the object of nostalgia, longing and fascination."[42] Judith Butler gives a voice to this disavowed longing: "I know very well that this cannot be but I desire this all the same." For Butler, white people's desire for their own repressed sexuality is at the very heart of the taboo on miscegenation. Although the colonial Other "claims that he would never associate with African-Americans, he requires the association and its disavowal for an erotic satisfaction that is indistinguishable from his desire to display his own racial purity."[43]

Since Aurelia Madison is the bad black Hagar in Hopkins's text, she is predictably the focus of Sumner's eroticized repressions. She is a part of the past that he cannot quite cancel out; she is the context of his hope that Jewel's "white" purity will help him forget past sexual liaisons (84); to be specific, he only hopes that "the purity and tenderness of Jewel's sweet face [will] blot out forever the summer splendor of Aurelia Madison's presence" (92). Aurelia is clearly the bad black passionate Hagar in the white Hagar canon, for the hallmark of the Hagar heroine is passion, and Aurelia Madison is a passionate adventuress to whom Sumner became briefly affianced—before she rejected him, much to his later relief and her later chagrin—after a passionate tryst one sultry summer.

That Aurelia is the sexualized bad heroine already split from white Hagar identity is signalled by Aurelia's dusky complexion—"dusky eyes" (90)—and her explicit sexuality—"voluptuous[ness]" (90). As with many Hagar heroines, Aurelia holds "rage and hatred in her heart" (93) toward Jewel, her rival for the affections of Sumner. Aurelia migrates to Washington as the daughter of the nefarious slave trader Walker/"Major" Madison. As part of the underbelly of the national myth, she is the threat to the pure white little girl Jewel that American nationalism has sworn to protect. Madison and Benson have become confidence men who operate out of "General" Benson's position in the government. Since the fate of Hagar's baby remains undiscovered, but one knows from the title of the book that she survives, one could surmise that Walker followed the current and recovered Hagar's daughter Aurelia as his own. Aurelia has certainly been tainted by her background. Not only has Benson been her lover (100, 158), but Walker and Benson conscript her in their monetary schemes. Aurelia herself is torn between her passion and her ambition to marry money.

Aurelia exceeds the Hagar type by tipping that delicate Hagar balance between good and bad womanly emotion. She notably lacks the creativity traditionally yielded from the good passion of the Hagar heroine, she does not participate as a mother—whose motherly love sometimes serves as an *apologia* for Hagar's passion—and she is not ultimately the good Hagar; she is closer to the night side and to evil.

Aurelia has been produced by white male perception; her caricatured sexuality and passion are an introjected effect of her a priori imprisonment within the white male gaze; her own actions arise from her loss of self in the male sexual economy. She sees her own sexuality as bad because self-definition is trapped in society's construction of her. Aurelia exploits her sexuality to survive and take revenge on the society that has exploited her.

Hopkins was perhaps aware of the century's sexually paranoic anti-Hagar novels, written largely by men, that demonized Hagar as a castrating mother. From the masculine point of view expressed in these novels, women's passion created chaos in a male-ordered and hierarchical world. Daniel Carson Goodman's later *Hagar Revelly* (1913) is characteristic. It portrays Hagar under the luridly naturalistic light of a seductress who debases her lover and then decides to abort her baby, only to have it rescued by the "good" Hagar, her sister, Thatah. Rescued from motherhood, Hagar thinks triumphantly, "Free again—free again—free again" (283).[44]

There is Hall Caine's *A Son of Hagar* (1894), in which Hagar's abandonment of an illegitimate child actually robs the legitimate son of his inheritance (social castration) through the manipulations of his unknown illegitimate pseudo-twin. It is in Pierce Egan's sexist and racist

Hagar's Lot; Or, The Fate of a Poor Girl (1882) that Hagar is a dark gypsy witch figure who threatens the death of a white child, Floret, who is not actually hers. Hagar is a grisly surrogate mother hired by Floret's real mother—a British countess who for various reasons wants to keep her motherhood a secret.

The notion of Hagar as terrifying—because sexualized and thus inevitably black—appears in southern writer Mary Jane Holmes's *Maggie Miller; Or, Old Hagar's Secret* (1859), in which the "hag" aspect always latent in the name "Hagar" (despite the lack of an etymological link) is fully exploited by description of Hagar's "dark, haggard face,"[45] which is "haggard and worn" (212). She is "an old hag of a woman, called Hagar" (259), "the old witch one" (263) who finally reveals to her granddaughter, "*Don't you know that I, the shrivelled, skinny hag, who tells you this,* AM YOUR OWN GRANDMOTHER!!" (404). The plot involves the British servant Hagar Warren, who had grown up in the family of her mistress and accompanied her matriarch to America. Although caste, not color, is the supposed dividing line and source of Hagar's envy, Holmes's novel eerily anticipates Mark Twain's *Pudd'nhead Wilson*: the closer Hagar comes to her fateful determination to switch her own baby granddaughter with the mistress's, the more Hagar is ethnicized with a "dark haggard face" (210): "her face, which was always dark, seemed to have acquired a darker, harder, look, while her eyes wore a wild startled expression, as if she were constantly followed by some tormenting fear" (215). Hagar's temptation is clinched when she "change[s] their clothes for once, just to see how fine cambrics and soft flannel would look upon a grandchild of Hagar Warren!" (211). Hagar lives with her fearful secret, which threatens to destroy her granddaughter, Maggie Miller. Her increased darkness seems part of the phantasmagoric dimension of Hagar, demonized almost into the devourer of children, as the dark gypsy surrogate-mother Hagar in Pierce Egan's *Hagar* tries to poison the little orphan called the "white floret."

The presence of such works within the Hagar canon suggests a backlash against the overt sexuality of the Hagar heroine. Post-psychoanalytical critic Madelon Sprengnether distinguishes between the term "mother," which "represents a fantasy of plenitude, an Edenic oneness with the body of the mother," and "(m)other," which "represents that which cannot be appropriated by the child's or infant's desire and hence signals a condition of division or loss." In Sprengnether's view, Freud imagines an oedipal tale in which the mother's desire for a penis is satisfactorily sublimated by her pleasure at producing a son, so that the mother's acquiescence to the oedipal drama, while "driv[ing] a wedge between the son and the object of his desire," is not seen as a "betray[al] [of] her son's infantile love."

The effect creates a double: "It preserves an image of mother as a source of unambivalent, albeit asexual love, at the same time as it engenders a dark female double, the woman who is object of desire, unstable and often degraded." Sprengnether further suggests that a triad of women is subsequently created in Western civilization, since the castration complex theoretically shields the son from his mother's radical otherness, her "power to withhold love, [which] appears to threaten his annihilation." From Freud's own terms, Sprengnether argues that it is "the body of the (m)other, both known and unknown, secret and familiar, [that] provides the prototype of the uncanny." Freud's repression of the mother's alienating features, however, "reinforces the split encoded in Western Christianity between woman as asexual mother (Mary) and as erotic object (Eve)." Most important to this analysis of the anti-Hagar novels is Sprengnether's remark that "the third and most terrifying aspect of the preoedipal (m)other, the autonomy of her desire, perceived by the infant as the threat of death, is frequently marginalized and scapegoated in the figure of the woman as witch" in order "to preserve a fantasy of maternal plenitude."[46]

It should not be surprising that women enculturated within a patriarchal world fall prey to a similar demonization of women's sexuality, or that in nineteenth-century racist America, Mary Jane Holmes embeds in her novel a fantasy of a dark-skinned Hagar crone figure who holds the secret to terrifying bloodlines, who represents, to her wealthy, proud granddaughter, the sign of sexuality that is the emblem of the granddaughter's own "otherness" or social "death."

The three Hagar heroines in Hopkins's novel represent the triad of Eve, the asexual mother, and the witch/death figure. Hagar is platonically reborn under the name of "Estelle," noted by onlookers as "a really beautiful woman, but too cold to please me. . . . a creature of snow and ice" (113–14). Jewel is the Eve character, although, as in antebellum Edenic myth, she is an innocent Eve, a white "angel." The terrifying aspect of Sprengnether's fragmented woman-icon, the witch-crone, Aurelia, now bears all the burden of the (m)other's sexual desire. Cuthbert Sumner, the white hero who relates to all these characters, is himself an orphan without a mother. His narcissistic need for an asexual mother to "complete" him is predictably transferred onto the wife that he will seek. Hopkins demonstrates as well that Sumner, the supposedly racially enlightened northern hero, is not only narcissistic but, more to the point of her story, racially narcissistic: witch women, fatal to men, are dark; angel-women are white. Hopkins's suggestive links between Aurelia and Hagar serve to lead the reader in the same direction—that same reader who, black or white, as pointed out by Giddings, might see the black woman as passionate and promiscuous, hence the Hagar type. Hopkins's narrative portrayal of Aurelia's sexuality is ironically filtered through white male paranoia. The reader's potential fall into the trap of Sumner's misogynist perceptions is a challenge thrown down as a gauntlet to test the alacrity of Hopkins's audience, so pervasively does Sumner's view guide the descriptions of Aurelia. It is probably unnecessary to remind the reader that these Hagar attributes have turned other Hagar heroines into creative goddesses who redeem not only themselves but those around them from potential excess.

These qualities in Aurelia, however, reduce her to a witch. Aurelia is not only promiscuous; she has been corrupted by her "father" and Benson into accepting risky speculation as the means to accumulating wealth. The clearest foil to Aurelia is the unambiguously African American heroine, Venus, who appears in Hopkins's subplot as the virtuous granddaughter of Aunt Henny. Venus's sacrifice of her own ambition to support her brother's college education through domestic service is not only the idealized behavior of the time for young African American women;[47] as the daughter of the "devil" Isaac—St. Clair's black conspirator against his own race for self-gain—Venus redeems her family history. In a parallel sense, Aunt Henny and her originally coquettish daughter Marthy ultimately domesticate Isaac. Venus is instrumental in uncovering Henson's scheme to frame Sumner for the murder of Henson's mistress and by recovering her grandmother and Jewel from their imprisonment in Henson's decayed southern mansion. But Venus's way, although replete with Hagar elements of independence—she changes into men's clothes and serves as a detective to foil St. Clair's plot and find her grandmother—nevertheless reencodes the late tone of the *Colored American* in which women were encouraged to forsake or forestall self-realization for the sake of black men.

Clearly the Hagar canon in the hands of white writers has not worked toward the empowerment of black women. Hopkins's Venus deviates from Hagar as a model for empowered black women. On the other hand, Hopkins portrays Aurelia/Hagar as "fixed" by the sexual longing of white men who make black women "erotic icon[s]," the "quintessential Other," "the hyperstatic alterity" of white male fantasy.[48] Through the extradiegetic narrator—that is, through this narrator's position outside the story—Hopkins dramatizes Cuthbert's process of shoring up defenses against ego fragmentation by inscribing lawful and virtuous chastity onto Jewel, and illegal, illegitimate sexuality onto Aurelia, whom one of Sumner's white friends calls "bewitching" (108).

Aurelia incited fascination and rapture during Sumner's earlier liaison with her at a summer resort. But "the purity and tenderness of Jewel's sweet face blotted out forever the summer splendor of Aurelia Madison's presence" (92). The narrative tip that Sumner acts out his sexual repression on the women who surround him comes shortly after this, in his response to two letters. Aurelia asks to see him; moments later he receives a reminder from Jewel about their evening arrangements. "'My little Blossom!' he said gently. But his little Blossom did not keep him from going to see Aurelia Madison. . . . Reluctantly and distastefully—but he went" (102).

Aurelia seeks to erode this platonic relationship by placing Sumner in a false position in plain sight of his fiancée. Aurelia "bewilders" (102); she is a witch because she is bewitching; she is a spider because she weaves webs (132) and ensnares men (130). Sumner feels "repulsion" (117) toward her when he discovers she is octoroon, that she is, reductively, a "Negress" (161) whom he barely escaped marrying. She is transformed into a death-dealing python in the nightmares of his unconscious that bear "a shadowy relation to the scenes through which he had just passed":

> In those uneasy slumbers he dreamed that he was in a deep, dark pit. Darkness blacker than the blackest night was all about him; but as he lay there . . . suddenly beneath his body he felt a movement as of a monstrous body—a regular undulating movement. Then it seemed borne in upon his mind that the pit was a snake's den; the monsters—three in number—pythons of immense size to whom human victims were offered as sacrifices. . . . Then he realized that he must act quickly. As he looked into the dense darkness a tremulous ray of light pierced the gloom of the pit and for an instant Jewel's face smiled upon him, then disappeared. In that instant of light he discerned a ladder leading to an opening at the top of the pit." (165)

Ironically, the three women are Aurelia, Estelle, and Jewel, although Sumner does not yet know it. At this point, Sumner fantasizes his sexual relation with a black woman, in the pit imagery, in the undulation, as monstrous; she is a "sacred reptile" (165) in her fantasized role as archetypal (m)other who is intent on devouring him. Jewel is connected with the symbol of platonism, the ladder, Sumner's way out of death through sexual transcendence. The crone image that Hagar has metamorphosed into, for Sumner, is even more apparent as he later confesses to Jewel that, even if he had loved Aurelia, "I think that the knowledge of her origin would kill all desire in me.... The mere thought of the grinning, toothless black hag that was her foreparent would forever rise between us" (271).

Here is the "grinning, toothless black hag," the death-dealing crone figure inflected by the white man as African American, partitioned off from his life-saving white women. Even the white stenographer, Elise Bradford, who has an illegitimate child with Benson, is forgiven her promiscuous sins by Sumner, who sees "a new dignity in her manner" and wants her to "know Jewel" (163). Significantly, Hopkins transfers the Hagar codes of "secret marriage" and "illegitimate child" onto a *white* woman, Elise, who essentially betrays Aurelia to Sumner by revealing the secret of Aurelia's ethnicity. Hopkins's white woman is the "fallen" Hagar in her text, which reverses the Hagar pattern of displacing illicit sexuality onto the black woman. In addition, Elise's fate, being poisoned to death by Benson, is surely a message that white women are not immune to white male abuse and that white feminists are foolish not to collaborate with black feminists in fighting issues of male-gendered sexual power.

Aurelia is not, ultimately, Hagar's daughter. It is Jewel, who was rescued from and adopted by Zenas Bowen and his wife. An heirloom locket and baby clothes discovered after Bowen's death provide the link. This satisfaction of the tragic mulatto storyline by the exposure of the near-white heroine and the complications that arise does not, however, do justice to the character of Aurelia, nor to the discussion of women's sexuality that is demanded by Hopkins's choice to write in the Hagar canon. Abandonment of Aurelia as the Hagar daughter discredits feminist empowerment, including women's sexuality, which is the hallmark of the Hagar canon.

For political reasons, Hopkins makes Jewel instead of Aurelia Hagar's daughter to remove the taint of sexual licentiousness from black women's identity. This was the taint enforced in texts by white women who rendered the overtly passionate Hagar covertly black. Hopkins does not endorse the eroticization of Aurelia by white male fantasy. She points out instead that white male fantasy—even when filtered through white women's fiction—commodifies the black woman as an eroticized "Hagar." Sumner threatens Aurelia that she must leave Washington or "God forbid that I should make you a social outcast!" (237). This is in effect what he does, and Aurelia vanishes from the text. White men from Abraham onward make Hagar a social outcast. And Washington, D.C., the seat of national identity, has allegedly protected the little white girl Jewel in her purity and innocence.

Hopkins deconstructs Sumner's white male fantasy by revealing that all three women, Estelle, Aurelia, and Jewel, are mixed-race. As Sprengnether suggests, the polarization of women as Eve, asexual mother, or hag/crone—certainly "Hagar" has all along carried with her the burden of "hag" despite the absence of an etymological link—is a false separation between the various unconscious perceptions of mother/woman. Sumner's determination to remain "unpolluted" (271) by refusing to recognize Estelle/Hagar as his mother-in-law represents the desperate shoring-up of his disintegrating ego by his repression of the intrusion of "blackness," but when his angelic white Jewel is disclosed as Hagar's daughter, Sumner's final defensive hesitation proves disastrous. Jewel fears that Sumner will "turn from her with loathing" (280). His absence for a day confirms her fears; she flees to Europe with her parents, where she dies of Roman fever, a prisoner of Sumner's feared perception of her and a self-imposed exile from the American dream of national identity. Certainly through the loss of these two women, Hopkins expresses "psychic rage at America for not trying to live up to the conditions of citizenship it promises in law and in spirit."[49]

Hopkins uses Hagar, Aurelia, and Jewel to show how black women in white culture are all potentially experienced as uncanny. The mystery surrounding where they come from foreshadows their symbolic role in the communal act of repression. The mystery surrounding each suggests a sexual aura that—in a sexually repressive society—can only be experienced as "unreal," estranged, as fantasy. Aurelia in particular displays a strangeness that nevertheless "seems familiar"; Jewel says this when she first sees her (91). They discover they do know each other through a shared convent experience in early adolescence, but Aurelia's uncanniness is never actually dispelled. One could as easily suppose that Jewel recognized Aurelia through a shadow imprint of Hagar's features upon Aurelia, an impression or "clue" that lingers despite Jewel's recognition of Aurelia on other grounds. Oddly enough, another "clue" to Aurelia's identity as Hagar's daughter is the repugnance that Estelle feels toward her when they first meet. The text notes that Hagar "was surprised and puzzled at the vague feeling of distrust and dislike that personal contact with her young guest brought to her." This discomfort is followed by Hagar's attempt to feel more sympathetic, which prompts her "ostensibly" fateful question, "How long since you lost your mother?" (107). Based on Hagar's initial self-loathing of her ethnicity and her burial of her identity through passing, her repulsion toward Aurelia could seem an instinctive recognition of herself in this young woman, hence a signal that Aurelia is Hagar's daughter. Finally, it is important to add that once Elise enters into the domain of sexuality, she also is the outcast Hagar.

It is not a coincidence that all three young women with Hagar markings—Elise, Aurelia, and Jewel—literally or figuratively die at the end of Hopkins's novel. White and black women are estranged from themselves and from each other under the terms of patriarchal society. In the beginning of the novel, Hagar returns to the South "almost a stranger after her long absence" (32). When Jewel first tours Washington with her stepmother in a Russian sleigh, "that she was a stranger to the crowd could be easily told from the questioning glances which followed the turn-out" (76). When Aurelia first appears publicly at an opera in Washington, she is labeled the "stranger" by Jewel (93), whose perception is preceded by her breathless question to Cuthbert, "Who is she?" (91), a trademark question applied to the Hagar heroine, who is estranged from herself through her objectification in the voyeuristic gaze.

Hopkins is caught in the irony that the perhaps richer and braver text—for claiming women's sexual rights—that might have occurred if Aurelia had been Hagar's daughter would have reinforced the social construction of black women as inherently more sexual. Hopkins's point seems to be that assigning sexuality through the ethnic filter of race is merely an alibi for casting *all* women under the male sign of prohibition. At a historical time when white feminists had abandoned black women, Hopkins's focus on the *process* of male sexual encoding argues the sheer stupidity of white women "splitting" from black women; she anticipates the loss of sexuality and passion for white women, who must imagine themselves sexually chaste to be emotionally free.

That risk becomes explicit in Mary Johnston's *Hagar* (1913), which marks the end of Hagar as American nineteenth-century readers had come to know her. Johnston's Hagar is the new southern white woman, although not actually so white. True to the Hagar paradigm, she is "a dark little girl" (1) called "Gipsy" (6), whose mother, "Maria"—suggested as an exotic presence in the South—dies imprisoned in the southern mansion where her husband abandoned her.

The use of "Maria" is not coincidental, since the Virgin Mary/Mary Magdalene split in Hagar identity had been dramatically present in Southworth's Hagar fiction, the most likely southern writer to whom Johnston tipped her hat by writing *Hagar*. The new southern Hagar rebels against Old South taboos. She knows about evolution, eagerly reads prohibited fiction such as *The Scarlet Letter*, and, unlike her mother, manages to escape the South and fulfill her life, Hagar-like, through her writing. But her most important contribution to her own feminist identity as the new Hagar is her choice of chastity as the path to a higher self-realization after her passionate relationship with a lover is sacrificed because of her admiration for her lover's feminist wife.

Although the end of Johnston's novel hints at Hagar's probable marriage to an equal, the message is clear in the novel that Hagar's prior rejection of men has allowed her to embrace intellectual freedom. She has become a suffragist, a pro-unionist, and a social activist. Sexual passion has become so easily controllable for the new white woman that sexual desire need not be imaginatively projected onto black women. The new southern white woman has the tools at her disposal to achieve her own freedom. Creativity arrives through the rejection rather than the embrace of sexual desire.

And what of Mary Magdalene, Southworth's archetypal black woman goddess, with whom southern white women had tenuously merged in Hagar fiction for the purposes of their self-empowerment? In Johnston's novel, she is shunted aside as "Mary Magazine," one of the black children Hagar plays with as a child, whose comical reduction through malapropistic misnomer is attributed to her own cultural illiteracy. Her identity is disclosed in a vaudevillian scene in which Hagar tries to convince her, much to Mary Magazine's own implicitly "ignorant" resistance, that she is actually named Mary Magdalene. Mary Magazine's colloquial intellect, according to the narrative, retains the name's religious significance, but in a distorted form that mocks the black woman's colloquial literacy: "My mammy done named me for de lady what took her cologne bottle somebody give her Christmas, an' poured it on her han' an' rubbed Jesus' feet" (32).

What is Mary Magazine's ultimate realization in Johnston's *Hagar*? Hagar hires her as her maid. The existence of "Mary Magazine" in Johnston's text is a remarkable gloss on how transparent Southworth's covert inflection of Mary Magdalene as black would have been for her southern women readers, for not only is Mary Magazine black but Johnston knew enough about her significance in the Hagar tradition to destroy her power. Within the context of the Hagar canon that precedes it, Johnston's text is a fantasized excoriation of black blood from the body of the southern white woman who no longer requires it.

The conclusion of the nineteenth-century American Hagar canon in Mary Johnston's *Hagar* deconstructs the implicit message in white Hagar fiction from its beginning. Black women, for these white southern writers, were an appropriatable but expendable commodity that could be exploited for the empowerment of white women.

Pauline Hopkins's *Hagar* exposes the real-world problematics of using Hagar as a model for African American empowerment as long as women can be subordinated—by virtue of their passion—by a masculinist world constructed to satisfy the repressive economics of white colonial sexual desire. In *that* world, black women are the particularized sexual scapegoats. Ironically, Hagar represents female power under the lock and key of white male mastery; as such, she models a "no way out" experience of domination under white male oppression. Her power as a myth—and it is great—is her archetypal site as the loss of female power in the world, and of course its possibility in a world reconstructed. Hence, she is our longing, our nostalgia, *and* our empowerment for a courageous resistance—for men and women—to the privileging of restraint, self-control, over the full range of emotion.

How she changes the world is through the power of articulation, which translates our longings into the actions by which we live. Homi Bhabha's insistence that we focus on the process rather than the content of mythification allows us to deconstruct the "myth" of female power as it became distorted and simplified as a tabooed black female presence in nineteenth-century America. The black-white twinning of women's identity in Pauline Hopkins's *Hagar's Daughter* represents the first genuine attempt at hybridization in Hagar fiction. Hopkins shows that the longings for female freedom that lie at the heart of the Hagar myth "twin" black and white women in America.

Conclusion

"What American Renaissance?"[1] "No More Separate Spheres!"[2] Literary criticism focusing on the American Renaissance has gone through sea changes in the last several years in reaction and counterreaction to shifting critical perspectives that alter how literature is judged. The fate of American Renaissance literature was challenged after Walter Benn Michaels, in *The Gold Standard and the Logic of Naturalism* (1987), implied that the texts of naturalism were the only authentic expressions of nineteenth-century literature because their innate materialism implicated them within the economic processes of American capitalism. From the perspective of new historicism, realist texts were irresponsibly bourgeois in claiming a position inside culture while their point of view was actually outside of it. American romance fiction was regarded as even more aloof from reality because of its detachment from historical particulars. The question became how literature was implicated within culture as new historicism shifted imperceptibly to cultural studies.

In the January 1992 issue of *PMLA,* Emily Miller Budick reclaimed prestige for American romanticism by resituating a classic romance text, *The Scarlet Letter,* within layered historical references that suggest the social value of Hawthorne's project as cultural and ideological discourse.[3] Suddenly—at least writ more forcefully into critical law—the aesthetic ironies embedded in romantic texts were reconstructed as social ironies, the aesthetic distance, being seen as an elaborate mask for historically specific social statements.[4]

The rhetorical strategy informing *American Literature*'s special issue "No More Separate Spheres!" (September 1998) seems to take a page out of Budick's recovery of the American classic romance in an attempt to recover or instate the still relatively uncanonized women's fiction of the American Renaissance on the grounds of its social complexity. Put bluntly, an essay such as Amy Kaplan's "Manifest Destiny," which rewrites domestic ideology as sinisterly complicit with Jacksonian imperial expansionism, implies the following: that domestic texts are as socioeconomically occult and ideologically suspect as *Moby-Dick* or *The House of the Seven Gables*. There *is* indeed no separate sphere; Sarah

Josepha Hale's *Liberia* (1852) could and should be taught alongside Melville's "Benito Cereno."[5]

Perhaps it is true that my study of nineteenth-century American Hagar fiction by women operates from a similar premise of justification. My work on uncanonized white women's fiction—for to a large degree Hopkins's *Hagar's Daughter* is approaching canonical status—became a mandate to deconstruct the historical reinvention and cultural identity formations of race by southern white women in nineteenth-century America. One of the issues not addressed in the stunning collection of essays that includes Kaplan's was the extent to which the principle of canonization per se funded the marginal works discussed. How close to the margins of unknowability were the texts discussed in the *American Literature* issue? How are authors such as Catharine Sedgwick, Sarah Orne Jewett, Sarah Josepha Hale, Catharine Beecher, and Harriet Beecher Stowe selected for the marriage vows between the male and female spheres of American romanticism? Is there an inbred canonization already in place in the selection of worthy women's novels, and have these decisions been already largely made?

Notably, only one of the novels that receives a central reading in *Dreaming Black/Writing White* is currently in print, *Hagar's Daughter*, which was, ironically, the only fiction in this study that did not originally appear in the form of a published book. It is valid to question the extent to which the books in this study deserve reading *because* of their racist appropriations of black female identity and the extent to which other principles need to be considered in determining what gets looked at and what gets republished.

Doubtless the American woman's canon has been formed by the recovery process of powerful critics such as Nina Baym who have—through sheer force of critical effort and magisterial criticism—seduced a number of teachers into seeking particular women's texts to teach, some of which, such as *Ruth Hall*, have even found their way into more traditional courses in American literature in undergraduate and graduate curriculums. *Dreaming Black/Writing White* is also organized by tracking a model. For Baym in *Woman's Fiction,* it was two plot paradigms that appeared continually through the various works that she examined. One suspects as well that her decision to focus on certain of these authors for further review was based on the relative degree of economic success—hence popularity—her major authors received, but as well to some extent on aesthetic judgment, since in *Novels, Readers, and Reviewers* Baym does not hesitate to endorse a particularly scathing contemporary review of a novel that she dismisses on similar grounds of distaste.

This preamble leads to a particular dilemma that I experienced in my research and composition for this Hagar project. The study came about through appreciation of two writers less known in more general circles, Pauline Hopkins and E.D.E.N. Southworth. I discovered the fascinating tales of Southworth serendipitously. It was the coincidental link that both Hopkins and Southworth wrote Hagar novels that aroused my curiosity to see if there might be more such novels to survey. My discovery that there were an abundance of such novels stunned me, especially since many were proslavery southern novels featuring the Hagar biblical character, who was universally known to be black. This discovery elicited the work of recovering and decoding the sociopolitical dimensions of Hagar texts.

If I were to rely on the implicit message in the *American Literature* issue on woman's domestic ideology, all of the books in my study deserve equal representation in print and an equal proportion of critical attention to their complex ideologies. I wonder, however, how many of these reintroduced works will earn a reprinting. They will perhaps remain in silence, memorialized only through their status in this book as racialized texts that expose white women's imagining of black female identity. They are historical testaments, certainly, to the betrayal of black women by white women in nineteenth-century America. They bear witness as well to the immense contribution that black women made to white female as well as American national consciousness. Finally, they serve as recovery documents of the Hagar tradition that provide an important context for reclaiming black female identity and deconstructing the white female apartheid in Hopkins's *Hagar's Daughter*.

Not only did the questions of "Who shall print these works" and "Should they be printed?" plague this study, but I found myself struggling as well with what seemed potentially "bad faith" questions about the driving force behind my inquiry. The original text was split. On one hand, I was negatively stunned by the racist configuration of black women's identity secretly lurking in these white feminist novels. On the other hand, in the process of recovering long-lost information on these generally unknown women authors, I was seduced into empathy with these complex women writers, unknown and unsung. To discover that the best shot at identifying Harriet Stephens was the brief mention of her in Sarah Josepha Hale's *Woman's Record,* informing the reader that Stephens was formerly a third-rate stage actress who wrote *Hagar the*

Martyr and *Home Scenes and Sounds,* led me to research tenaciously the available theatre annals to recover her final performance. Through this looking glass into her life, I was seduced into research about how theatre actresses such as Stephens sought to climb upward through careers as writers, a fascinating phenomenon that connected Marion Stephens's *Hagar* to its performative aspects.

The recovery of these obscure women writers felt very much like the celebratory recovery work that has unified the feminist scholars who are researching the literary world of the domestic woman's novel. In fact, the ideological split in the original draft of my Hagar manuscript predicts a possible split in future critical work on American women's fiction. Critics of women's novels in general celebrate the ideological enlightenment of the woman's text as it resists the patriarchal colonialism of canonized texts. It is upon that basis in general that an alternative tradition of the American woman's novel has crept into traditional studies of the American Renaissance. This Hagar study raises the question of how we celebrate texts (and authors) that embed racism in their dominant discourse. A countermovement whose rationale is based on the moral enlightenment of Renaissance women—as opposed to male—authors loses momentum if there are "no more separate spheres."

How can we both celebrate and remonstrate? In a sense, this Hagar study moves with lightning speed. It both urges "Here, read this fascinating book that I have just read and just imagine this author" and chastens "Do not be innocent, fair reader, for here lies disturbing racism." There is an ironic disparity between the long-instated male canonized texts that can withstand and flourish under the more skeptical gaze of the most recent critical perusal: It can be argued that these books are still clever although indelibly ethically flawed. On the other hand, the marriage between cultural studies and the woman's novel of the American literary Renaissance barely gets the woman's novel to the altar to say "I do" before it is sued for divorce.

It goes without saying that critical canniness cannot be timed to accommodate the rhetorical aging necessary to instate a feminist canon. But I think it is important to note that women's novels have a right to be read. For some, the novels of E.D.E.N. Southworth are more engaging and fascinating than many canonical novels. Their ideology is embedded within adventurous tales about women struggling in a patriarchal world. They recreate one's point of view in corrective measure to Judith Fetterley's lament that the history of the American canon has coerced the female reader to construct herself as male.[6] The aesthetic values that emerge from reading domestic fiction featuring women's struggles talk back to the authoritative values we generally attribute to the inherent greatness of the American white male canon.

To assume that "liking" a Southworth text is not merely a guilty pleasure but an aesthetic experience is a dividend of reading women's fiction. One's immersion in a form shifts the reading paradigm in subtle ways that sneak up unexpectedly. The rarely articulated aesthetic values that determine "great literature" have some place here. One may read impatiently through the stilted prose of Charlotte Clark's *Modern Hagar* yet feel the vibrations of keen attention in the complex and compelling texts of E.D.E.N. Southworth or Susan Warner, where the master stroke of the storyteller holds sway.

The bipolarity of praising and condemning an author produces an uneasy sensation one learns to live with in order to experience literature at more than a superficial level. Deep diving is one thing that distinguishes those books that we treasure, no less in women's domestic fiction than in the white male canon that has previously directed our reading experience of the American Renaissance. Why, one might ask, did this study devote such goodly space to individual readings instead of privileging, in abbreviated form, defining textual moments and then focusing on theory? My response would be that I did not want readers to miss the pleasure of the text. I believe that a text's ethical convolutions can be sounded only through close navigation of textual movement. We should also, I think, be seduced by the life-paradox of a woman such as E.D.E.N. Southworth whose struggle with racism is staged through the virtual heave of the tangled ideologies that blight her fantasy. This is worth reading—for the experience of the text.

Nevertheless, in the final draft of this book I consciously subordinated the pleasure of the text and the engagement with authors to the larger history revealed in the Hagar canon. I assumed that many readers will not share my pleasure in these texts—not because these readers are closed to appreciation of a wider range of aesthetics but because the texts may seem so implicitly offensive that their value will lie more in the lesson than in the reading. And it is a lesson that should be passed on. What does it mean that white women still dream black women? Why is Hagar still such a powerful archetype? What we learn from the nineteenth-century American Hagar canon is the dream basis upon which America was built. Blackness—at least the imagination of blackness—is at the heart of American identity. If white people deny that fact, it is a betrayal and blockage of the path to cultural hybridity and cultural enlightenment. If we learn nothing else from the texts in this book, it should be the lesson that if one must affirm her identity based on the denial of the "other," she is indeed a fragile vessel with no "ballast" of her own.

Notes

For full information on works cited, see Bibliography.

1. Hagar and John Audubon: American Hybridity

1. Dorman, "John James Audubon," xii.
2. Patricia Hill Collins employs this term to identify one of four negative nineteenth-century stereotypes of black women in *Black Feminist Thought,* 77.
3. For a discussion of the exclusionary properties of the white Edenic myth, see Greene, *Blacks in Eden,* 1–11.
4. Herrick, *Audubon the Naturalist,* 65–68, vii.
5. Ibid., xliii.
6. Herrick (1) notes the public stigma attached to illegitimacy.
7. Driskell, *Two Centuries of Black American Art,* 38.
8. Reviewers of Driskell's book do not remark on the inclusion of Audubon. See, for example, *Atlantic Monthly* 339 (April 1977): 93; *American Historical Review* 83 (June 1977): 726; *Library Journal* 101 (December 1976): 2472; *New Yorker* 53 (June 20, 1977): 119. *Village Voice* (21 [December 13, 1976]: 71) notes simply that Audubon is "the most famous" artist included.
9. Herrick, *Audubon the Naturalist,* 56.
10. Gobineau is quoted from Young, *Colonial Desire,* 116.
11. Bhabha, *Location of Culture,* 60.
12. Ibid., 241.
13. Ibid., 26, 66.
14. Ford, *John James Audubon,* 23.
15. Ford, *Biography,* 22.
16. Young, *Colonial Desire,* 181.
17. Ford, *Biography,* 17; idem, *John James Audubon,* 6.
18. *The New Standard Alphabetical Indexed Holy Bible (Authorized or King James Version).* All biblical citations in the text refer to this edition.
19. Williams, *Sisters in the Wilderness,* 2, 245n. 2.
20. Heller, *Black Names in America,* iii; Fox-Genovese, *Within the Plantation Household,* 130; Williams, *Sisters in the Wilderness,* 245n. 2.
21. Greene, *Blacks in Eden,* 84–85.
22. Reynolds, *Faith in Fiction,* 1, 5.
23. These include John Rollin Wells's *Hagar: A Dramatic Poem in Three Acts* (New York: Broadway Publishing Co., 1903); C.P. Flockton's *Hagar and Ishmael: A Drama Founded on the Bible Story in Three Acts* (New York: Van

Fleet, 1898); and Ernest E. Hanham's *Hagar: A Play in One Act* (Portsmouth: Frampton, 1891).

24. These also include George Kibbe Turner's *Hagar's Hoard* (New York: Alfred P. Knopf, 1920); Cothburn O'Neal's *Hagar* (New York: Crown Publishing, 1958); and Lois T. Henderson's *Hagar: A Novel* (San Francisco: Harper & Row, 1978). Recent Hagar poems appear in Rosanna Warren's *Stained Glass* (New York: W.W. Norton, 1993), and in poet Alicia Ostriker's *The Nakedness of the Fathers: Biblical Visions and Revisions* (New Jersey: Rutgers University Press, 1994).

25. Baym, *Woman's Fiction,* xxxviii.

26. Baym, *Novels, Readers, and Reviewers,* 107–8.

27. Stephens, *Hagar the Martyr,* 115.

28. See, for example, Jones, *Tomorrow Is Another Day,* 3–5, 9, 14–15.

29. Baym, *Woman's Fiction,* 27–28.

30. Woodman, *The Pregnant Virgin,* 121, 124, 126. Woodman more specifically discusses the entrapping relationship between mother and daughter as a result of the white male's prohibitive construction of female sexual desire and the mother's consequent anger at the loss of her virginity.

31. Teubal, *Hagar the Egyptian,* xxi.

32. Teubal interprets from the Old Testament Documentary Theory, in which folksy, story-telling strains in the Old Testament are identified with "J" editors who call God "YHWH." For her dating and discussion of the "J" text's patriarchal treatment of Hagar, see Teubal, 14, 20–21, 35–48 passim.

33. Cvetkovich, in *Mixed Feelings* (1–13) suggests a continuum of women's feelings from platonic emotion through sexual passion.

34. See, for example, M. Goshgarian, *To Kiss the Chastening Rod,* 52–53.

35. Marzio, *Chromolithography,* 1. Engraving on Bavarian limestone proved to be a far less expensive means of reproduction than copper or steel engraving, which faded with each reprinting. The chromo involved the application to a print of at least three different colors from three separate stones. First introduced in America in 1840, chromolithographs reached their height of popularity in the 1870s. See also Carey, "American Lithograph," and Twyman, *Lithography.*

36. Art Institute of Chicago, *Corot,* 19.

37. Waters and Hutton, *Artists of the Nineteenth Century,* 1:19. The first American lithographic firm of Barnet and Doolittle, for example, began with an early plate by Frenchman J. Milbert; Barnet studied lithography in Paris. See Carey, "American Lithograph," 62.

38. Since West himself was a lithographer, it seems possible that his paintings would have been known to other lithographers. This circle of influence makes it more likely that an engraving of this painting might have been produced. See Twyman, *Lithography,* 27.

39. *Southern Literary Messenger* 6 (April 1840): 303.

40. *Godey's* 34 (June 1847): 313.

41. Bal, *Reading "Rembrandt,"* 214.

42. Robertson, *Sir Charles Eastlake*, 269. Eastlake's later painting was done for William Marshall, M.P., of Eaton Square, but apparently a copy of this painting was made for an American named Carey, probably Edward Carey, president in 1845 of the Philadelphia Academy of Fine Arts. Robertson speculates that this painting remained unfinished because of Eastlake's other concerns at the time. The American copy was finished, however; it appeared in an exhibition at the Philadelphia Academy in 1847, according to *Godey's*, which notes that it had appeared even earlier for the Artist's Fund in Philadelphia. *Godey's* assumes that it was the same one that Eastlake exhibited at the Royal Academy in 1843, the one apparently done for Marshall. This Philadelphia Academy painting is mentioned by John Sartain in the *Union Magazine of Literature and Art* 5:3 (September 1849): 189, as the source for the *Diadem* engraving.

43. Neumann, *The Great Mother*, 120, 18–19, 42. See Neumann's chapter 10, 120–46, for his discussion of women goddesses as vessel statuary.

44. See, for example, Warner's discussion of chastity ethics as a product of patriarchal Christianity: "In the case of Artemus . . . and Hippolyte . . . and of Athene Parthenos . . . their sacred virginity symbolized their autonomy, and had little or no moral connotation." *Alone of All Her Sex*, 48.

45. Neumann, *The Great Mother*, 48.

46. Butler, *Bodies That Matter*, 40, 41, 42, 43.

47. Ibid., 9.

48. Butler, *Bodies That Matter*, 62, 84. Although Butler disagrees with Luce Irigaray on the question of essentializing the female phallus, she acknowledges her use of Irigaray to deconstruct patriarchal phallic logocentrism.

49. Teubal, *Hagar the Egyptian*, 46.

50. Bal, *Reading "Rembrandt,"* 187.

51. Goshgarian, *To Kiss the Chastening Rod*, 51, 59.

52. Neumann, *The Great Mother*, 269–70.

53. Warner, *Alone of All Her Sex*, 43, 52, 77, 235, 225, 274; Woodman, *The Pregnant Virgin*, 121–22.

54. See Showalter, "Syphillis, Sexuality," 88–115.

2. Hagar: The Nineteenth-Century Myth

1. The first Hagar title published in America may have been the play *Hagar in the Desert*, by French Countess Stéphanié Felicité de Genlis for "the use of children." It emphasizes Hagar's virtue as a self-sacrificial mother. It was published by Isaiah Thomas in 1785 in Worcester, Massachusetts..

2. Cather, "Old Mrs. Harris," 604–5, 602, 611.

3. Unsigned, *Boston Recorder*, Nov. 23, 1822, 1.

4. Unsigned, *Christian Parlor Magazine* 1 (June 1844): 33.

5. See, *Desire and the Sign*, 39.

6. Stowe, *Uncle Tom's Cabin*, 109.

7. Stowe, *Woman in Sacred History*, 42, 43.

8. See Mott, *History of American Magazines,* 1:495. Mott (2:166) notes that Willis's popularity was waning by 1850.

9. Hagar was also a popular figure in periodical poetry of the time. Although the poem "Hagar," published by "J.L.N." in the *Southern Literary Messenger* of April 1840 still repeats the earlier model of Hagar as self-sacrificial mother, in the 1850s the Hagar poems in *Graham's* (45:1 [July 1854]: 19) and *Gleason's Pictorial and Drawing-Room Companion* (5:2 [July 1853]: 19) show Willis's shift to a dual focus on Hagar's role as mother and her symbolic status as an exotic woman in defiance of patriarchal and colluding matriarchal forces. The conflict between Hagar's dual identities as sacred mother and rebellious woman is illustrated in Anne Lynch's "Hagar," where Hagar, although a mother, is a "dark-browed child of Egypt" with "woe and shame to hide." More radical still is the absence of a reference to motherhood in Eliza Poitevent Nicholson's poem "Hagar," a lengthy blank-verse poem that is an imagined soliloquy recreating Hagar's passionate imprecations against Abraham.

10. Willis, "Hagar in the Wilderness," 22, 21. Willis's Hagar poem actually objectifies womanhood through the male gaze as the poet/narrator proceeds to fantasize about Hagar's love for her dominant master. The feminist implications of this, and the possible link between this Hagar poem and the earlier contrasting Hagar poem in the *Boston Recorder,* which may also have been written by Willis, are not examined within the parameters of this study.

11. Hedrick, *Harriet Beecher Stowe,* 363, 368.

12. "Hagar in the Wilderness" first appeared in Willis's *Sketches.* With minor emendations, it reappeared in *The Memorial Giftbook* (1829), in *Sacred Poems* (1843, reprinted through 1873), and in *Poems, Sacred, Passionate, and Humorous* (1844, reprinted through 1873).

13. The only Hagar woman's novel that clearly eschews passion is T.T. Purvis's novella *Hagar: The Singing Maiden.* "T.T" is ambiguously gendered. Purvis's little Hagar never departs adolescence.

14. Teubal, *Hagar the Egyptian,* 20.

15. Ibid., xxxvi, 82–84, xxiii.

16. Woodman, *The Pregnant Virgin,* 121, 31–32.

17. Clark, *History and Myth,* 20.

18. Woodman, *The Pregnant Virgin,* 121.

19. "Hagar's predicament involved slavery, poverty, ethnicity, sexual and economic exploitation, surrogacy, rape, domestic violence, homelessness, motherhood, single-parenting and radical encounters with God" (Williams, *Sisters in the Wilderness,* 4).

20. Ibid., 31.

21. Bhabha, 74.

22. Baird, *Ishmael,* 83, 59.

23. Morrison, *Playing in the Dark,* 5.

24. As quoted from Melville, *Pierre* (89) in Baird, *Ishmael* (94): "Yet was this feeling entirely lonesome, and orphan-like. Fain, then, for one moment,

would he have recalled the thousand sweet illusions of Life; tho' purchased at the price of Life's Truth; so that once more he might not feel himself driven out an infant Ishmael into the desert, with no maternal Hagar to accompany him."

    25. Herzog, *Women, Ethnics, and Exotics,* xxi, 7–16, 16, 17.
    26. Erlich, *Family Themes and Hawthorne's Fiction,* 2.
    27. The author was actually John Foxe (with an "e"), who was educated at Oxford but resigned as a fellow when he could not conform to Magdalen College's religious strictures. His argument for religious tolerance, the 1554 *Commentarii,* or *Actes and Momuments,* went through revisions and became popularly known as the *Book of Martyrs.*
    28. Southworth, *The Deserted Wife,* 22.
    29. Hawthorne, *The Scarlet Letter,* 52.
    30. Baym, *Woman's Fiction,* xxxviii.
    31. Ibid., 49.
    32. Greene, *Blacks in Eden,* 6. Critic Brian Davis and colonialist William Bradford, respectively, are quoted in Greene, 13, 84.
    33. Ibid., 1–2.
    34. Ibid., 13.
    35. For a compelling discussion of Ishmael's complex role as victim and colonial agent, see Dimock, *Empire for Liberty,* 109–39.
    36. Giddings, *When and Where I Enter,* 88–89, 125–26.

3. The Resurrected South: Hagar in Southworth's THE DESERTED WIFE

    1. Jan Bakker, Alan Dowty, Elizabeth Moss, and Anne Jones do not include Southworth in their lists of "Old South" southern writers: Bakker, "Twists of Sentiment," 3; Dowty, "Urban Slavery in Pro-Southern Fiction," 37; Moss, *Domestic Novelists,* 12; Jones, *Tomorrow Is Another Day,* xi. Since Southworth can lay claim to the South as her home as much as any of the authors these scholars consider southern, it is probably her overt loyalty to the Union cause that excludes her from most lists.
    2. In fact, many New England periodicals were either neutral or sympathetic to slavery. See Mott, *History of American Magazines,* 1:590. *Godey's,* for example, prohibited Civil War references.
    3. Boyle, *Mrs. E.D.E.N. Southworth,* 8, 16, 15. It was actually Southworth who encouraged Stowe to publish *Uncle Tom's Cabin* in the *National Era* (Boyle, 15).
    4. See chapter 1, note 48, above.
    5. Harris, *Nineteenth-Century American Women's Novels,* 120.
    6. Neumann, *The Great Mother,* 144. See also Johnson, *Lady of the Beasts,* 124–31, 134–35.
    7. Perry, *Image of the Indian,* xiii, 35, 36, 37. An ambiguous exception to

this was John Singleton Copley's "Watson and the Shark" (1788), discussed in Boime's *Art of Exclusion,* 20–36.

8. The nineteenth-century theologian Samuel Roberts, for example, alludes to a widely circulated folkloric belief that gypsies were "probably a mixture of Egyptians and Ethiopians" (*Parallel Miracles,* 146).

9. Irwin, *American Hieroglyphics,* 3–5.

10. Frederickson, *Black Image in the White Mind,* 12–14.

11. Buick, "Ideal Works of Edmonia Lewis," 18.

12. Young, *Colonial Desire,* 126, 127, 124.

13. Roberts, *Parallel Miracles,* 146. Samuel Roberts was a Welsh minister who opposed slavery in Britain, a position that became more ambiguous after he emigrated to Tennessee. There his embroilment in land disputes occupied most of his time, although he did debate in opposition to a friend's abolitionist views. Later opponents of Roberts called him a "slave-owner." See Shepperson, *Samuel Roberts,* 118, 9, 99, 100, 123.

14. Nott, "Two Lectures on the Natural History of the Caucasion and Negro Races" (1844), as quoted in Young, *Colonial Desire,* 129.

15. For a more complete discussion of nineteenth-century racist genetics, see Frederickson, *Black Image in the White Mind,* and Young, *Colonial Desire,* 118–41. For a specific discussion of Agassiz, see Wallis, "Black Bodies, White Science."

16. I am grateful to Diana Miles for her discussion with me on the limits of white women's "imagination" of black women. For a discussion of contradictions between white women's use of the slave metaphor and minority ethnic concerns, see Yellin, *Women and Sisters,* 25–26, and Sanchez-Eppler, "Bodily Bonds."

17. Claudia Tate, "Pauline Hopkins: Our Literary Foremother," in *Conjuring Black Women: Fiction and Literary Tradition,* ed. Marjorie Pryse and Hortense J. Spillers (Bloomington: Indiana University Press, 1985), 60. Gillman ("The Mulatto, Tragic or Triumphant?" 232) points out that Hopkins's Reuel in *Of One Blood* is olive-complexioned.

18. Southworth's Ishmael series includes *Ishmael; or, In the Depths* and *Self-Raised, or, From the Depths* (serialized from 1863 to 1864 in *The New York Ledger*), rept. T.B. Peterson & Brothers, 1876.

19. Fox-Genovese, *Within the Plantation Household,* 148; Ries, "Mammy: A Story."

20. Bakker, "Twists of Sentiment," 3–13. On Southworth's "blood" typology see Boyle, *Mrs. E.D.E.N. Southworth,* 77–78, 89–98.

21. Neumann, *The Great Mother,* 296.

22. Bardes and Gossett discuss the importance for Southworth of "giving women legal control of their property" (88) in "The Discarded Daughter" in *Declarations of Independence,* 88–99.

23. Bercovitch, *American Jeremiad,* 162.

24. See Greene, 36–37, 84–85.

25. Bercovitch, 162.

4. Hagar's Demise in Southworth: VIRGINIA AND MAGDALENE

1. The frequent testimony that a great number of white plantation children were nursed by black slaves in the antebellum South is challenged by McMillen's "Mothers' Sacred Duty." McMillen alleges that more than 85 percent of the 78 nineteenth-century upper- and middle-class women whose comments she consulted nursed their own babies (336). She argues that white women were socially pressured to provide the best nurturance possible. McMillen also attributes the origin of the "myth" of black women nursing white babies to the post–Civil War South, with its sentimentalization of the antebellum days "when the devoted black mammy often became a symbol of a time when blacks allegedly knew their place" (334).

It can be argued that McMillen's anecdotal evidence is countered by antebellum, as opposed to postbellum, fiction unexamined by McMillen. The nurturing "mammy" was *not* an invention of post–Civil War times. She is ever-present in southern antebellum texts by white women. If McMillen is right that white women were ashamed of not nursing their own babies, such antebellum texts would seem the least likely place to portray surrogate nursing. In Southworth's *The Deserted Wife* (1849), Hagar alludes to her own nursing by a black woman. In Mary Jane Holmes's *Tempest and Sunshine* (1854), set in Kentucky, a long-lost older brother returns home unrecognized by his very own brother but is immediately recognized by the black housekeeper "Aunt Katy," whose name is suddenly transformed into "Mammy" by the returning brother, who exclaims, "Katy, dear old mammy Katy," while "Mammy" Katy responds, "and didn't I nuss him, and arter his mother died, didn't I larn him all his manners?" (115–16). Beyond the fictive context, Harriet Jacobs, in *Incidents in the Life of a Slave Girl* (1860), relates how her grandmother ceased weaning her own child to nurse her mistress's white infant (New York: Oxford University Press, 1988), 16. In Pauline Hopkins's *Contending Forces* (1900), a vernacular character remarks how squeamish northerners are about touching black people, while "'Down South the big white folks has nussed so meny black mammies thet they don't known nuthin' else for their chillun,'" 192. Granted, Hopkins writes during the post-Reconstruction period, but she may be recollecting real-life experiences of antebellum black women.

Only when white women were ill after childbirth, suggests McMillen, did they feel constrained to resort to a wet nurse. It is certainly the case that white female invalidism was valued in Victorian culture as the sign of a "lady." Whether or not white women were sick or simply pretended to be so, if they were unable to nurse their own babies then they would hardly rush to testify to this, in light of McMillen's suggestion that it was a source of shame or chagrin not to nurse one's own baby. Black women would have been thought the most likely nursing surrogates, since "black women were represented in both scientific and historical tracts as being either excessively sexualized or as enduringly strong," and "nineteenth-century physicians . . . argued that black people were ideally suited to difficult physical labor." Herndl, "The Invisible (Invalid) Woman," 557, 564.

In the context of my contention that Southworth sets up a white mother/black mother nursing reciprocity to transform black female labor into love discourse, the text illustrates Southworth's wish to dramatize the white mother's nursing as unusual, based on her frailty. The mother's choice is also a feminist resistance to a white patriarchal system in place that would clearly prohibit her action. Southworth portrays a white woman nursing a metaphorically black baby in the frame of a fairytale, which suggests that many more black women in reality nursed white babies than McMillen's findings suggest.

2. Williams, *Sisters in the Wilderness*, 62, 38.

3. Toni Morrison's disturbing portrayal of the violence done to Sethe through the appropriation of her milk by white men in *Beloved* deconstructs Southworth's familial reading of black women nursing white children.

4. Fox-Genovese, *Within the Plantation Household*, 198.

5. See Dearborn, *Pocahontas's Daughters*, 72. Young, in *Colonial Desire*, notes that "class was increasingly thought of in terms of race" in Britain in the nineteenth century (96).

6. Fox-Genovese, *Within the Plantation Household*, 119–20.

7. Young, *Colonial Desire*, 165, 173.

8. Southworth was a great admirer of the southern intellectual William Wirt, upon whose life she based her sequel Hagar novels, the *Ishmael* series. Wirt defended the Cherokees against land dispossession that he felt was in opposition to the presidential philosophies of Washington, Jefferson, Madison, Monroe, and John Quincy Adams. See Kennedy, *Memoirs of the Life of William Wirt*, 2: 259, 296.

9. Dimock, *Empire for Liberty*, 116.

10. In Duvall, "Uncle Tom's Cabin," 165–66.

11. Fox-Genovese, *Within the Plantation Household*, 134.

12. This rosy picture is challenged by Frederick Douglass's account of the time between Christmas and New Year's for the African American plantation slave, when, he says, slaveowners encouraged drunkenness "to disgust the slave with freedom." Also slaves "almost universally say they are contented and that their masters are kind" because "the slaveholders have been known to send in spies among their slaves, to ascertain their views and feelings in regard to their condition." *Narrative*, 77, 20.

13. Quoted in Fox-Genovese, *Within the Plantation Household*, 198.

14. Boyle, *Mrs. E.D.E.N. Southworth*, 2–3

15. Jephtha vowed to sacrifice to God the first who emerged from his household after his victorious return from defeat of the Ammonites. His daughter was portrayed in the nineteenth century as a martyr. See DeJong, "God's Women," 246–49.

16. Moss, *Domestic Novelists in the Old South*, 16.

17. William Bradford, quoted in Barnett, *The Ignoble Savage*, 80, 81.

18. Ibid., 9.

19. Woodman, *Pregnant Virgin*, 122, 126. Interestingly, both Southworth and Woodman use "gypsy" and "outcast" to describe Hagar.

20. As quoted in Boyle, *Mrs. E.D.E.N. Southworth*, 84.

21. The fate of Magdalene's legal status as "married" or not is also dependent on the whimsy of Englishman Sir Clinton Carey, who ravishes Magdalene in a secret marriage which he then abandons to court her foster-sister Virginia for her inheritance. This puts Magdalene in the symbolic role of the African American mistress.

22. I am indebted for this observation to Jan Bakker's reading of *Retribution* in "Twists of Sentiment in Antebellum Southern Romance."

23. Frederickson, *Black Image in the White Mind*, 121.

24. Ibid., 278.

5. The Scandal of Race: Stephen's HAGAR THE MARTYR

1. Bank, "Howard Athenaeum Company," 283. Francis Drake, in *Dictionary of American Biography*, 17:56, lists 1851 as Stephens's final acting year.

2. Kendall, *Golden Age of the New Orleans Theatre*, 347, 349.

3. For expanded discussion of sexual promiscuity and the nineteenth-century theatre, see Johnson, *American Actress*.

4. For a good discussion of nineteenth-century American women's anxieties about authorship, see Wood, "The 'Scribbling Women,' 3–24.

5. One famous actress, Charlotte Cushman, published a short story in *Godey's* that proved her "a worthy, cultivated woman." Cushman continued this "promotional publishing" of poems and short pieces throughout her career. Dudden, *Women in the American Theatre*, 82.

6. Minor stage actresses were in fact paid better than other women laborers, such as seamstresses, tobacco packers, and book folders. Actually, a famous actress could make double what a famous woman author of the time made. See Johnson, *American Actress*, 129. Stephens knew she would never be a famous actress, so she went for the social status of a domestic "lady" writer.

7. J.L.M., "Hagar"; anon., "Hagar in the Wilderness"; Lynch, "Hagar"; Allen, "The Departure of Hagar,"; Hayden, "Hagar"; and Alexander, "Hagar." Carey's book was published by Redfield (New York) in 1852.

8. Baym, *Novels, Readers, and Reviewers*, 107–8.

9. Cvetkovich, *Mixed Feelings*, 24.

10. Cohen, *Sex Scandal*, 2.

11. Ibid., 2; Cvetkovich, *Mixed Feelings*, 22.

12. Young, *Colonial Desire*, 146–47.

13. Cvetkovich uses these words to describe "the immorality of feeling itself" illustrated in the dramatization of women's affect in the sensationalist novel (*Mixed Feelings*, 20). Sexual feeling intermingled with blackness provides an intensification of the proscriptive dynamics Cvetkovich examines in tabooed women's feeling.

14. Young, *Colonial Desire*, 115.

15. As quoted in Cvetkovich, *Mixed Feelings*, 18.

16. Gilman, "Black Bodies, White Bodies," 221, 229. Gilman notes that these "scientists" determined that prostitutes and black women had abnormally large genitalia. For an additional discussion of the racist sexualization of black women, see Giddings, *When and Where I Enter*. See in particular chapters 2, 3, and 4 in Giddings.

17. Canova was a late eighteenth- to early nineteenth-century Italian neoclassical sculptor, given to sensuous sculpture, even in religious subjects, including "The Penitent Magdalene." See Licht and Finn, *Canova*.

18. From Edward Long's *History of Jamaica* (1774) as quoted in Young, *Colonial Desire*, 150.

19. See Showalter, "Syphilis, Sexuality," 88–115.

20. Gilman, "Black Bodies, White Bodies," 231.

21. Collins uses this term to designate one of four controlling negative stereotypes of black women from the nineteenth century. *Black Feminist Thought*, 77.

22. John Berger as quoted in Kappeler, *Pornography of Representation*, 45.

23. Wilson, *History of American Acting*; Dudden, *Women in the American Theatre*, 101.

24. *Graham's*, 280. *Graham's* also published a sarcastic review of Southworth's *The Curse of Clifton* in 1853 (Boyle, *Mrs. E.D.E.N. Southworth*, 57).

25. Cvetkovitch, *Mixed Feelings*, 22.

26. Cohen, *Sex Scandal*, 5.

27. Berzon, *Neither White Nor Black*, 96, 120.

28. Sanchez-Eppler, "Bodily Bonds," 98, 99.

29. Gilman, "Black Bodies, White Bodies," 209.

30. Cohen, *Sex Scandal*, 22.

31. Baym, *Woman's Fiction*, 262.

32. Moss notes that post–Civil War feminist resistance to patriarchal force was a northern rather than a southern phenomenon, since women's submission as passive ladies was essential to the structure of proslavery mythology. See, for example, *Domestic Novelists in the Old South*, 15–16.

33. Stephens's subplot borrows heavily from *Romance and Reality; or, The Young Virginian*, by Irish American playwright John Brougham. Published in 1856, it was nevertheless on the bill for Brougham's 1851–52 season at his short-lived Lyceum Theatre Stock Company in New York City. He was also at the Howard Athenaeum in 1851–52 when Stephens was there, and the resemblances suggest Stephens's appropriation. See Ryan, "Brougham's Lyceum Theatre Stock Company," 131; and Moody, *Dramas from the American Theatre*, 283. Brougham's New York Lyceum opened in late December of 1850, but obviously Brougham was adept at simultaneous tasks. Moody notes that "he was the first performer to attempt playing in New York and Philadelphia on the same evening" (400).

6. Hagar Splitting: Clark's MODERN HAGAR

1. Bhabha, *Location of Culture*, 66.
2. Barthes, *Mythologies*, 121.
3. Chesnut, *Diary from Dixie*, 29.
4. Fox-Genovese, *Within the Plantation Household*, 202.
5. See Gabler-Hover, "North-South Reconciliation Theme," and Kaplan, "Spectacle of War."
6. For the discontinued use of slavery emblems, hence of slavery analogies in the white feminist movement, see Yellin, *Women and Sisters*, 171–72, especially the discussion of the white Bugler Girl who "merits analysis in relation to turn-of-the-century imperialism and the white racism rampant in the feminist movement" (172). For a concise discussion of the exclusion of black women from the white feminist movement after the Civil War, see Carby, "Introduction" to *Iola Leroy*, xiv-xv.
7. Ransom, *Conflict and Compromise*, 93, 96, 124–27, 150, 155. For a full discussion of the congressional compromise that preceded the Civil War, consult this source.
8. But by 1691, severe punishment was enforced on any white who intermarried; Ballagh, "History of Slavery in Virginia," 57.
9. Ridgely uses this phrase in *Nineteenth-Century Southern Literature*.
10. Slotkin, *Fatal Environment*, 19.
11. For example, one of Southworth's favorite southern proslavery politicians, William Wirt, defended Cherokees against the federal government and, in his *Letters of the British Spy* (1803), venerated Pocahontas as the veritable mother of Virginia's noble family of southern white aristocrats (Ridgely, *Nineteenth-Century Southern Literature*, 34–36).
12. Estergreen, *Kit Carson*, 69, 76, 77. For a discussion of Kit Carson's more complex relationship with Indians, including his violence against them, which Charlotte Clark suppresses, see for example McCutcheon, *Kit Carson*.
13. Coacooche actually went to Washington in 1844 to plead for governmental protection of Seminole blacks. In Clark's text, Coacooche is on his way to Mexico, an allusion to actual attempts made from 1846 onward to establish an Indian and "Negro" colony in Mexico, to circumvent the "hungry hounds [who] have tracked the Seminoles from Florida to Arkansas ... [and] find safety for ... the brave black tribe that grew up beneath the shade of his father's lodge" (1:32). McReynolds, *The Seminoles*, 257.
14. Irving, "Philip of Pokanoket": "He was a patriot, attached to his native soil—a prince true to his subjects, and indignant of their wrongs—a soldier, daring in battle, firm in adversity, patient of fatigue, of hunger. . . . he lived a wanderer and a fugitive . . . without a pitying eye to weep his fall, or a friendly hand to record his struggle" (232–34, 222). Clark also quotes Irving's "Traits of Indian Character" (*Sketch Book Crayon Papers*) in the epigraph to chapter 3. Reading Irving selectively is itself an example of forming a "usable past." While

Slotkin finds Irving a champion of white colonial imperialism in *Astoria* and *Captain Bonneville* (*Fatal Environment,* 204, 122), Charlotte Clark finds an Irving who is distressed with New England colonial times as when Irving laments that "it is painful to perceive . . . how the footsteps of civilization may be traced in the blood of the aborigines." "Philip of Pokanoket," 220.

15. See Clark, 1:223, and Irving's "Philip of Pokanoket," 223.

16. For a full discussion of Hentz and Eastman's staging of this antebellum scene, see Hunter's "Maids and Mammies," chapters 2 and 3.

17. Smith, *Oxford Spy Wed,* 3–4.

18. Mentioned in ibid., 14, and Bakeless, *Spies of the Confederacy,* 146.

19. For fuller discussions of the Copperheads, Clement Vallandigham, and the activities of Lincoln and General Burnside in relation to him, see Axelrod, *War between the Spies,* 214; Klement, *Copperheads in the Middle West*; and Gray, *Hidden Civil War.*

20. Klement, *Copperheads in the Middle West,* 90, 6, 9.

21. Gray, *Hidden Civil War,* 45.

22. Axelrod, *War between the Spies,* 31.

23. Smith, 7.

24. For an account of the Sumner incident involving the beating of Massachusetts Senator Charles Sumner by South Carolina Representative Preston Brooks after Sumner's personal attack on Brooks's cousin Andrew P. Butler, see Ransom, *Conflict and Compromise,* 152–53.

25. Smith, *Oxford Spy Wed,* 8.

26. Although "sachem" can refer to any Indian chief, the fact that Clark consciously uses "Philip of Pokanoket" in which Irving refers ceremoniously to Philip as "sachem" (220) suggestively connects Carson as a sachem with Philip. This is reinforced by the link between Carson's son and Philip.

27. Neumann, *The Great Mother,* 80, 288. One also thinks of Freud's crone figure, which enters the male child's perception when faced with the autonomy of his mother's desire and thus of his own separateness and ultimate demise.

28. Giddings notes in *When and Where I Enter* that even prominent black men such as William Wells Brown contended that slave women had been degraded with their consent (61).

29. Textual references are from Johnston, *Hagar.*

30. See Giddings for an explicit discussion of how Susan B. Anthony, Elizabeth Cady Stanton, and their white feminist sisters devised suffrage strategies exclusive of the interests of black men and women and championed southern suffragists such as Carrie Chapman Catt, who argued "the usefulness of woman suffrage . . . as a means of legally preserving White supremacy in the South" (*When and Where I Enter,* 88–89).

31. Sprengnether, "(M)other Eve," 305.

32. This defense of the black mother by the white daughter foreshadows the plot of *Imitation of Life* in its most famous 1959 remake of the Fanny Hurst novel. In the movie, the white daughter, Sandra Dee, is appalled at how the black

maid (Juanita Moore) is rejected by her "passing" mixed-race daughter (played by Susan Kohner).

7. Prodigal Daughters: Hopkins's HAGAR'S DAUGHTER and Black Female Identity

1. Foster, *A Brighter Coming Day*, 218. I am indebted to Berlant's use of this quotation in *The Queen of America Goes to Washington City* (235), which called Harper's statement to my attention.

2. Carby notes that Hopkins "both adopts and adapts popular fiction formulas" for deeper purposes of "political and social critique" (Introduction to *Magazine Novels of Pauline Hopkins*, xl, xxxvii). Brooks argues the ethical "undecidability" of Hopkins's use of minstrel caricatures in the subplot of *Hagar's Daughter* ("Mammies, Bucks, and Wenches," 119–57).

3. "Sculptors, writers, poets, scholars, preachers [including Paul Lawrence Dunbar, Richard Wright, E. Franklin Francis, Frances Harper, Francis P. Reid, Toni Morrison, and Maya Angelou] and just plain folks have passed along the biblical figure Hagar to generation after generation of black folks" (Delores Williams, *Sisters in the Wilderness*, 2, 245n. 2).

4. As quoted in Hunter, "Maids and Mammies," 244.

5. As quoted in Giddings, *When and Where I Enter*, 58.

6. See for example Braithwaite, "Negro America's First Magazine," 22; also W.E.B. Du Bois's account of this editorship in "The Colored Magazine in America," 33, and Charles Johnson, "Rise of the Negro Magazine," *Journal of Negro History* 13 (January 1928), 12, 325. The argument for Hopkins's early editorship is made also by Johnson and Johnson, "Away from Accommodation." See also Hazel V. Carby's introduction to *The Magazine Novels of Pauline Hopkins*, xxx-xxxvi.

7. The stories referred to here from *CAM* include, in order of discussion: Scales, "Beth's Triumph"; Stewart, "The Wooing of Pastor Cummings"; idem, "Aunt 'Ria's Ten Dollars"; and Mossell, "Mizeriah Johnson."

8. Terborg-Penn, "Mossell, Gertrude E.H. Bustill."

9. Significant accounts of Washington's acquisition of the *Colored American Magazine* and the probable firing of Pauline Hopkins include Meier, "Booker T. Washington and the Negro Press," and Johnson and Johnson, "Away from Accommodation."

10. Braithwaite, "Negro America's First Magazine," 25; Joyce, *Black Book Publishers in the U.S.*, 82.

11. See Tate's groundbreaking work *Domestic Allegories of Political Desire*, 161. See also Susan Gillman's argument that tragic mulatto fiction "fuse[s] . . . familial love disrupted and restored with the political project of imagining a viable biracial community" ("The Mulatto, Tragic or Triumphant?" 225).

12. Campbell, "Pauline Elizabeth Hopkins," 187.

13. Murray, "Educated Colored Men and White Women," 94, 95; "Why Men Don't Marry," 329; Giddings, *When and Where I Enter*, 61.

14. Such views were supported by women contributors, including Johnson, "Home Life," 135, and Graves, "Motherhood."

15. DeJong argues that "Jephthah's Daughter," along with Hagar, was one of the four most common Victorian biblical heroines ("God's Women," 240, 242).

16. This portrait of Hester by Hugues Merle is in the Walters Art Gallery in Baltimore and is reproduced in the Washington Square Press edition of *The Scarlet Letter* (New York: Pocket Books, 1994). The portrait bears a stunning resemblance to the Hagar/Ishmael representation by Christian Koehler.

17. Giddings, *When and Where I Enter*, 61.

18. Ibid., 32, 82. As quoted in Giddings, 114.

19. Hall, "Hagar and Ishmael," 302, 303.

20. Nicholson, "Hagar."

21. Dickson Bruce notes the frequency with which the tragic mulatta heroine was forced to face death rather than remission into the brutalities of slavery for herself and her child (*Black American Writing*, 43). Other plot elements that lead to the disclosure of Hagar's mixed-race ethnicity are typical of the tragic mulatto story. Hagar's birth is shrouded in mystery; she is adopted by a Maryland plantation couple who die early but raise Hagar in St. Louis and send her to a young ladies' seminary in the North, from which the heroine returns to the patrimonial plantation at the novel's beginning. These elements set up the plausibility that the mulatta heroine's identity may be unknown to her and her ultimate exposure by a willful proslavery villain.

22. See the discussion of Hagar as an African American survivor in Williams, *Sisters in the Wilderness*, chapter 2.

23. In *Contending Forces*, British relatives of an African American family represent racially enlightened white people. In Hopkins's second serial novel, *Winona*, both Canada and Britain are strategically presented as racially tolerant.

24. Bhabha, *The Location of Culture*, 86.

25. Ibid.

26. "Edmonia Lewis," curator's files, National Museum of Art, 3.

27. Driskell, *Two Centuries of Black American Art*, 48.

28. Fine, *Afro-American Artist*, 64.

29. Buick, "Ideal Works of Edmonia Lewis," 10, 11.

30. Bhabha, *Location of Culture*, 88.

31. Yellin notes that several of the prominent features of antislavery emblems, such as the Wedgewood medallions "Am I Not a Man and a Brother" (1787) and "Am I Not a Woman and a Sister" (1836) are postures of supplication, including the kneeling position of the supplicant and the supplicant's upraised glance and praying hands. These elements "freeze the subject into a position of subordinacy" (*Women and Sisters*, 110–12).

32. See my discussion of Delores Williams and Savina Teubal, respectively,

in chapter 2, above.

33. Bhabha, *Location of Culture*, 34.
34. Kappeler, *Pornography of Representation*, 45.
35. Rimmon-Kenan, *Narrative Fiction*, 87.
36. Benstock, "Authorizing the Autobiographical," 1041.
37. Quoted from psychoanalytical literary critic Donna Przybylowicz, *Desire and Repression*, 22–23.
38. For an overview, see Greene's Introduction in *Blacks in Eden*, 1–11.
39. Berlant, *Queen of America*. See, for example, chapter 1, "The Theory of Infantile Citizenship."
40. Milton, "Paradise Lost," Book I, ll. 752–57. Textual variants in Hopkins's use include occluding lines and changing Milton's "Trumpets souns" to "trumpet Sound." Either Hopkins had a different edition or she was quoting from memory.
41. Axelrod discusses the assassination plot in *The War between the Spies*, 12–22.
42. Young, *Colonial Desire*, 115.
43. Butler, *Bodies That Matter*, 171–72.
44. Goodman, *Hagar Revelly*.
45. Holmes, *Dora Deane*, 210.
46. Sprengnether, "(M)other Eve," 300, 302, 303, 304, 305.
47. A late nineteenth-century African American convention in Philadelphia resolved to "recommend to our mothers and our sisters to use every honorable means to secure for their sons and brothers places of profit and trust in stores and other places of business, such as will throw a halo around this proscribed people." As quoted in Giddings, *When and Where I Enter*, 60.
48. du Cille uses the terms I quote to describe white perception in "The Occult of True Black Womanhood," 592.
49. Berlant, *Queen of America*, 235. Berlant notes that in *Iola Leroy*, Harper tries to "solve the problem of America for itself" (238) by suggesting the African American community as a new force to create healthy citizenship. Hopkins's vernacular "Aunt Henny" not only holds her family together but is the custodian of the capital in more ways than one. She testifies in court, exposing the graft of corrupt politicians that stands in direct opposition to her own return of the one million dollars of graft money she discovered while she was sweeping in the Capitol building. But Aunt Henny's symbolic redemption of the capital is imperilled by her tainted race status, which is used to suggest that she is not a reliable witness (256–59).

Conclusion

1. This is the main title of an essay by Avallone that challenges the exclusion of minorities from the American Renaissance canon.

2. The title of the special issue of *American Literature* on domestic ideology (70:3 [September 1998]).

3. Budick, "Sacvan Bercovitch, Stanley Cavell, and the Romance Theory of American Fiction."

4. Critical works with a similar mission include Dimock's *Empire for Liberty* and Bercovitch's *Office of the Scarlet Letter*.

5. Kaplan, "Manifest Destiny."

6. See Fetterley, *Resisting Reader*.

Bibliography

Alexander, William. "Hagar." *Graham's Magazine* 45:1 (July 1854): 19.
Allen, Catharine. "The Departure of Hagar." *Peterson's Magazine* 22 (September 1852): 115.
"And Hagar Sat Over Against Him and Wept." *Boston Recorder* 7 (November 23, 1822): 188.
Art Institute of Chicago. *Corot: An Exhibition of His Paintings and Graphic Works*. Foreword by S. Lane Faison Jr., notes on Corot by James Merrill. Chicago: R.R. Donnelley and Sons, 1960.
Avallone, Charlene. "What American Renaissance? The Gendered Genealogy of a Critical Discourse." *PMLA* 112:5 (October 1997): 1102–20.
Axelrod, Alan. *The War between the Spies: A History of Espionage during the American Civil War*. New York: Atlantic Monthly Press, 1992.
Baird, John. *Ishmael: A Study of the Symbolic Mode in Primitivism*. Baltimore: Johns Hopkins University Press, 1956.
Bakeless, John. *Spies of the Confederacy*. Philadelphia: J.B. Lippincott, 1970.
Bakker, Jan. "Twists of Sentiment in Antebellum Southern Romance." *Southern Literary Journal* 26:1 (fall 1993): 3–13.
Bal, Mieke. *Reading "Rembrandt": Beyond the Word-Image Opposition*. New York: Cambridge University Press, 1991.
Ballagh, James Curtis. "A History of Slavery in Virginia." In *Early Studies of Slavery by States*. Foreword by Donald Franklin Joyce. Northbrook, Ill.: Metro Books, 1972. 1:1–147.
Bank, Rosemarie K. "Boston Museum Company." In *American Theatre Companies, 1749–1887*, ed. Weldon B. Durham. New York: Greenwood Press, 1986. 68–75.
———."Howard Athenaeum Company." In *American Theatre Companies, 1749–1887*, ed. Weldon B. Durham. New York: Greenwood Press, 1986. 281–84.
Bardes, Barbara, and Suzanne Gossett. *Declarations of Independence: Women and Political Power in Nineteenth-Century American Fiction*. New Brunswick, N.J.: Rutgers University Press, 1990.
Barnett, Louise K. *The Ignoble Savage: American Literary Racism, 1790–1890*. Westport, Conn.: Greenwood Press, 1975.
Barthes, Roland. *Mythologies*. Trans. Annette Lavers. New York: Hill and Wang, 1972.
Baym, Nina. *Novels, Readers, and Reviewers: Responses to Fiction in Antebellum America*. Ithaca: Cornell University Press, 1984.

———. *Woman's Fiction: A Guide to Novels by and about Women in America, 1820–70*. 2d ed. Urbana: University of Illinois Press, 1993.
Benstock, Shari. "Authorizing the Autobiographical." In *Feminisms: An Anthology of Literary Theory and Criticism*, ed. Robyn R. Warhol and Diane Price Herndl. New Brunswick, N.J.: Rutgers University Press, 1991. 1040–57. Reprinted from *The Private Self: Theory and Practice of Women's Autobiographical Writings*, ed. Shari Benstock. Chapel Hill: University of North Carolina Press, 1988.
Bercovitch, Sacvan. *The American Jeremiad*. Madison: University of Wisconsin Press, 1978.
———. *The Office of the Scarlet Letter*. Baltimore: Johns Hopkins University Press, 1991.
Berlant, Lauren. *The Queen of America Goes to Washington City*. Durham, N.C.: Duke University Press, 1997.
Berzon, Judith R. *Neither White Nor Black: The Mulatto Character in American Fiction*. New York: New York University Press, 1978.
Bhabha, Homi K. *The Location of Culture*. London: Routledge, 1994.
Boime, Albert. *The Art of Exclusion: Representing Blacks in the Nineteenth Century*. Washington, D.C.: Smithsonian Institution Press, 1990.
Boyle, Regis Louise. *Mrs. E.D.E.N. Southworth, Novelist*. Washington, D.C.: Catholic University of America Press, 1939.
Braithwaite, William Stanley. "Negro America's First Magazine." *Negro Digest* 6 (December 1947): 21–26.
Brooks, Kristina. "Mammies, Bucks and Wenches: Minstrelsy, Racial Pornography, and Racial Politics in Pauline Hopkins's *Hagar's Daughter*. In *The Unruly Voice: Rediscovering Pauline Elizabeth Hopkins*, ed. John Cullen Gruesser. Urbana: University of Illinois Press, 1996. 119–57.
Bruce, Dickson D., Jr. *Black American Writing from the Nadir: The Evolution of a Literary Tradition, 1877–1915*. Baton Rouge: Louisiana State University Press, 1989.
Budick, Emily Miller. "Sacvan Bercovitch, Stanley Cavell, and the Romance Theory of American Fiction." *PMLA* 107:1 (January 1992): 78–91.
Buick, Kirsten P. "The Ideal Works of Edmonia Lewis: Invoking and Inverting Autobiography." *American Art* 9 (summer 1995): 5–19.
Butler, Judith. *Bodies That Matter: On the Discursive Limits of "Sex."* London: Routledge, 1993.
Caine, Hall. *A Son of Hagar: A Romance of Our Time*. New York: A.L. Burt, 1894.
Campbell, Jane. "Pauline Elizabeth Hopkins." In *Afro-American Writers before the Harlem Renaissance."* Vol. 50 of *Dictionary of Literary Biography*, ed. Trudier Harris and Thadious M. Davis. Detroit: Bruccoli Clark, 1986. 182–89.
Carby, Hazel V. "Introduction." In Frances E.W. Harper, *Iola Leroy, or Shadows Uplifted*. Black Women Writers Series. Boston: Beacon Press, 1987. ix-xxx.

———. "Introduction." In *The Magazine Novels of Pauline Hopkins*. The Schomburg Library of Nineteenth-Century Black Women Writers. General Ed. Henry Louis Gates. New York: Oxford University Press, 1988. xxix-l.
Carey, Alice. *Hagar: A Story of Today*. New York: Redfield, 1852.
Carey, John Thomas. "The American Lithograph from Its Inception to 1865: With Biographical Considerations of Twenty Lithographers and a Check List of Their Works." Thesis. Ohio State University, 1954.
Cather, Willa. "Old Mrs. Harris." In *American Women Regionalists, 1850–1910: A Norton Anthology*, ed. Judith Fetterley and Marjorie Pryse. New York: W.W. Norton, 1992. 597–638.
Chesnut, Mary Boykin Miller. *A Diary from Dixie*. Ed. Ben Ames Williams. Boston: Houghton Mifflin, 1949.
Clark, Charlotte Moon (Charles M. Clay, pseudonym). *The Modern Hagar: A Drama*. 2 vols. New York: George W. Harlan, 1882.
Clark, Robert C. *History and Myth in American Fiction, 1832–52*. New York: St. Martin's Press, 1984.
Cohen, William A. *Sex Scandal: The Private Parts of Victorian Fiction*. Durham: Duke University Press, 1996.
Collins, Patricia Hill. *Black Feminist Thought: Knowledge, Consciousness, and the Politics of Empowerment*. New York: Routledge, 1990.
Cvetkovich, Ann. *Mixed Feelings: Feminism, Mass Culture, and Victorian Sensationalism*. New Brunswick, N.J.: Rutgers University Press, 1992.
Dearborn, Mary. *Pocahontas's Daughters: Gender and Ethnicity in American Culture*. New York: Oxford University Press, 1986.
DeGenlis, Countess Stéphanié Felicité. *Hagar in the Desert*. Worcester, Massachusetts: Isaiah Thomas, 1785.
DeJong, Mary. "God's Women: Victorian American Readings of Old Testament Heroines." In *Old Testament Women in Western Literature*, ed. Raymond-Jean Frontain and Jan Wojcik. Conway, Arkansas: UCA Press, 1991. 238–60.
Dimock, Wai-chee. *Empire for Liberty: Melville and the Poetics of Individualism*. Princeton: Princeton University Press, 1989.
Dorman, James H. "John James Audubon: The Man and His Milieu." In *Audubon: A Retrospective*, ed. James H. Dorman. Lafayette: Center for Louisiana Studies, University of Southwestern Louisiana, 1990. ix–xiv.
Douglass, Frederick. *Narrative of the Life of An American Slave: Written by Himself*. Boston: Anti-Slavery Office, 1845. Reprint: New York: Doubleday, 1989.
Dowty, Alan. "Urban Slavery in Pro-Southern Fiction of the 1850's." *Journal of Southern History* 32 (1966): 25–41.
Drake, Francis S. "Stephens, Mrs. Harriet Marion." In *Dictionary of American Biography*, supplement, vol. 17. Ed. Francis S. Drake. Boston: James R. Osgood, 1872.

Driskell, David C. *Two Centuries of Black American Art*. Los Angeles County Museum of Art. New York: Alfred A. Knopf, 1976.
Du Bois, W.E.B. "The Colored Magazine in America." *Crisis* 5 (November 1912): 33–35.
du Cille, Ann. "The Occult of True Black Womanhood: Critical Demeanor and Black Feminist Studies." *Signs* 19:3 (spring 1994): 591–629.
Dudden, Faye E. *Women in the American Theatre: Actresses and Audiences, 1790–1870*. New Haven: Yale University Press, 1994.
Duvall, Severn. "Uncle Tom's Cabin: The Sinister Side of the Patriarchy." In *Images of the Negro in American Literature*, ed. Seymour L. Gross and John Edward Hardy. Chicago: University of Chicago Press, 1966. 163–80.
"Editor's Table." *Graham's Magazine* 46:2 (February 1855): 280–82.
"Edmonia Lewis." In curator's files. National Museum of American Art. Washington, D.C.
Egan, Pierce. *Hagar Lot; or, The Fate of the Poor Girl*. New York: Dick and Fitzgerald, 1876[?].
Erlich, Gloria C. *Family Themes and Hawthorne's Fiction: The Tenacious Web*. New Brunswick, N.J.: Rutgers University Press, 1984.
Estergreen, M. Morgan. *Kit Carson: A Portrait in Courage*. Norman: University of Oklahoma Press, 1962.
Fetterley, Judith. *The Resisting Reader: A Feminist Approach to American Fiction*. Bloomington: Indiana University Press, 1978.
Fine, Elsa Hong. *The Afro-American Artist: A Search for Identity*. New York: Holt, Rinehart and Winston, 1973.
Ford, Alice. *John James Audubon*. Norman: University of Oklahoma Press, 1964.
———. *John James Audubon: A Biography*. New York: Abbeville Press, 1988.
Foster, Frances Smith, ed. *A Brighter Coming Day: A Frances Ellen Watkins Harper Reader*. New York: Feminist Press, 1990.
Fox-Genovese, Elizabeth. *Within the Plantation Household: Black and White Women of the Old South*. Chapel Hill: University of North Carolina Press, 1988.
Frederickson, George M. *The Black Image in the White Mind: The Debate on Afro-American Character and Destiny, 1817–1914*. New York: Harper and Row, 1971.
Gabler-Hover, Janet. "The North-South Reconciliation Theme and the 'Shadow of the Negro' in *Century Illustrated Magazine*." In *Periodical Literature in Nineteenth-Century America*, ed. Kenneth R. Price and Susan Belasco Smith. Charlottesville: University Press of Virginia, 1995. 239–56.
Giddings, Paula. *When and Where I Enter: The Impact of Black Women on Race and Sex in America*. New York: William Morrow and Company, 1984.
Gillman, Susan. "The Mulatto, Tragic or Triumphant? The Nineteenth-Century American Race Melodrama." In *The Culture of Sentiment: Race, Gender, and Sentimentality in Nineteenth-Century America*, ed. Shirley Samuels. New York: Oxford University Press, 1992. 221–43.

Gilman, Sander L. "Black Bodies, White Bodies: Toward an Iconography of Female Sexuality in Late Nineteenth-Century Art, Medicine, and Literature." *Critical Inquiry* 12:1 (autumn 1985): 204–42.

Goodman, Daniel Carson. *Hagar Revelly.* New York: Mitchell Kennerly, 1913.

Goshgarian, G.M. *To Kiss the Chastening Rod: Domestic Fiction and Sexual Ideology in the American Renaissance.* Ithaca: Cornell University Press, 1992.

Graves, Mrs. A. "Motherhood." *Colored American Magazine* 14 (September 1908): 495.

Gray, Wood. *The Hidden Civil War: The Story of the Copperheads.* New York: Viking Press, 1942.

Greene, J. Lee. *Blacks in Eden: The African American Novel's First Century.* Charlottesville: University Press of Virginia, 1996.

"Hagar." In *African Fundamentalism: A Literary and Cultural Anthology of Garvey's Harlem Renaissance.* New Marcus Garvey Library, No. 5. Ed. Tony Martin. Dover, Mass.: Majority Press, 1991.

"Hagar in the Wilderness." *Christian Parlor Magazine* 1 (June 1844): 33–34.

Hall, Charles Winslow. "Hagar and Ishmael." *Colored American Magazine* 2:4 (February 1901): 302–6.

Harper, Frances Ellen Watkins. *Iola Leroy, or Shadows Uplifted.* Boston: Beacon Press, 1987.

Harris, Susan. *Nineteenth-Century American Women's Novels: Interpretive Strategies.* New York: Cambridge University Press, 1990.

Hawthorne, Nathaniel. *The Scarlet Letter.* In *The Centenary Edition of the Works of Nathaniel Hawthorne.* Vol. 1. Ed. William Charvatt, Roy Harvey Peace, and Claude M. Simpson. Columbus: Ohio State University Press, 1962.

Hayden, Caroline A. "Hagar." *Gleasons' Pictorial Drawing-Room Companion* 5:2 (July 9, 1853): 19.

Hedrick, Joan. *Harriet Beecher Stowe: A Life.* New York: Oxford University Press, 1994.

Heller, Murray, ed. *Black Names in America: Origins and Usage.* Collected by Newbell Niles Puckett. Newbell Niles Puckett Memorial Gift, Cleveland Public Library. Boston: G.K. Hall, 1975.

Herndl, Diane Price. "The Invisible (Invalid) Woman: African-American Women, Illness, and Nineteenth-Century Narrative." *Women's Studies* 24 (1995): 553–72.

Herrick, Francis Hobart. *Audubon the Naturalist: A History of His Life and Time.* New York: D. Appleton-Century 1913, 1938. Reprint, New York: Dover Publications, 1968. Vol. 1.

Herzog, Kristin. *Women, Ethnics, and Exotics.* Knoxville: University of Tennessee Press, 1983.

Holmes, Mary Jane. *Maggie Miller; or, Old Hagar's Secret.* In *Dora Deane; or The East India Uncle: And Maggie Miller; or, Old Hagar's Secret.* New York: C.M. Saxton, 1959. 199–474.

———. *Tempest and Sunshine*. In *Tempest and Sunshine and The Lamplighter*. Ed. Donald A. Koch. New York: Odyssey Press, 1968. 3–212.
Hopkins, Pauline. *Contending Forces: A Romance Illustrative of Negro Life North and South*. Boston: Colored Co-operative Publishing Company, 1900. Reprint, New York: Oxford University Press, 1988.
———. *Hagar's Daughter*. In *Colored American Magazine 1901–1902*. Reprint in *The Magazine Novels of Pauline Hopkins*. Schomburg Library of Nineteenth-Century Black Women Writers. New York: Oxford University Press, 1988.
Hunter, Lee. "Maids and Mammies: Black Women in White Fiction." Ph.D. diss., Georgia State University, 1998.
Irving, Washington. "Philip of Pokanoket. An Indian Memoir." *Sketch Book Crayon Papers*. New York: Fred DeFau and Company, n.d. 219–33.
Irwin, John T. *American Hieroglyphics: The Symbol of the Egyptian Hieroglyphics in the American Renaissance*. New Haven: Yale University Press, 1980.
J.L.M. "Hagar." *Southern Literary Messenger* 6 (April 1840): 303–4.
Johnson, Abby Arthur, and Ronald M. Johnson. "Away from Accommodation: Radical Editors and Protest Journalism, 1900–1910." *Journal of Negro History* 62 (October 1977): 325–38.
Johnson, Alice. "Home Life." *Colored American Magazine* 12:2 (February 1907): 135–36.
Johnson, Buffie. *Lady of the Beasts: Ancient Images of the Goddess and Her Sacred Animals*. San Francisco: Harper and Row, 1981.
Johnson, Charles. "Rise of the Negro Magazine." *Journal of Negro History* 13 (January 1928): 7–21.
Johnson, Claudia. *American Actress: Perspectives on the Nineteenth Century*. Chicago: Nelson-Hall, 1984.
Johnston, Mary. *Hagar*. Boston: Houghton Mifflin, 1913.
Jones, Anne Goodwyn. *Tomorrow Is Another Day: The Woman Writer in the South, 1859–1936*. Baton Rouge: Louisiana State University Press, 1981.
Joyce, Donald Franklin. *Black Book Publishers in the U.S.: An Historical Dictionary*. New York: Greenwood Press, 1991.
Kaplan, Amy. "Manifest Destiny." *American Literature* 70:3 (September 1988): 581–606.
———. "The Spectacle of War in Crane's Revision of History." In *New Essays on 'The Red Badge of Courage,'* ed. Lee Clark Mitchell. Cambridge: Cambridge University Press, 1986.
Kappeler, Susanne. *The Pornography of Representation*. Minneapolis: University of Minnesota Press, 1986.
Kendall, John S. *The Golden Age of the New Orleans Theatre*. Baton Rouge: Louisiana State University Press, 1952.
Kennedy, John P. *Memoirs of the Life of William Wirt*. 2d ed., 2 vols. Philadelphia: Lea and Blanchard, 1850.

Klement, Frank L. *The Copperheads in the Middle West.* Chicago: University of Chicago Press, 1960.
Licht, Fred, and David Finn. *Canova.* New York: Abbeville Press, 1983.
Lynch, Anne Charlotte. "Hagar." In *Diadem for 1845: A Present for All Seasons.* Philadelphia: Carey and Hart, 1845. 97–98.
Macknight, James Arthur. *Hagar.* New York: Belford, Clark, 1889.
Marzio, Peter C. *Chromolithography, 1840–1900: The Democratic Art: Pictures for a 19th-Century America.* Boston: David R. Godine, 1979.
McCutcheon, Gordon, ed. *Kit Carson: Indian Figher or Indian Killer?* Niwot, Colo.: University of Colorado Press, 1996.
McMillen, Sally. "Mothers' Sacred Duty: Breast-Feeding Patterns among Middle- and Upper-Class Women in the Antebellum South." *Journal of Southern History* 51:3 (August 1985): 333–56.
McReynolds, Edwin C. *The Seminoles.* Norman: University of Oklahoma Press, 1957.
Meier, August. "Booker T. Washington and the Negro Press: With Special Reference to the *Colored American Magazine.*" *Journal of Negro History* 38 (January 1953): 67–90.
Melville, Herman. *Pierre; or, The Ambiguities.* Chicago: Northwestern University Press and Newberry Library, 1971.
Milton, John. *The Complete Poetry of John Milton.* Ed. John T. Shawcross. Garden City, N.Y.: Anchor Books, 1971.
Moody, Richard. *Dramas from the American Theatre, 1762–1909.* New York: World Publishing Company, 1966.
Morrison, Toni. *Playing in the Dark: Whiteness and the Literary Imagination.* Cambridge: Harvard University Press, 1992.
Moss, Elizabeth. *Domestic Novelists in the Old South: Defenders of Southern Culture.* Baton Rouge: Louisiana State University Press, 1992.
Mossell, Gertrude. "Mizeriah Johnson: Her Arisings and Shinings." *Colored American Magazine* 4:3 (January and February 1902): 229–33.
Mott, Frank Luther. *A History of American Magazines.* 5 vols. Cambridge: Harvard University Press, 1939. Vols. 1 and 2.
Murray, George Henry. "Educated Colored Men and White Women." *Colored American Magazine* 8:2 (February 1905): 93–95.
Neumann, Erich. *The Great Mother: An Analysis of the Archetype.* Trans. Ralph Manheim. Bollingen Series XLVII. Princeton: Princeton University Press, 1974.
New Standard Alphabetical Indexed Holy Bible (Authorized or King James Version), The. Chicago: John A. Hertel, 1963.
Nicholson, Eliza Poitevent. "Hagar." *Cosmopolitan* 16:1 (November 1893): 10–13.
"Notices of the Fine Arts. The Exhibition." *Godey's Lady's Book* 34 (June 1847): 313–14.
Perry, Ellwood. *The Image of the Indian and the Black Man in American Art, 1590–1900.* New York: George Braziller, 1974.
Przybylowicz, Donna. *Desire and Repression: The Dialectic of Self and Other in*

the Late Works of Henry James. University, Ala: University of Alabama Press, 1986.

Purvis. T.T. *Hagar: The Singing Maiden with Other Stories and Rhymes.* Philadelphia: Walton and Co., 1881.

Ransom, Roger L. *Conflict and Compromise: The Political Economy of Slavery, Emancipation, and the American Civil War.* Cambridge: Cambridge University Press, 1989.

Review of *Hagar the Martyr*, by H. Marion Stephens. *Godey's Lady's Book* 50 (February 1855): 276.

Reynolds, David. *Faith in Fiction: The Emergence of Religious Literature in America.* Cambridge: Harvard University Press, 1981.

Ridgely, J.V. *Nineteenth-Century Southern Literature.* New Perspectives on the South, ed. Charles P. Roland. Lexington: University Press of Kentucky, 1980.

Ries, Adeline F. "Mammy: A Story." *Crisis* 13 (January 1917): 117–18. Reprinted in *Short Fiction by Black Women*, ed. Elizabeth Ammons. New York: Oxford University Press, 1991. 520–23.

Rimmon-Kenan, Shlomith. *Narrative Fiction: Contemporary Poetics.* London: Methuen, 1983.

Roberts, Samuel. *Parallel Miracles: Or, The Jews and the Gypsies.* London: J. Nisbet, 1830.

Robertson, David. *Sir Charles Eastlake and the Victorian Art World.* Princeton: Princeton University Press, 1978.

Ryan, Pat M. "Brougham's Lyceum Theatre Stock Company." In *American Theatre Companies, 1749–1887*, ed. Weldon B. Durham. Westport, Conn.: Greenwood Press, 1986. 129–34.

Sanchez-Eppler, Karen. "Bodily Bonds: The Intersecting Rhetorics of Feminism and Abolition." In *The Culture of Sentiment: Race, Gender, and Sentimentality in Nineteenth-Century America*, ed. Shirley Samuels. New York: Oxford University Press, 1992. 92–114.

Sartain, John. "Editorial. Arts and Artists." *Sartain's Union Magazine of Literature and Art* 5:3 (September 1849): 189.

Scales, Anne Bethel. "Beth's Triumph." *Colored American Magazine* 1:3 (August 1900): 152–59.

See, Fred G. *Desire and the Sign: Nineteenth-Century American Fiction.* Baton Rouge: Louisiana State University Press, 1987.

Shepperson, Wilbur A. *Samuel Roberts: A Welsh Colonizer in Civil War Tennessee.* Knoxville: University of Tennessee Press, 1961.

Showalter, Elaine. *Sexual Anarchy: Gender and Culture at the Fin de Siècle.* New York: Penguin, 1990.

———. "Syphilis, Sexuality, and the Fiction of the Fin de Siècle." In *Sex, Politics, and Science in the Nineteenth-Century Novel*, ed. Ruth Bernard Yeazell. Baltimore: Johns Hopkins University Press, 1986. 88–115.

Sjoo, Monica, and Barbara Mor. *The Great Cosmic Mother: Rediscovering the Religion of the Earth.* San Francisco: Harper and Row, 1987.

Slotkin, Richard. *The Fatal Environment: The Myth of the Frontier in the Age of Industrialization, 1800–1880.* New York: Atheneum, 1985.

Smith, Ophia D. *Oxford Spy Wed at Pistol Point: A True Story . . . More Exciting Than Fiction.* Oxford, Ohio: Cullen Print Company, 1962.

Southworth, E.D.E.N. *The Deserted Wife.* New York: D. Appleton, 1850.

———. *Virginia and Madgalene; or, The Foster-Sisters.* Philadelphia: A. Hart, 1852.

Sprengnether, Madelon. "(M)other Eve: Some Revisions of the Fall in Fiction by Contemporary Women Writers." In *Feminism and Psychoanalysis,* ed. Richard Feldstein and Judith Roof. Ithaca, N.Y.: Cornell University Press, 1989. 298–322.

Stephens, H. Marion. *Hagar the Martyr; or, Passion and Reality: A Tale of the North and South.* Boston: W.P. Fetridge, 1855.

Stewart, Georgia F. "Aunt 'Ria's Ten Dollars." *Colored American Magazine* 3:2 (June 1901): 105–8.

———. "The Wooing of Pastor Cummings." *Colored American Magazine* 3:4 (August 1901): 273–76.

Stowe, Harriet Beecher. *Uncle Tom's Cabin; or, Life among the Lowly,* 1852. Library of America. New York: Vintage Books, 1991.

———. *Woman in Sacred History.* New York: J.B. Ford, 1873.

Tate, Claudia. *Domestic Allegories of Political Desire: The Black Heroine's Text at the Turn of the Century.* New York: Oxford University Press, 1992.

———. "Pauline Hopkins: Our Literary Foremother." In *Conjuring Black Women: Fiction and Literary Tradition,* ed. Marjorie Pryse and Hortense J. Spillers. Bloomington: Indiana University Press, 1985. 53–66.

Terborg-Penn, Rosalyn. "Mosell, Gertrude E.H. Bustill (1855–1948)." In *Black Women in America: An Historical Encyclopedia,* ed. Darlene Clark Hine. Brooklyn: Carlson Publishing, 1993. 1:820.

Teubal, Savina J. *Hagar the Egyptian: The Lost Tradition of the Matriarchs.* San Francisco: Harper and Row, 1990.

Twyman, Michael. *Lithography, 1800–1850.* London: Oxford University Press, 1970.

Wallis, Brian. "Black Bodies, White Science: Louis Agassiz's Slave Daguerreotypes." *American Art* 9 (summer 1995): 39–61.

Warner, Marina. *Alone of All Her Sex: The Myth and the Cult of the Virgin Mary.* New York: Vintage, 1983.

Waters, Clara Erskine, and Laurence Hutton. *Artists of the Nineteenth Century and Their Works.* Vol. 1. New York: Arno Press, 1960.

"Why Men Don't Marry." *Colored American Magazine* 13:5 (November 1907): 328–29.

Williams, Delores S. *Sisters in the Wilderness: The Challenge of Womanist God-Talk.* Maryknoll, N.Y.: Orbis Books, 1993.

Willis, Nathaniel Parker. "Hagar in the Wilderness." In *Sketches.* Boston: S.G. Goodrich, 1827. 20–25.

Wilson, Garff B. *A History of American Acting*. Bloomington: Indiana University Press, 1966.
Wood, Ann D. "The 'Scribbling Women' and Fanny Fern: Why Women Wrote." *American Quarterly* 23 (1971): 3–24.
Woodman, Marion. *The Pregnant Virgin: A Process of Psychological Transformation*. Toronto: University of Toronto Press, 1985.
Yellin, Jean Fagin. *Women and Sisters: The Antislavery Feminists in American Culture*. New Haven: Yale University Press, 1989.
Young, Robert J.C. *Colonial Desire: Hybridity in Theory, Culture, and Race*. London: Routledge, 1995.

Index

References to figures are in italicized type

Alcott, Louisa May, 82
Angelou, Maya: "The Mothering Blackness," 7
Anthony, Susan B., 37, 175n. 30
anti-Hagar novels, 148–50; *Hagar Revelly*, 148; *Hagar's Lot*, 148–49; *A Son of Hagar*, 148. *See also* Hagar paradigm, rejection of
Atwood, Margaret: *The Handmaid's Tale*, 7
Audubon, John James, 1–6; disavowal of racial hybridity, 1–5; family relations of, 2–6; illegitimacy of, 1–2; legacy as white of, 1, 2, 3–4; mixed race identity of, 1–4; *Ornithological Biography*, 2

Bailey, Gamaliel, 38
Baird, James, 32
Bal, Mieke, 15, 21
Ballagh, James, 102
Barnett, Louise K., 69
Barocci [?]: "Hagar and Ishmael." *See* Hagar artwork
Barthes, Roland, 96
Baym, Nina, 9, 34–35, 89, 159–60; *Novels, Readers, and Reviewers*, 9, 159; *Woman's Fiction*, 9, 159
Beecher, Catharine, 159
Beecher, Henry Ward, 110
Benstock, Shari, 139
Bercovitch, Sacvan, 53, 54
Berlant, Lauren, 142
Berzon, Judith, 86
Bhabha, Homi, 3–4, 24, 50, 86, 95, 96, 134, 137, 140, 157; *Location of Culture*, 24, 86

Braithwaite, William Stanley, 125
Brown, William Wells, 129, 131–32, 175n. 28
Bruce, Dickson, 177n. 21
Bryant, William Cullen, 84
Budick, Emily Miller, 158
Buick, Kirsten, 135, 137
Butler, Judith, 18, 20, 22, 39, 147

Caine, Hall: *A Son of Hagar*, 148. *See also* anti-Hagar novels
Carey, Alice: *Hagar: A Story of Today*, 8, 29, 77, 81, 89–90, 95
Castiglione, Giovanni Benedetto: "Hagar and the Angel." *See* Hagar artwork
Cather, Willa, 25–26
Champollion, Jean-François, 41
Chesnut, Mary, 97
Child, Lydia Maria, 69, 87
Chopin, Kate: *The Awakening*, 125
Clark, Charlotte Moon, 88; family life of, 108–10; political views of, 109–10
—, *Baby Rue*, 99
—, *Modern Hagar*, 8, 95–121, 123, 130, 132, 141, 145, 146; disseminated southern space in, 100–110 *passim*, 113; exposure of blackness in, 96–97, 98–99, 111, 112, 114; insanity as Hagar splitting in, 88, 96, 114, 130; marginalization of black women in, 100, 114; mythification of Kit Carson in, 103–4, 110–11; northern violence against minorities in, 100–103, 104, 105, 107–8, 111; patriarchal southern benevolence in, 106–7, 111, 119, 121; Rue as positive Hagar

in, 99, 105; and tragic mulatto fiction, 111, 118; and white southern womanhood, 97, 98, 114, 115. *See also* Edenic myth; Hagar paradigm; slave imagery, appropriation of
Clark, Robert, 30, 32
Clitherall, Elizabeth, 7
Cohen, William, 85, 88, 89
Collins, Patricia, 164n. 2, 173n. 21
Collins, Wilkie, 78
Colored American Magazine, 122, 124–26, 127, 129, 151; black woman's sexuality in, 126, 129; empowered portrayal of black women in, 124–25; motherhood in, 124, 125–26; and Pauline Hopkins, 122, 124–25
Cooper, James Fenimore, 1, 69
Corot, Jean-Baptiste-Camille: "Hagar in the Wilderness." *See* Hagar artwork
Cvetkovich, Ann, 84, 172n. 13

DeJong, Mary, 129
Dimock, Wai-chee, 62
Douglass, Frederick, 171n. 12
Driskell, David, 1, 2, 3, 135
Dunbar, Paul Laurence, 6

Eastlake, Charles: "Hagar." *See* Hagar artwork
Eastman, Mary, 106, 107
Edenic myth, 35–36, 41; and the American Adam, 35; in Clark, 106; exclusionary properties of, 7, 35–36, 38, 52–54, 140, 164n. 3; in Hagar fiction, 35; in Hopkins, 140, 142, 150; and the South, 35–36, 38, 52–54; in Southworth, 38, 39, 42, 44, 51–53, 58, 62, 64, 67
—, and proslavery apologism: in Clark, 100, 104–10 *passim*, 113, 119; in Hagar fiction, 8, 9, 10, 23, 24, 37, 134, 160; in Southworth, 38–39, 48, 55–64 *passim*, 95, 174n. 11. *See also* Greene, J.L.; Jefferson, Thomas
Egan, Pierce: *Hagar's Lot*, 148–49. *See also* anti-Hagar novels

feminism: white women's abandonment of black women, 37, 100, 122, 155, 160, 174n. 6, 175n. 30. *See also* slave imagery
Fern, Fanny. *See* Parton, Sara
Fetterley, Judith, 161
Field, James T., 82
Fine, Elsa, 135
Ford, Alice, 3, 4–5
Fox-Genovese, Elizabeth, 48, 60, 98
Frazier, E. Franklin, 123
Frederickson, George, 72
Freud, Sigmund, 3, 20, 118, 140, 149, 150, 175n. 27

gender stereotypes:
—, black women: in antebellum domesticity, 58–60, 65, 170–71n. 1. *See also* racist stereotypes
—, white women: as chaste, 6, 22, 23, 65–66, 129; as mothers, 22
—, women: as no thing, 20, 39
Giddings, Paula, 37, 126, 129, 151
Gilman, Sander, 78, 79, 88
Godey's Lady's Book, 12, 28, 77, 166n. 42
Goodman, Daniel Carson: *Hagar Revelly*, 148. *See also* anti-Hagar novels
Goshgarian, G.M., 22
Greene, J. Lee, xi–xii, 2, 7, 35–36, 53, 140

Hagar, biblical story of, 6, 10, 15, 24, 29–31, 52
Hagar art, 1, 6, 7, 10–18, 21, 25; barren landscape in, 15, 18; bow/archer imagery in, 11, 15, 20, 21; desert/wilderness scene in, 11, 15, 21; desexualization of Hagar in, 10–11, 21–22, 26; exploitation of blackness in, 1; farewell scene in, 11, 15, 21; Hagar depicted as white in, 7, 10, 11, 39; and patriarchal repression, 10–11, 22; water vessel imagery in, 11, 15–16, 18, 21, 137; by white artists, 7, 39. *See also* Hagar artwork; Hagar paradigm

Hagar artwork: Barocci's [?] "Hagar and Ishmael," xii, 12, *14*; Castiglione's "Hagar and the Angel," 11; Corot's "Hagar in the Wilderness," xii, 11, 12, 18; Eastlake's "Hagar," xii, 12–21 *passim*, 26, 166n. 42, *16*; Eastlake's Hagar portrait (earlier), 21; Koehler's "Hagar and Ishmael," 15, 16, *17*, 22; Lewis's "Hagar in the Wilderness," xii, 135, *136*; lithograph in Cather's "Old Mrs. Harris," 25, Meile's illustration of Hagar, 127, *128*; *Peterson's Ladies' Magazine's* "Departure of Hagar," xii, 15, 18, *19*; Prud'hon's *Christian Parlor* illustration, xii, 12, *15*, 18; Rembrandt's "Hagar's Dismissal," 21; Skeete's *Hagar's Daughter* illustration, 132, *133*; West's "Hagar and Ishmael," xii, 12, *13*, 18

Hagar fiction, 7, 8, 164n. 23, 165n. 24; anti-Hagar novels 148–50; exposure of blackness in, 96; and female dispossession, 25; and racism in, 159; relation to sensationalism of, 9, 95; relation to woman's novel of, 9, 10, 34–35; and white male audience, 23; by white southern women, 8, 9, 24, 25, 123, 134; by white women, 8, 9–10, 18, 23–4, 25, 28, 36–37, 159. See also Edenic myth; Hagar paradigm

Hagar paradigm:

—, artistic creativity: in Hagar art, 18, 21–22, 26; in Hagar fiction, 9, 23, 24, 35, 39, 95, 151; in Hopkins, 126, 148, 151; in Johnston, 156; in Southworth, 40, 43, 49–50, 67, 68, 69, 70; in Stephens, 76, 82

—, as black: in African American tradition, 6–7; in biblical account, 6, 7, 24, 30; in Clark, 96, 97, 98, 99, 111, 112, 113, 117; in Hagar art, 1, 6; in Hagar fiction, 6, 8–9, 23, 24, 37, 123, 153; in Hall, 127, 129; in Hopkins, 122, 130–31, 135, 139, 141; in Johnston, 155; in Lewis, 135, 137; in Southworth, 39, 47, 48, 49, 50, 57, 58, 70–71, 72, 73–74, 96, 98; in Stephens, 76, 77–78, 85, 86, 93, 94; in Stowe, 26, 27, 29; in Willis, 28

—, empowerment: in biblical account 29–31; in Clark, 96, 107, 117, 121; in Hagar fiction, 9, 10, 22, 35, 36, 39, 95, 96, 123, 134, 142, 151, 156, 157; in Hall, 129; in Hopkins, 122, 134, 151, 153, 157; in Southworth, 39, 50, 52, 55, 68, 70, 95, 156; in Stephens, 80, 81, 84, 87, 92; in Willis, 28

—, equestrian skills: in Clark, 99, 145; in Hagar fiction, 35; in Hopkins, 127, 145; in Southworth, 48, 145; in Stephens, 82, 92

—, feminist resistance: in Hagar fiction, 8–9, 10, 23, 24, 39, 123, 143; in Hopkins, 123, 126–27, 130, 132; in Southworth, 42, 44, 47–48, 49, 56, 65–74 *passim*, 95, 161; in Stephens, 86, 93, 94

—, goddess archetype: in biblical account 30; in Clark, 96, 99, 113, 117; in Hagar art, 10, 26; in Hagar fiction, 31, 32, 95, 96, 123, 151; in Hopkins, 151; in Southworth, 39, 40, 49–51, 68, 70, 81, 95, 156; in Stephens, 81

—, hunter: in Hagar fiction, 35; in Southworth, 81; in Stephens, 81

—, hybridity/mixed ethnicity: in Clark, 99, 123; in Hagar fiction, 8, 9, 36, 123; in Hopkins, 37, 123–24, 130, 143, 146, 157; in Southworth, 39, 43, 46, 47, 51, 57, 58, 66, 67–68, 74, 95, 96, 123; in Stephens, 9, 77, 123

—, masculinity: in Clark, 99; in Hagar fiction, 9; in Southworth, 68

—, motherhood: in anti-Hagar novels, 148; in Clark, 114, 115; in Hagar art, 11, 21, 26; in Hagar fiction, 166n. 1, 167n. 9; in Hall, 129; in

Hopkins, 126, 127, 148; in Lewis, 137; in Southworth, 51; in Stowe, 26, 27; in Willis, 28, 167n. 9
—, orphanhood: in Clark, 99, 111; in Hagar fiction, 9, 35; in Southworth, 39; in Stephens, 81
—, rebellion: in Clark, 105; in Hagar fiction, 35, 39, 123; in Hopkins, 126; in Southworth, 71, 73, 74
—, Sanitte Bouffard as, 6
—, self-reliance: in Clark, 105; in Hagar fiction, 9, 35; in Hopkins, 145; in Southworth, 67, 68, 69; in Stephens, 82
—, sexual passion: in biblical account 29–31; in Carey, 29, 95; in Clark, 99, 111, 117; in Hagar art, 26; in Hagar fiction, 8–9, 23, 24, 34–35, 37, 39, 95–96, 123, 149, 167n. 13; in Hall, 129–30; in Hopkins, 126, 130, 138, 140, 145, 147–48, 151, 155; in Johnston, 156; in South-worth, 29, 43, 48, 49, 50, 67, 69, 70, 81, 82, 88, 95; in Stephens, 82, 88, 92, 93; in Stowe, 26, 29; in Willis, 28, 29
—, survival: in biblical account, 30–31, 138; in Clark, 105, 120; in Hagar fiction, 142; in Hopkins, 131, 132, 135
—, victim: in biblical account 31, 138; in Hagar art, 18; in Clark 96, 100; in Hopkins, 132; in Southworth, 51
—, warrior: in Clark, 99; in Hagar fiction, 35, 142. *See also names of individual authors*
Hagar paradigm, rejection of:
—, chastity: in Clark, 117; in Hagar fiction, 37; in Hopkins, 127, 138, 141, 145, 147, 152, 155; in Johnston, 37, 156; in Southworth, 65, 67; in Stephens, 78, 80, 94
—, erasure/disavowal of blackness: in Clark, 96, 106, 113, 118–19, 121, 132; in Hagar art, 1, 10–11, 39; in Hagar fiction, 6, 9, 36–37, 134, 135, 146; in Holmes (Lizzie), 37; in Johnston, 37; in Southworth, 39, 48, 50–53, 54, 55, 74, 75, 95, 96, 106; in Stephens, 87, 93–94
—, Hagar splitting: in Clark, 88, 96, 99, 100, 117; in Hagar fiction, 37, 50, 96, 123, 138, 143; in Hopkins, 144–45, 146, 147; in Southworth, 50, 68, 88; in Stephens, 81, 86, 92–93, 96; in Stowe, 29
—, illicit sexuality: in anti-Hagar novels, 148; in Carey, 89–90; in Clark, 96–97, 98–99, 111, 116–17, 118, 120; in Hagar fiction, 23, 39, 50, 123, 138, 141, 150; in Hall, 129; in Hopkins, 123, 130, 138–57 *passim*; in Southworth, 49, 50, 66, 67, 69, 70; in Stephens, 78, 79, 80–81, 84, 87–88, 93–94, 138; in Stowe, 28
—, male violence: in Clark, 117; in Southworth, 43–46, 47, 72; in Stephens, 80, 86
—, witch figure: in anti-Hagar novels, 149, 150; in Clark, 113, 118; in Holmes (Mary Jane), 149; in Hopkins, 150–51, 152, 153, 154. *See also names of individual authors*
Hagar poetry, 6, 7, 26, 28, 29, 77, 98, 131, 165n. 24, 167n. 9
Hale, Sarah Josepha, 158–59, 160; *Liberia*, 158–59; *Woman's Record*, 160
Hall, Charles Winslow: "Hagar and Ishmael," 127, 129–30
Hall, James, 69
Harper, Frances Ellen Watkins, 122, 132; *Iola Leroy*, 132
Harris, Susan, 39
Hawthorne, Nathaniel, 36, 77; *The House of the Seven Gables*, 158; *The Scarlet Letter*, 33–34, 127, 156, 158
Hedrick, Joan, 29
Hentz, Caroline, 106, 107
Herrick, Francis Hobart, 2, 3, 4
Herzog, Kristin, 33
Holmes, Lizzie, 37
Holmes, Mary Jane, 77; *Maggie Miller*, 8, 149, 150

Hopkins, Pauline: and *Colored American Magazine*, 122, 124–25, 176nn. 6, 9; feminism of, 124–25, 138
—, *Contending Forces*, 125
—, *Hagar's Daughter*, xi, 122–57, 159, 160; asexual mother figure in, 150, 154; Eve figure in, 140–41, 150–51, 154; and passing, 134–35, 144; race mimicry in, 134, 135, 137, 144, 145; reclamation of Hagar as black in, 8, 122, 123, 126; as response to white women's Hagar fiction, 8, 122, 127, 134, 135, 137, 139, 144–45, 153; and tragic mulatto fiction, 122, 131, 132, 134, 146, 153, 177n. 21; use of white male focalizer in, 138–48 *passim*, 151–57 *passim*; the West as tolerant in, 132, 145
—, *Of One Blood*, 46, 169n. 17
—, *Winona*, 46. See also Edenic myth; Hagar paradigm

Irving, Washington: "Philip of Pokanoket," 104, 174–75n. 14, 175n. 26
Ishmael: biblical account of, 6, 20–21; as black, 7, 32; depiction in Hagar art of, 20–21; exclusion from Eden of 53; hybridity of, 32; in *Moby-Dick*, 32, 36

Jacobs, Harriet, 170n. 1
Jefferson, Thomas, 2, 35, 53, 62, 103, 108
Jewett, Sarah Orne, 159
Johnston, Mary, 37; *Hagar*, 8, 81, 117, 155–57
Joyce, Donald, 125
Jungian archetypes and race, 18–32 *passim*. See also race theory

Kaplan, Amy, 158, 159
Kappeler, Susanne, 80, 138
Koehler, Christian: "Hagar and Ishmael." See Hagar artwork

Lacan, Jacques, 20

Laurence, Margaret: *Stone Angel*, 7
Lewis, Edmonia, xii, 135–37
—, "Hagar in the Wilderness," xii, 135, *136*; Hagar coded as black in, 135, 137; interpretations of, 135, 137; mimicry in, 137; overt whiteness in 135, 137
—, "The Death of Cleopatra," 135
—, "Old Arrow Maker," 135. See also Hagar artwork; Hagar paradigm
Lynch, Anne Charlotte: "Hagar," 6

Melville, Herman, 32–33, 36; "Benito Cereno," 159; *Moby-Dick*, 32, 36, 158; *Pierre*, xi, 32; "Two Temples," 32
Merle, Hugues, 127; illustration of Hagar, 127, *128*; illustration of Hester Prynne, 127, 177n. 16. See also Hagar artwork
Michaels, Walter Benn, 158
Mor, Barbara, 30
Morrison, Toni, 7, 32; *Song of Solomon*, 7
Moss, Elizabeth, 67
Mossell, Gertrude, 124–25
Mowatt, Anna Cora, 77, 82

Native Americans. See Pocahantas; racist stereotypes, Native Americans
Neumann, Erich, 18, 22, 50. See also Jungian archetypes and race
Nicholson, Eliza Poitevent: "Hagar," 131, 167n. 9

Page, Thomas Nelson, 105
Palmer, Phyllis Marynick, 123
Parton, Sara (pseud. Fanny Fern), 28; *Ruth Hall*, 28, 159
Peabody, Elizabeth, 82
Perry, Ellwood, 40
Peterson's Ladies' Magazine: "Departure of Hagar." See Hagar artwork
Plato, 20, 39
Pocahontas, 62, 102, 174n. 11
Powers, Hiram, 135, 137; "Greek Slave," 137

Prud'hon, Pierre-Paul: *Christian Parlor* illustration. *See* Hagar artwork
Purvis, T.T.: *Hagar, The Singing Maiden*, 81

race theory: and Agassiz (Louis), 42; and Cleopatra, 41, 129, 135; and Creole status, 3, 4; and diseases, 79–80; and the Egypt-Africa debate, 6, 41–42, 48; and Gliddon (George), 42; and Gobineau (Joseph), 3; and miscegenation, 36, 42, 72, 78, 79, 87, 88, 102, 144, 147; and Morris (Robert T.), 23–24; and Morton (Samuel), 42; and Nott (Josiah), 42; and Roberts (Samuel), 41, 169n. 13
racist stereotypes:
—, black men: inappropriate sexuality of, 45–46
—, black women: inappropriate sexuality of, 2, 5–6, 23–24, 50, 70, 78, 95–96, 123, 129, 173n. 16; as Jezebels, 2, 80, 164n. 2; as mammies, 48, 57; as no thing, 5; as objects of colonial gaze, 5, 32, 79, 80
—, mulattos: as degenerate, 72, 73, 74, 88, 94
—, Native Americans: as "The Bad Indian," 69; inappropriate sexuality of, 24; as "Noble Savages," 62, 63, 69
—, whites: myth of superiority of, 2, 4, 5, 31, 32, 39, 96. *See also* race theory
Rembrandt: "Hagar's Dismissal." *See* Hagar artwork
Ries, Adeline, 48
Rimmon-Kenon, Shlomith, 138

Sanchez-Eppler, Karen, 87
Sedgwick, Catharine, 69, 159
See, Fred G., 26
Sjoo, Monica, 30
Skeete, Alexander: *Hagar's Daughter* illustration. *See* Hagar artwork
slave imagery, appropriation of: by Clark, 115–16; by Southworth, 43, 45–46, 48, 49, 51, 97; by Stephens, 86–87, 92, 94
Southworth, E.D.E.N. [Emma Dorothy Eliza Nevitte], 105, 127, 160, 161–62; feminism of, 38, 64, 76; public abolitionist views of, 38–39, 58, 168n. 1
—, *Broken Pledges*, 70
—, *Deserted Wife*, xi, 8, 36, 38–54, 74, 77, 82, 89, 97, 141; covertly black Hagar in, 8, 39–40, 55, 57, 68; Egyptian imagery in, 40–41, 42, 43, 48, 49; erasure of slave labor in, 53, 55, 62, 102; instability of racial color in, 47, 49, 51; New Testament *caritas* in, 56; Old Testament punitive patriarch in, 56; possible influence on *Scarlet Letter* of, 33–34; quest imagery in, 39, 50
—, *Ishmael*, xi, 38
—, *Retribution*, 71
—, *Self-Raised*, 38
—, *Virginia and Magdalene*, 50, 54, 55–75, 141; benevolent Old Testament God in, 56, 63–64, 66; erasure of white blame in, 56, 62, 71; fear of slave insurrection in, 62, 71–72, 73, 74; forgiveness in, 56, 64, 66, 67, 75, 88; Indian splitting in, 68; mariological paradigm in, 53, 65–67, 88, 156; Mary Magdalene as Native American in, 58, 68–70, 71, 72; Mary Magdalene encoded as Black in, 57, 58, 70–71, 72, 73–74; milk as commodity in, 57, 60–61, 62, 64, 71, 92; milk as love in, 57–58, 59, 60–61, 64; Native Americans blamed for slavery's oppression in, 56, 62, 64, 71; patriarchal repression in, 65; patriarchal white benevolence in, 63, 66, 71; punitive Old Testament God in, 56, 63–64, 66; slave labor as love in, 56–65 *passim*, 171n. 1; slave labor as no thing in, 56, 58–60, 64, 65; stereotyping of Native Americans in, 58, 62, 63, 69. *See also* Edenic

myth; Hagar paradigm; slave imagery, appropriation of

Sprengnether, Madelon, 149–50, 154

Stephens, Harriet Marion: acting career of, 76–77, 82, 160–61; and Charlotte Cushman, 76, 81, 82; social shunning of, 76–77, 82; southern background of, 76, 90–91

—, *Hagar the Martyr*, 8, 9, 34, 76–94, 123, 141, 160–61; atonement in, 89–90, 93; benevolent plantation patriarchy in, 90–91; exploitation of black sexuality in, 76, 78–79, 80, 85–86, 87; exposure of blackness in, 96, 97; negative reviews of, 83–84; race and diseases in, 79–80; relation to sensationalism, 77, 78, 83; revenge in, 76, 81; sexual scandal in, 77–78, 81, 85, 89, 94; and tragic mulatto fiction, 85–86, 87; used for social mobility, 76–77, 83, 161, 172n. 6; and white male audience, 80, 81, 83–85, 86, 89, 91, 93, 124. *See also* Hagar paradigm; slave imagery, appropriation of

—, *Home Scenes and Sounds*, 161

stereotypes, gender. *See* gender stereotypes

stereotypes, racist. *See* racist stereotypes

Stewart, Georgia F., 124

Stowe, Harriet Beecher, 26–29, 38, 159; accused impropriety of, 28–29

—, *Lady Byron Vindicated*, 28–29

—, *Uncle Tom's Cabin*, 7, 26–29, 168n. 3; and abolition, 26, 28; Hagar as symbol of racial injustice in, 26; Hagar desexualized in, 26, 27

—, *Woman in Sacred History*, xii, 15, 19, 27–28; condemnation of Hagar in, 27–28. *See also* Hagar paradigm

Stowe, Lyman Beecher, 26

Suarez, Francisco, 23

Tate, Claudia, 46, 125, 126

Taylor, Susie King, 7

Terborg-Penn, Rosalyn, 125

Teubal, Savina, 10, 18, 20–21, 29–30, 31, 37, 116, 138, 145

tragic mulatto fiction, 46, 85–86, 87, 111, 118, 122, 131–32, 134, 146, 153, 176n. 11, 177n. 21

Twain, Mark: *Huckleberry Finn*, 2; *Pudd'nhead Wilson*, 149; *Tom Sawyer*, 25

Warner, Marina, 22–23, 166n. 44

Warner, Susan, 162

Washington, Booker T., 125, 176n. 9

Wells, H.G., 117

West, Benjamin: "Hagar and Ishmael." *See* Hagar artwork

Wharton, Edith: *Summer*, 125

Whitman, Walt, 105

Whittier, John Greenleaf, 38

Williams, Delores, 6, 10, 30–32, 36, 57, 105, 167n. 19

Williams, Fannie Barrier, 129

Willis, Nathaniel Parker: "Hagar in the Wilderness," 28, 29, 167n. 10. *See also* Hagar paradigm

Wirt, William, 53, 171n. 8, 174n. 11

Woman's Fiction, 9–10, 159

Woodman, Marion, 10, 23, 30, 70

Young, Robert J.C., 3, 4, 41, 61, 78, 147